Brainstorms & Thunderbolts

Brainstorms &

OTHER BOOKS BY THE AUTHORS

The Macmillan Illustrated Almanac for Kids

BY ANN ELWOOD

Windows in Space (with Linda Wood)

Thunderbolts

How Creative Genius Works

Carol Orsag Madigan & Ann Elwood

Macmillan Publishing Company

New York

Macmillan Publishing Company
866 Third Avenue, New York, N.Y. 10022
Collier Macmillan Canada, Inc.

Library of Congress Cataloging in Publication Data
Madigan, Carol Orsag.
Brainstorms & thunderbolts.
1. Creative ability—Biography. 2. Genius—Biography.
I. Elwood, Ann. II. Title. III. Title: Brainstorms and
thunderbolts.
BF408.M223 1983   155   83-18731
ISBN 0-02-579160-5

10 9 8 7 6 5 4 3 2 1

Designed by Jack Meserole

Printed in the United States of America

To Betty, John, Brook, and Johnny

with love and gratitude

C.O.M.

To my friends, family, and Puppy

with thanks for their encouragement

A.E.

CONTENTS

4. *Dreams and Drugs*

5. *On Death*

Contents | xi

INTRODUCTION

What supernatural incident inspired Adolf Hitler to seize power in Germany? Where did Jules Verne get the idea for *Around the World in Eighty Days*? What essay led both Charles Darwin and Alfred Russel Wallace, working independently, to the theory of natural selection? Where did *MAD* magazine find a face for the cover boy Alfred E. Neuman? What conversation caused Hiram Maxim to develop the Maxim machine gun? Who was the real Goldfinger? These questions are the basis for just a few of the many stories we present in this book. As you will see, inspirations spring from a multitude of sources: from visions, drugs, dreams, love, and death to a toothache, a grapefruit, a dust storm, and a lily pad.

Some creators—those who were able to refine their flashes of insight into masterful products—worked in a highly agitated, almost intoxicated state. Harriet Beecher Stowe wept uncontrollably as she penned the chapters of *Uncle Tom's Cabin*. Emma Goldman turned her emotions, which were "too horrible for tears," into an anarchistic crusade. Archimedes was so excited that he ran naked into the streets, shouting, "Eureka!" ("I have found it!"). Scientist Nikola Tesla experienced a flash in a Budapest park at sunset and felt his body sway and his arms rise in a frenzy of movement. Alexander Graham Bell, upon a new discovery, broke into a Mohawk war dance.

Some geniuses—Elias Howe, Samuel Taylor Coleridge, Mary Shelley, Robert Louis Stevenson—awoke abruptly from a dream or dreamlike state to frantically capture on paper what had been revealed to them while asleep. Some subjects found inspiration while in the midst of pain, suffering, and noise: Blaise Pascal had a toothache, Lewis Carroll endured migraine headaches, Alfred Russel Wallace shivered in a feverish fit, and Martin Luther was inspired on the privy during a bout of constipation.

Many creators, though their inspirations were intense, did not cry, whirl about, or tear out locks of hair. Their stories, nonetheless, are just as exciting. Joan of Arc heard sweet, humble voices that commanded and guided her in battles against the English. King C. Gillette methodically and diligently searched his mind for a useful, disposable product and came up with the safety razor. Shy and reclusive Elizabeth Barrett Browning quietly penned the passionate *Sonnets from the Portuguese.* William Booth's unwavering convictions led him to form the Salvation Army. Dante turned everyday occurrences into an epic, the *Divine Comedy.*

Not all of the creations mentioned in this book are undeniably original—as evidenced in the chapter "Creative Thievery." Many innovators had historical or contemporary help. For example, the ancestor of the fastening tape Velcro came from the Jura Mountains in Switzerland. The lyrics for "The Star-Spangled Banner" were written by Francis Scott Key, but the melody for the American national anthem came from a rather decadent source. In the chapter "People: Real and Ideal" are the real people who inspired some of today's favorite characters: Auntie Mame, Dracula, Bluebeard, "A Boy Named Sue," and others.

"Fakes, Mistakes, and Accidents" chronicles the lucky, serendipitous moments that gave birth to scientific principles and theories as well as products such as rayon and Ivory Soap. In addition, we could not resist including a number of contrived inspirations: Watt and his teakettle, L. Frank Baum and the naming of Oz, and Newton and the falling apple.

A number of writers, from psychologists and scientists to philosophers and sociologists, have written scores of volumes on the subject of creativity in an attempt to solve the mystery of what constitutes the creative mind. As yet, no one has been able to come up with a definitive answer. Some point to biological, hereditary influences. Others claim that environmental factors are the key to the solution. Most would agree that certain elements are desirable for creativity: curiosity, intuitiveness, enthusiasm, flexibility, intelligence, and independence.

Most books on creativity are bogged down with technical jargon, complicated diagrams, and complex theories. From time to time the reader finds a few sentences, perhaps a paragraph, about a writer, an inventor, a composer—and how he or she came to create a great work. But those hints of a story, those teasers, leave much unsaid. We have attempted to fill in the gaps, weaving into the story the personalities, the quirks, the high and low points of the lives of our subjects.

Brainstorms and Thunderbolts is a collection of stories about people who experienced an inner awakening that moved them to create. The experience might be supernatural—a vision, a voice, a dream; an intuitive flash or trigger; an emotional response to an intense love or a devastating death; a self-induced state from drugs; a bit of creative copying.

Our cast of characters falls into an array of categories: rich to poor; egotistical to humble; beautiful to homely; robust to sickly; spirited and witty to shy and retiring. We find comfort in the fact that humankind, with all its technological know-how and problem-solving gadgetry, has not found a way to accurately label some of us creative and some uninspired. Walter Winchell once wrote of inventor Rube Goldberg: "Generations of Americans have roared at Rube Goldberg machines—but the combined scientists of the world cannot and never will produce a machine which laughs at a man." We heartily agree.

CAROL ORSAG MADIGAN
ANN ELWOOD

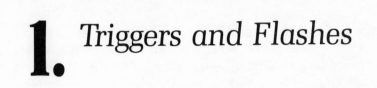

1. Triggers and Flashes

Chance favors the prepared mind," Louis Pasteur said. A recent study of more than two hundred scientists bears out his statement. It concludes that successful hunches burst upon the scientists during a lazy period following concentrated hard work on the problems they were trying to solve. Though creators often debunk the moment of discovery as a brilliant but frivolous firework less significant than the more mundane realm of thought and hard work, most of them, driven to the wall, admit that few feelings are more ravishing than that final pyrotechnic explosion in the mind. Scientist Nikola Tesla called it a "thrill going through the human heart."

Triggers of the great inspirational thunderbolt vary from the sublime (a trance following a beautiful sunset), to the painful (an excruciating toothache), to the trivial (a newspaper ad). The trigger often has far less importance than the idea it generates. The page of a book fluttering in the wind inspired the life work of Mark Twain, for instance. A trigger can be just the right combination of circumstances waiting for someone of perception to seize upon it—for example, two men, Charles Darwin and Alfred Russel Wallace, independently arrived at similar ideas upon reading a book written decades earlier. Creation often results from a probability in which the dice are loaded in favor of discovery. But sometimes the opportunity was always there. How many sat in a bathtub before Archimedes had his great flash?

Eureka! (I Have Found It!)

ARCHIMEDES, the greatest of ancient Greek scientists, was a man consumed by his work, often forsaking food, drink, and social companionship for it. Mesmerized by his own thoughts, he was often observed alone, in a trancelike state, drawing figures in the sand or in ashes on the hearth, or in the oil which covered and softened his body. Appropriately enough, this otherworldliness led to both his greatest discoveries and his death.

One of his most important discoveries resulted from a request from his cousin, King Hieron II. Hieron, ruler of the city-state of Syracuse, suspected that his new gold crown was not solid gold—that the goldsmith had mixed in some silver and pocketed a portion of the gold. To prove his theory, the king called upon his cousin, the great mathematician and inventor Archimedes. Solve the problem, Hieron commanded, but do not melt down or disfigure the crown.

For weeks Archimedes struggled to find a solution. One afternoon the answer came—swift, clear, and definitive—as he stepped into a tub at the public baths. As he immersed himself, the water overflowed, and the more he submerged himself, the less his body seemed to weigh.

Realizing that a submerged body displaces water according to its volume, Archimedes knew he had found a way to test the authenticity of the gold crown. Elated by the unexpected discovery, he ran naked into the streets, shouting, "Eureka! Eureka!" ("I have found it! I have found it!")

As soon as he got home, he submerged a weight of gold, identical to the crown's, into a container of water and noted how much water it displaced. He followed the same procedure with silver. It displaced more water than the gold, so he knew that silver occupied more volume per weight than gold. Finally, he placed the crown in the water. The water rose, but the crown displaced a greater amount of water than the gold. The king's suspicions were correct: the crown was alloyed with silver, and the goldsmith was a crook. Today we call his discovery Archimedes' Principle: "A body immersed in a fluid loses as much in weight as the weight of the fluid it displaces."

The introspective scientist was never interested in the practical applications of his discoveries. He was intrigued only by pure science—how to understand the complex workings of the universe. However, at the request of King Hieron, Archimedes did turn back to the earthly world to invent some war machinery to defend Syracuse against the advancing armies of Roman general Marcus Claudius Marcellus. So, at age seventy-five, Archimedes found himself at war.

The year was 212 B.C., and the Roman assault came from both land and sea. Archimedes' war machines were particularly successful against the sea assault, for behind the harbor walls built by the Greeks for protection Archimedes placed catapult machines that hurled heavy stones at

Roman ships. Even more ingenious were two cranes he had devised. One dropped huge lead weights onto the Roman ships and sank them instantly. The other held a hook that caught a ship, raised it high into the air, and smashed it against the rocks. The Romans, amazed and bewildered, were in awe of the scientist turned military genius. But the military strategy, effective as it was, could not put a stop to the food and supplies blockade that the Romans imposed. It was not long before the citizens of Syracuse surrendered.

Marcellus, eager to meet the great Archimedes, issued orders that he was not to be harmed. But, as the Roman soldiers overran the city, his orders were inadvertently disobeyed: During the invasion one Roman soldier happened upon a simply dressed, unpretentious old man who was totally absorbed in solving a mathematical problem that he had outlined in the sand. The soldier commanded him to rise and be taken before Marcellus for questioning. The Greek, obviously a scientist of some sort, refused and asked to be left alone; he needed only a few more moments to resolve his problem. Angered by the old man's indifference to the mayhem around him, the impatient soldier struck him down. Archimedes died instantly.

The Two Inspirations for Jules Verne's Around the World in Eighty Days

TO HIS LAST DAYS, French author Jules Verne claimed that the idea for *Around the World in Eighty Days* came to him in 1871 while he was working in Paris. One day, as he strolled on the Place de la Madeleine, he read a newspaper advertisement for the Thomas Cook Travel Agency. "The paragraph that caught my attention," he recalled, "mentioned the fact that nowadays it would be quite possible for a man to travel around the world in eighty days, and it immediately flashed into my mind that the traveler, profiting by a difference of meridian, could be made to either gain or lose a day during that period of time."

As all Verne fans will recall, Phileas Fogg bets his friends at the Reform Club of London that he can travel around the world in eighty days. After a nonstop chase full of adventures, Fogg disappointedly returns to London one day late. He quickly discovers, however, that by traveling west to east he gained a day and has actually arrived in London on time. Fogg and his loyal valet, Passepartout, rush to the Reform Club, arriving with only ten minutes to spare, and collect the bet.

There is, however, another, perhaps stronger inspiration for the geographic twist to the novel. It originated in an Edgar Allan Poe short story called "Three Sundays in a Week." In the story, an old man refuses his daughter's hand to a suitor until there is a week with three Sundays. Verne was so impressed by Poe's geographical plotting that he even read a paper on the subject to the Société de Géographie in Paris. And he adapted the plot to fit *Around the World*—but never admitted using it.

Malthus, Darwin, Wallace—
The Curious Connection

WITHOUT conscious volition, three shy, gentle men jostled God's throne and faced the wrath of believers. They did it all with ideas. And between their ideas was a curious connection.

In 1798, the thirty-two-year-old curate of Okewood, a parish of poor cottagers in Surrey, England, had a conversation verging on argument with his father about "Avarice and Profusion," an essay by the anarchist philosopher William Godwin. In the essay Godwin claimed that "myriads of centuries of still-increasing population may pass away, and the earth be yet found sufficient for the support of its inhabitants." When the day came that the earth was full of people, Godwin claimed, population growth would become static. How? No one would die, and no one would be born. No one would make love, either, for the sex urge would be conquered by reason. This was Godwin's idea of utopia, his later love affairs with Mary Wollstonecraft and other ladies notwithstanding. Reading the essay, the curate, T. Robert ("Bob") Malthus, could not imagine such an eventuality. Nor did he believe that it would take "myriads of centuries" before population increase, if unchecked, would cause dire distress to human beings, particularly the poor whom he saw every day leading their mean lives. So, we must suppose, he argued with his father.

The conversation inspired him to write an essay of his own: "Essay on the Principle of Population, as It Affects the Future Improvement of Society, with Remarks on the Speculations of Mr. Godwin, M. Concordet, and Other Writers." He published it anonymously. In the essay, he skewered Godwin and other utopians with ironic praise for their "beautiful phantoms of the imagination," their wistful picturing of a rosy human future. He proposed "two postulata":

"First, that food is necessary to the existence of man.

"Secondly, that the passion between the sexes is necessary, and will remain nearly in its present state."

The "two postulata" led Malthus to the nub of his theory: that no matter how humane civil institutions may be, nature will overcome human happiness because "the power of population is indefinitely greater than the power in the earth to produce subsistence for man." There were inexorable laws: 1) that population, unchecked, grows in geometrical ratio, and 2) subsistence grows in arithmetical ratio. The "checks" on population varied—disease, famine, war . . . or, far more humane in Malthus's eyes, late marriage. (Byron later sneered at this last solution, saying that Malthus was "turning marriage into arithmetic.")

The essay, its author soon identified, caused a furor. Malthus was accused of defying God's command to multiply and replenish the earth. Providence, some religious people said, would not allow such a law as Malthus proposed to exist. In his later versions of his "Essay on Population," Malthus prefaced his name with "Reverend."

On the other hand, many atheists also derided him. Karl Marx, long after Malthus was dead, sarcastically called him "Parson Malthus" and a "shameless sycophant of the ruling classes." Romantic poets like Shelley and Coleridge saw him as a mean-spirited capitalist.

In 1837, already tall and gangly, fourteen-year-old Alfred Russel Wallace was sent to live in London with his brother. His father, a business failure, could no longer afford to send Alfred to school. The two brothers went to meetings at London's Hall of Science, a workingman's club, where members hotly discussed the theories of utopian socialist Robert Owen. Owen disagreed with the theories of Malthus, still a controversial figure though three years dead, and said he believed that educated people could produce more food than they could consume. The utopians were still sniping at Malthus, and Wallace, then converted to socialism, heard their arguments.

In 1838, naturalist Charles Darwin, aged twenty-nine, returned from his five-year, around-the-world trip to South America on the English ship *Beagle* and went to live in a comfortable London house with his wife. He had already started a notebook "for facts in relation to the origin of species," a question that obsessed nineteenth-century scientists, even before Darwin. How, they asked, had the earth's animal and plant population changed so much over the millennia? For instance, why had mammoths, first found preserved in ice in 1799, died out? Why did elephants so resemble them? The predominant theory was that such species rose by an act of "special creation" and that any resemblances between fossils and living things were coincidental. According to the "law of the succession of types," species went totally extinct, probably because of some catastrophe like the Flood, and were replaced by new and improved ones. But Darwin had seen some curious likenesses among species in South America, particularly on the "enchanted" Galapagos Islands, with their distinct yet very similar species of land birds, particularly finches, lizards, and tortoises.

One day, while in the midst of pondering these questions, Darwin read "for amusement" Malthus's "Essay."

In 1844, Wallace, now an obscure schoolmaster in his early twenties, read the same "Essay" in the Leicester Library. Already an amateur naturalist, he had taught himself botany from a book. Joining in the nineteenth-century mania for pinning nature to a board, Wallace had become a plant collector when he had been a land surveyor for a few years before. At Leicester, however, a fellow collector, Herbert W. Bates, a hosiery manufacturer's son, acquainted him with another passion: collecting beetles and butterflies.

About that same time, Darwin, who had been experimenting with artificial selection by breeding barnacles and ornamental chickens, was still wrestling with difficult questions: How did species become modified? What made them change? By now he was convinced that species evolved through infinitesimal changes so slow that they were imperceptible to humans, whose brief lives were after all, winks in millennial time. (This idea, incidentally, was not new. Lucretius, a philosopher of ancient Rome, had considered a version of it.)

By then Darwin and his wife had moved to a country estate, Down House, in Kent. One day he was out traveling about, thinking about Malthus's book. He later recalled, "and I can remember the very spot in the road, whilst in my carriage, when to my joy the solution occurred to me. . . ." That solution was this: Animals reproduce in great numbers—many more are born than the environment can support, as Malthus said. Those best able to survive in that environment (and environments change) are *naturally selected*—they live while others die. This flash of inspiration, stemming from Malthus, occurred sometime between 1842, when he wrote a "pencil sketch" of his theory, and 1844, when he enlarged it to 230 pages. He did not publish the theory. As he wrote to his friend Sir Joseph Hooker, a botanist and director of Kew Gardens, "At last gleams of light have come, and I am almost convinced (quite to the contrary of the opinion I started with) that species are not (it is like confessing to a murder) immutable." A murder? Yes. It was the murder of religious fundamentalist belief: that God created each species for all time as related in Genesis. Darwin, like Malthus, had created an idea that shook the throne of the traditionalists' Creator, and he knew it.

In 1858, Wallace, who had become a specimen collector, or "flycatcher," as the scientific elite would sneeringly call him, was shivering with fever in his thatched bungalow at Ternate on a volcanic island in the Malay Archipelago when, "muffled in blankets," he suddenly remembered the Malthus essay he had read more than a decade before:

> While again considering the problem of the origin of species, something led me to think of Malthus's "Essay on Population" . . . and the "positive checks"—war, disease, famine, accident, etc.—which he adduced as keeping all savage populations nearly stationary. It then occurred to me that these checks must also act upon animals and keep down their numbers. . . . Then it suddenly flashed upon me that this self-acting process would necessarily *improve the race*, because in every generation the inferior would inevitably be killed off and the superior would remain. . . .

A change in the environment, he saw, would engender such modifications in species, favoring mutant variations that would be able to survive. He later said: "In the two hours of my fit I had thought the *main points of the theory*." Impatiently, he waited for the fever attack to abate so that he could make notes for a paper on the idea. As he recalled later, "The same evening I did this pretty fully, and on the two succeeding evenings wrote it out carefully in order to send it to Darwin by the next post, which would leave in a day or two. . . ."

The paper Wallace wrote, "On the Tendency of Species to Depart Indefinitely from the Original Type," was twenty handwritten pages (3,764 words) long. He sent it off by Dutch cargo vessel to Singapore, where it was picked up by an English packet boat. Darwin received the essay in June. As Wallace remarked some fifty years later, "My letter, with the enclosed essay, came upon him like a thunderbolt from a cloudless sky!"

Crushed, Darwin wrote to geologist Charles Lyell, "So my originality is smashed, though my book, if it will have any value, will not be deteriorated, as all know the labor exists in the application of the theory."

In an elegant solution to a bad problem (who should claim to be the first discoverer of the theory?), Hooker suggested that Wallace's essay and Darwin's 1844 essay both be read at a meeting of the Linnean Society. And so it was done.

A chagrined Darwin speeded up the writing of his *Origin of Species*, published in 1859. In one day its entire first printing of 1,250 copies sold out. Wallace and Darwin became correspondents, and when Wallace came back to England in 1862, the two men became personal friends. Though they came from different backgrounds—Darwin of upper-class gentry, Wallace from a professional family—they had much in common besides their use of Malthus's "Essay" as a source of inspiration.

• Both had been collectors since they were young. Darwin collected all sorts of things, shells, seals, franks, coins, and minerals, as a child, and as a college student, like Wallace at Leicester, he collected beetles. Wallace later said, "It is this superficial and almost childlike interest in the outward forms of living things, which, though often despised as unscientific, happened to be *the only one* that would lead up towards a solution of the problem of species. . . . When, as in the case of Darwin and myself, the collectors were of a speculative turn of mind, they were constantly led to think upon the 'why' and the 'how' of all this wonderful variety in nature—this overwhelming and, at first sight, purposeless wealth of specific forms among the very humblest forms of life."

• Both men traveled in strange and marvelous lands which had plants and animals unknown in Europe. Darwin's trip to South America as a young naturalist on the *Beagle* from 1831 to 1836 was the seedbed from which his later work sprang. Wallace, after his schoolteaching stint in Leicester, left with his beetle-collector friend Bates for Brazil in 1848. While there, a sojourn that lasted four years, Wallace collected thousands of specimens and began to develop rudimentary evolutionary theories. Later he went to the Malay Archipelago, another exotic place, where he experienced his fever-induced flash of inspiration and collected 156,660 specimens. He also traveled fourteen thousand miles, sometimes in native boats with rat-eaten sails. Collecting still thrilled him. Of the capture of a rare butterfly, he said, "It is one thing to see such beauty in a cabinet, and quite another to feel it struggling between one's fingers, and to gaze upon its fresh and living beauty, a bright gem shining out amid the silent gloom of the dark and tangled forest."

• Both were meticulous, as befits collectors. Darwin, of course, spent twenty years painstakingly putting together the pieces of the theory and proving it with example after example. Wallace—who untied parcels rather then cut the string, then folded up the string—was equally careful.

* * *

The fruit of the publication of their theory was bitter.

After the publication of *Origin of Species*, while Wallace was still off in the Far East, the first monkey trial was held by the British Association for the Advancement of Science at Oxford, with the famous debate between Bishop Samuel Wilberforce and Darwin's defender, scientist T. H. Huxley. Seven hundred people heard the Bishop claim, "There is nothing in the idea of evolution: rock-pigeons are what rock-pigeons have always been," and then ask Huxley through which grandparent he claimed descent from a monkey. Huxley's rebuttal: "I should feel it no shame to have risen from the origin of a monkey, but I should feel it a shame to have sprung from an ignorant bishop." (Only four years before, in 1856, the fossil remains of an early form of Homo sapiens had been found in the Neanderthal valley in Germany—the first of many discoveries of creatures representing the evolution from ape to man.)

Religious fundamentalists were no happier with the theory of natural selection than their forebears had been with Malthus's "Essay." They believed it negated the teachings of the Bible, including Genesis and the story of the Flood. Yet Darwin, who was an agnostic, wrote at the end of *Origin of Species*: "There is grandeur in this view of life, with its several powers, having been originally breathed by the Creator into a few forms or into one; and that, whilst this planet has gone cycling on according to the fixed law of gravity, from so simple a beginning endless forms most beautiful and wonderful have been, and are being, evolved."

While the Romantic poets had objected directly to Malthus's ideas as insulting to the lower classes, such objections came more indirectly to Darwin and Wallace. The theory of evolution was picked up by others and applied in ways that appalled them both. Herbert Spencer, who coined the term "survival of the fittest," and others like him promoted what became known as Social Darwinism: the idea that good things come to the "fittest," or most privileged, humans by natural law. Of course they were ignoring the obvious advantages of material inheritance and social position, neither genetically transmitted, in obtaining the advantages of life. Wallace, as a lifelong socialist, was particularly enraged that his theories were being used to justify the knavery of the robber barons of the nineteenth century.

So it was that one seeker of truth unknowingly inspired two others, that the truths that they discovered shook at least one concept of God's work, and that all three were sadly misinterpreted. Those are the morals of this chronology.

A Genius in the Age of Electricity

NIKOLA TESLA, the Yugoslavian-American scientist who ushered in the modern age of electricity with his alternating current (AC) power transmission system, was a willing slave to his prodigious mind—a mind overloaded with ideas and inventions waiting to be born. Throughout most of his adult life he worked twenty-hour days, controlled by a herculean self-discipline that forbade relaxation, recreation, women, and love. But his inventions, the payment for the personal sacrifices, were more than enough compensation. As Tesla once said, "I do not think there is any thrill that can go through the human heart like that felt by the inventor as he sees some creation of the brain unfolding to success. . . . Such emotions make a man forget food, sleep, friends, love, everything."

Born in the village of Smiljan, Croatia (now Yugoslavia), in 1856, Tesla became a full-fledged inventor at age five when he designed a small paddlewheel waterwheel. Also on his list of boyhood inventions were pop guns (made in several sizes and sold to his friends), fishing hooks, and a motor powered by sixteen June bugs (the bugs, glued to the apparatus, beat their wings and created a force that gave the engine its turning power).

His aptitude for math, science, and all things mechanical was very evident in school. At age nine, when he studied the principles behind various kinds of machinery, including the water turbine, Tesla proved very adept at building his own turbines and found great satisfaction in operating them. It was at this time that he first read about Niagara Falls.

As he later wrote, "I was fascinated by a description of Niagara Falls I had perused and pictured in my imagination a big wheel run by the falls. I told my uncle that I would go to America and carry out this scheme. Thirty years later I saw my ideas carried out. . . ."

After attending the Technical University at Graz, Austria, and the University of Prague, Tesla accepted a draftsman position at the Central Telegraph Office in Budapest, Hungary. Although the pay was minimum, the twenty-five-year-old electrical engineer was nonetheless optimistic and enthusiastic about the job, especially since the telegraph office was to oversee a new American invention just being introduced to the area—Alexander Graham Bell's telephone. Even when Tesla was busy with everyday job responsibilities, his thoughts constantly detoured to a problem that had occupied his mind since his school days at Graz. It was there that he first became acquainted with a Gramme dynamo, a direct-current machine that could be used both as a generator and as a motor. Disturbed by the many shortcomings of the direct-current system, Tesla was convinced that he could devise an entirely new electrical system based on alternating current (AC). But first he would have to invent an AC motor, a device which many scientists had tried but had failed to build successfully. However, Tesla was committed to solving the problem and was confident that the answer lay somewhere in the deep recesses of his brain.

The design for the AC motor came to him one day in February 1882, as he was walking with a friend, Anital Szigeti, in a park in Budapest. The sunset with its panorama of brilliant colors filled the sky, moving Tesla to recite a passage from Goethe's *Faust*:

> The glow retreats, done is the day of toil;
> It yonder hastes, new fields of life exploring;
> Ah, that no wing can lift me from the soil,
> Upon its track to follow, follow soaring . . .

As he spoke, his body swayed from side to side, his arms waved about in the air. Suddenly he became immobile and fell into a trancelike state. He later recalled the overpowering experience: "As I uttered these inspiring words the idea came like a flash of lightning, and in an instant the truth was revealed. . . . The images I saw were wonderfully sharp and clear and had the solidity of metal and stone, so much so that I told him [Szigeti], 'See my motor here; watch me reverse it.' I cannot begin to describe my emotions. Pygmalion seeing his statue come to life could not have been more deeply moved. A thousand secrets of nature which I might have stumbled upon accidentally I would have given for that one which I had wrested from her against all odds."

A year passed before Tesla constructed a working model of his AC induction motor. He built it without the aid of any blueprints, with no rough sketches, with nothing except his memory to guide him. Gifted with amazing mental powers, Tesla was able to "see" a machine in his mind, take a mental photograph of it, store the information in his brain, and recall it at will. The parts for his motor were exactly sized from mathematical calculations worked out in his mind and fit together precisely as he had pictured them. When the motor was ready to be tested, he confidently threw a switch, the machine obeyed his commands, and Tesla knew he had a system that would revolutionize technology around the world.

Filled with high expectations, Tesla emigrated to the United States in 1884. After brief employment with Thomas Edison (who was promoting direct-current systems and refused to be converted to Tesla's AC theories), the Yugoslavian inventor joined forces with George Westinghouse, head of the Westinghouse Electric Company, who eventually purchased all the patent rights to Tesla's alternating-current system. Tesla was soon to become a very recognized and highly respected name. As Margaret Cheney, one of Tesla's most perceptive biographers, wrote: "He conceived of such practical alternating-current motors as polyphase induction, split-phase induction, and polyphase synchronous, as well as the whole polyphase and single-phase motor system for generating, transmitting, and utilizing electric current. And indeed, practically all electricity in the world in time would be generated, transmitted, distributed, and turned into mechanical power by means of the Tesla Polyphase System. What it signified was vastly higher voltages than could be obtained through direct current, with transmission possible over hundreds of miles—a new age of electric light and power everywhere."

Tesla's mental capacities did not diminish with age. By the time he died at age eighty-six, he had secured 112 U.S. patents and had blazed trails in the fields of radio, television, robotry, and guided missiles. In an interview titled "Making Your Imagination Work for You" by M. K. Wisehart, published in the April 1921 issue of *American Magazine*, Tesla outlined his creative processes:

> Some people, the moment they have a device to construct or any piece of work to perform, rush at it without adequate preparation, and immediately become engrossed in details, instead of the central idea. They may get results, but they sacrifice quality.

Here, in brief, is my own method: After experiencing a desire to invent a particular thing, I may go on for months or years with the idea in the back of my head. Whenever I feel like it, I roam around in my imagination and think about the problem without any deliberate concentration. This is a period of incubation.

Then follows a period of direct effort. I choose carefully the possible solutions of the problem I am considering and gradually center my mind on a narrowed field of investigation. Now, when I am deliberately thinking of the problem in its specific features, I may begin to feel that I am going to get the solution. And the wonderful thing is that, if I do feel this way, *then I know I have really solved the problem and shall get what I am after.*

The feeling is as convincing to me as though I already had solved it. I have come to the conclusion that at this stage the actual solution is in my *subconscious*, though it may be a long time before I am aware of it *consciously*.

Before I put a sketch on paper, the whole idea is worked out mentally. In my mind I change the construction, make improvements, and even operate the device. Without ever having drawn a sketch, I can give the measurements of all parts to workmen, and when completed all these parts will fit, just as certainly as though I had made the actual drawings. It is immaterial to me whether I run my machine in my mind or test it in my shop.

The inventions I have conceived in this way have always worked. In thirty years there has not been a single exception. My first electric motor, the vacuum tube wireless light, my turbine engine, and many other devices have all been developed in exactly this way.

Despite his undisputed genius, Tesla's ever-present financial difficulties, eccentric behavior (which included a number of phobias—fear of germs among them), and several outlandish claims (that he had invented a "death ray" and that there was intelligent life on Mars) stirred up unfavorable publicity that portrayed him as a mad scientist, a utopian dreamer. His last few years were relatively quiet, spent mostly in the company of the thousands of pigeons he had befriended. Without fail, as long as his health permitted, he would enjoy a daily midnight stroll up New York City's Fifth Avenue, stopping at various spots to let out a low whistle that would summon the birds. It was a private moment that even his closest friends were not invited to share. Passersby, however, were touched by the scene—a tall, lean, impeccably dressed old man, birds perched on his arms and shoulders, scattering about a ration of seed.

Mark Twain "Meets" Joan of Arc

I like the *Joan of Arc* the best of all my books: and it *is* the best; I know it perfectly well. And besides, it furnished me seven times the pleasure afforded me by any of the others: twelve years of preparation and two years of writing. The others needed no preparation, and got none.   —MARK TWAIN

DURING a walk on a dreary afternoon in his early teenage years, Mark Twain had a chance literary encounter with Joan of Arc—an emotional experience that became the turning point in his life. After it he suddenly became interested in history, writing, and learning languages; the encounter also led him to write *Personal Recollections of Joan of Arc*, which he considered the best of all his books. But he hadn't always been such an avid student, nor had he seemed destined for literary greatness.

At fourteen, Samuel Langhorne Clemens (who later wrote under the name Mark Twain) was apprenticed to a printer in Hannibal, Missouri. He had dropped out of school, which he hated with a passion, at the age of twelve following the death of his father. A sandy-haired boy with a fair complexion and large blue-gray eyes, Sam was serious-minded and diligent while on the job, always reporting to the office on time and always pulling his fair share of the work load.

Luckily these early adult responsibilities did nothing to dampen the spirits of the highly imaginative Sam, who enjoyed a full measure of childhood adventures. (Years later, many of them showed up in his books, especially *Tom Sawyer* and *Huckleberry Finn*.) When his working day ended at three in the afternoon, he was usually off to the river to swim or fish or navigate a boat, "borrowed" from an unsuspecting owner, with the skill of an experienced pilot. Dressed in hand-me-down clothes ("I had to turn the trousers up to my ears to make them short enough"), Sam Clemens was a boy whose wit and devil-may-care nature made him very popular with his teenage friends, including more than just a few ribboned-and-laced girls.

Though he was a good speller, Sam showed little interest in reading or writing. However, since his job included setting type for a daily paper, he did proofread a variety of articles and was exposed to all the current news of the day. When forced to admit to reality, Sam said that his ambition was to become a competent journeyman printer. But in his fantasy-filled mind, he dreamed of becoming a pirate, a bandit, or a trapper-scout. Writing books, or any other type of literary endeavor, was not even a remote possibility. But all that was changed one day when Sam encountered Joan of Arc. The experience was written up many years later by his official biographer, Albert Bigelow Paine:

> He was on his way from the office to his home one afternoon when he saw flying along the pavement a square of paper, a leaf from a book. At an earlier time he would not have bothered with it at all, but any printed page had acquired a professional interest for him now. He caught the flying scrap and examined it. It was a leaf from some history of Joan of Arc. The "maid" was described in the cage at Rouen, in the fortress, and the two ruffian English soldiers had stolen her clothes. There was a brief description and a good deal of dialogue—her reproaches and their ribald replies. . . .
>
> There arose within him a deep compassion for the gentle Maid of Orleans, a burning resentment toward her captors, a powerful and indestructible interest in her sad history. It was an interest that would grow steadily for more than half a lifetime and culminate at last in that crowning work, the *Recollections*, the loveliest story ever told of the martyred girl.
>
> The incident meant even more than that: it meant the awakening of his interest in all history—the world's story in its many phases—a passion which became the largest feature of his intellectual life and remained with him until his very last day on earth. From the moment when that fluttering leaf was blown into his hands, his career as one of the world's mentally elect was assured. It gave him his cue—the first word of a part in the human drama.

Personal Recollections of Joan of Arc was first published as a serial in *Harper's Magazine* in 1895, forty-six years after Mark Twain first succumbed to the charms of the beautiful saint. He had put his soul into the book, never once complaining about the endless hours of historical research that it required. He often read chapters aloud to his family and usually cried when reciting one of Joan's moving speeches. Afraid that the book would not be taken seriously ("People always want to laugh over what I write and are disappointed if they don't find a joke in it"), Twain asked to have it printed anonymously in the magazine. However, when it came out as a book a year later, Twain's name was on the cover.

Sales of the book were at first disappointing as book reviewers handed out only lukewarm plaudits. In time the book did rise in stature, taking a respectable place in the list of the author's many well-loved works. While it never came close in popularity to *Huckleberry Finn* or *Tom Sawyer*, Mark Twain didn't care. He had once said, "Possibly the book may not sell, but that is nothing—it was written for love."

Blaise Pascal: A Vision and a Toothache

ON AUGUST 19, 1662, several days after the death of French mathematician, physicist, and religious philosopher Blaise Pascal, a manservant who was packing away his clothes and other belongings noticed a swelling in the lining of Pascal's doublet. After ripping open the seam of the coat, he discovered two secret documents, both in Pascal's handwriting. One was a piece of paper with hastily scribbled writing; the other was a sheet of parchment with neat, meticulous script. They had essentially the same verse, the parchment obviously a carefully copied duplicate of the other, more frayed paper. These papers shed new light on Pascal's somewhat abrupt conversion from secular scientist to theologian. They contained an account of the mystical revelation he had experienced eight years earlier which caused him to relinquish most of his possessions, turn his back on what he considered a vain, selfish world, and most importantly, abandon the mathematical studies which had allowed him to solve problems that many scientists could hardly fathom.

Born on June 19, 1624, at Clermont-Ferrand, France, Pascal was an infant prodigy who never went to school but was tutored at home by his father, Etienne Pascal. While he was very young, Pascal used to hear his learned father talk at length with friends about geometry. He begged his father to teach him geometry, but Etienne refused. One afternoon, in his playroom, the precocious eleven-year-old boy took a piece of charcoal and drew circles and triangles all over the floor. Mystified and excited by these diagrams, he began to formulate rules that governed his creations. Before long he had discovered many of Euclid's theorems, including the thirty-second theorem which states that the sum of the angles of a triangle is equal to two right angles. When Etienne entered the room and saw the galaxy of drawings and notations, his son burst into an explanation of his findings. Since Blaise hadn't been schooled in proper mathematical terminology, he talked of "bars" instead of "straight lines" and "rounds" instead of "circles." His father, very impressed and quite proud, agreed immediately to teach him geometry.

At sixteen Pascal published an essay on conic sections that astounded scientist René Descartes and caused him to declare that the complex findings could not possibly have been written by one so young. And the essay was only the start of an impressive, distinguished career.

Pascal's studies of atmospheric pressure proved the existence of the vacuum and improved upon the barometer which was the creation of Italian physicist Evangelista Torricelli. Among Pascal's inventions are the syringe, the hydraulic press, and the first calculating machine (to aid his father, a local administrator who was responsible for levying taxes). In addition, he formulated Pascal's Law, which states that pressure applied to a confined liquid is transmitted undiminished through the liquid in all directions regardless of the area to which the pressure is applied. His greatest contribution to mathematics evolved out of a gambling problem presented to him by a friend. With the aid of another great mathematician, Pierre de Fermat, Pascal solved the problem and in the process formulated the "theory of chances"—later developed into the theory of probability.

After his religious vision in 1654, Pascal devoted his life to religious studies and writings; these include his two most famous works, *Les Provinciales* and *Pensées*. Still interested in mathematics, he sometimes discussed various theories with friends and former associates. But it was not until the spring of 1658 that a common ailment, a toothache, regenerated his scientific genius and enabled him to solve a problem that Galileo proclaimed insoluble: the mathematics of the cycloid (the curve generated by a point on the circumference of a circle that rolls on a straight line). One night Pascal lay in bed, unable to sleep because his head was throbbing from an agonizing toothache. His sister Gilberte recalled: "There came uninvited into his mind some thought on the problem of the cycloid. It was followed by another, and that by another, a whole crowd of thoughts leading on and showing him, as though in spite of himself, the proof of all these things, even to his own surprise."

For the next two years Pascal was again working at breakneck speed; his major works were *A History of the Cycloid* and six long treatises on geometrical subjects, until for a second and final time he rejected his scientific life for religion. He wrote to a friend: "To speak frankly about geometry, I find it the highest exercise of the mind, but at the same time I recognize it as so useless, that I make little difference between a man who is only a geometer and a skillful artisan. . . . I would not take two steps for geometry's sake." Until his death in 1662 he never again indulged in mathematics.

P. T. Barnum, the Great Practical Joker

AS A BOY, P. T. Barnum adored his maternal grandfather Phineas Taylor. The bespectacled, crafty Taylor "would go further, wait longer, and contrive deeper to carry out a practical joke than for anything else under heaven," he later wrote. Certainly Taylor waited a long time—more than six years—for the punch line of one of his jokes. The butt of it was his own grandson.

From the time the boy was quite small, his family regaled him with tales of his inheritance from his grandfather. "My grandfather always spoke of me (in my presence) to the neighbors and to strangers as the richest kid in town, since I owned the whole of Ivy Island, one of the most valuable farms in the state. My mother and father frequently reminded me of my wealth and hoped I would do something for the family when I attained my majority. The neighbors professed to fear that I might refuse to play with their children because I had inherited so large a property."

The young Phineas was hardly averse to being rich—hard physical labor never appealed to him. When he was ten or twelve and the family finally agreed to take him to his estate, he was on tenterhooks. The reality brought him down with a crash. Ivy Island was a worthless snake-and-hornet-infested bog covered with sickly ivy and awash with water. The adults solemnly told him he was foolish to be surprised. Wouldn't one expect a place named Ivy Island to grow ivy? Weren't islands always surrounded by water?

P. T. Barnum, the great trickster-to-be, had been humbugged for the first time. It inspired the rest of his life, for thereafter he tried to hoist others by their own petards as he had been. Most of the time he succeeded, but more than once he was the loser.

Joice Heth—Old, Old, Old (?) Lady

The sharp-dealing, hard-bargaining Barnum was selling groceries in 1835 when New Englander Coley Bartram came in his store and in the course of conversation told how he had just sold his interest in Joice Heth, a 161-year-old slave who had supposedly been George Washington's nurse. Barnum was intrigued, so intrigued that he went to Philadelphia where R. W. Lindsay, Heth's owner and Bartram's former partner, was exhibiting her. The old lady "might as well have been called a thousand years old as any other age," said Barnum. Partially paralyzed, she had four-inch-long fingernails on her left hand, and her legs were drawn up into her body. Lindsay showed Barnum her ancient-looking yellowed papers, a bill of sale from 1729 showing her age then as fifty-four.

Barnum bought her by selling out his interest in the grocery store. His exhibition campaign was carefully planned with the help of an indolent but sharp Yankee lawyer, Levi Lyman. The two plastered New York with posters and issued a pamphlet about the amazing Heth, who was "the first person to put clothes on the unconscious infant [George Washington]." Heth, on exhibition, brought in $1,500 a week, even though the tiny pipe-smoking woman was described by the press as a "loathsome old wench" and "an animated mummy." But she could tell stories of the Washington family and sing old Baptist hymns, and the public loved her.

After her New York appearance, Barnum took her on tour. When attendance dropped off in Boston, Barnum engaged in a clever bit of humbug. He planted a letter in the paper intimating that Heth was not human but a robot of "whalebone, india rubber, and numberless springs, ingeniously put together and made to move at the slightest touch, according to the will of the operator." Her voice? A ventriloquist. Curious about the truth of the letter's allegation, people came in droves to see the old lady, who turned out to be all too real: she died in 1836.

Surgeon David L. Rogers, who did an autopsy on her, stated that she could not have been more than eighty because there was no ossification in the arteries near her heart. In an editorial, the *New York Sun* vilified Barnum for the hoax. Had he known that the bill of sale was false? The question remains unanswered.

Lyman then told James Gordon Bennett of the *New York Herald* that the autopsied body had belonged to one Aunt Nelly, not Heth at all. The *Herald* published the story. Bennett, later realizing he had been taken, asked for the true story, so Lyman told him Barnum had found Heth in Kentucky, had her teeth pulled to make her look older, and rehearsed her in the Washington story. Bennett, hoodwinked for the second time, published the story.

The Fee-Jee Mermaid

The mermaid that Moses Kimball of the Boston Museum bought from a sailor in 1842 had a colorful history. The sailor's father had found the mermaid in Calcutta in 1817; he claimed that she had been captured off the coast of Japan in 1817. She was not beautiful: Her body was scaly and fishlike, her head and hands humanoid. Barnum, who adored the grotesque, described her ecstatically: "The animal was an ugly, dried-up, black-looking, and diminutive specimen, about three feet long. Its mouth was open, its tail turned over, and its arms thrown up, giving it the appearance of having died in great agony."

Kimball offered to lease the mermaid to Barnum, who agreed eagerly and proceeded to develop a scheme for selling her to the public. In the summer of 1842, letters from southern papers (behind-the-scenes Barnum setups) began to appear in the New York papers. They described a mermaid brought to the United States by a London naturalist, Dr. Griffin, who was, of all people, our old friend Levi Lyman. Once in New York, however, Griffin refused to exhibit the mermaid, saying he did not want to do so anywhere but London. Barnum ordered three woodcuts of romantic mermaid scenes and offered them to the papers, claiming that they were worthless because Griffin (Lyman) refused to display his half-and-half protégé. On July 17, 1842, editors printed the woodcuts and Barnum distributed a penny pamphlet on the authenticity of mermaids. Finally, supposedly egged on by scientists, Griffin agreed to a one-week exhibit of the Fee-Jee Mermaid at Concert Hall for an admission of twenty-five cents. It was a grand success, grossing over $1,000 a week. After that the mermaid found her way to the American Museum, owned by Barnum, and receipts tripled.

Ivy Island Reapppears

Scudder's American Museum, at the corner of New York's Broadway and Ann streets, was for sale and Barnum wanted it. One problem: He lacked credit. The owner of the building, Francis Olmsted, said he would give credit to Barnum only if he could put up unencumbered real estate. All Barnum had of that description was Ivy Island, and Olmsted, not knowing what it was like, was only too happy to accept it. After many machinations, Barnum ended up owning the museum.

Clock Company—Barnum Meets His Match

Barnum hoped to build a city in his hometown of Bridgeport, Connecticut. Part of his plan was to attract industry to the area. In 1855, the owners of Jerome Clock Company intimated that they might be induced to move to Bridgeport if Barnum would extend a loan to offset temporary setbacks. Barnum obliged and, $60,000 later, went bankrupt.

White Elephant

Barnum bought a white elephant which turned out to be gray. He said it was a "technical white elephant, as white as the Lord makes 'em." Competitor Adam Forepaugh had a white elephant, too. Its name was "Light of Asia," and it had been whitewashed. Even so, it was more popular than Barnum's authentic elephant.

Egress

On Saint Patrick's Day, crowds of people jammed the American Museum, and the sale of tickets had to be stopped. Barnum erected a sign saying "To the Egress" over a door leading to the outside. People, thinking it was an animal that they hadn't seen, exited.

Barnum did *not* say "There's a sucker born every minute." He *did* say "The American people like to be humbugged" and "The bigger the humbug, the better the people will like it." Yet, strangely, his own reaction to being humbugged belied his estimate of human response to trickery.

The Origin of Tarzan: It All Started . . .

THE LEAD STORY for the October 1912 issue of *All-Story Magazine* was "Tarzan of the Apes—a Romance of the Jungle." Pictured on the cover was the handsome, muscular Ape Man whose powerful right arm was locked around the neck of a gargantuan lion, while his left hand held a dagger poised and ready to strike. The success of the article led to a book, and for the next thirty-five years author Edgar Rice Burroughs turned out an entire library of Tarzan books—twenty-eight in all.

Where did Burroughs get the idea for Tarzan? Since so many people were curious about Tarzan's origins, Burroughs tried to give them an honest answer. In a letter to Rudolph Altrocchi, a professor of Italian at the University of California who was on a literary search for the "folkloristic and narrative motifs" of Tarzan, Burroughs wrote: "I have tried to search my memory for some clue to the suggestions that gave me the idea, and as close as I can come to it, I believe that it may have originated in my interest in mythology and the story of Romulus and Remus [the twin brothers who were suckled by a she-wolf and founded Rome]. I also recall having read many years ago the story of the sailor who was shipwrecked on the coast of Africa and who was adopted by and consorted with great apes to such an extent that when he was rescued a she-ape followed him into the surf and threw a baby after him. Then, of course, I read Kipling, so that it probably was a combination of all these that suggested the Tarzan idea to me. The fundamental idea is, of course, much older than Mowgli [the boy who lived with wild animals in Rudyard Kipling's *The Jungle Book*] or the story of the sailor, and probably antedates even Romulus and Remus, so that after all there is nothing new or remarkable about it. I am sorry that I cannot tell a more interesting story concerning the origin of Tarzan."

But in 1932, Burroughs concocted an origins story that more than made up for Tarzan's lackluster beginnings. However, this tale was not about a fictional character, it was about Burroughs himself. The autobiographical sketch was outrageous, preposterous, hilarious—and hardly a phrase in it was true. Perhaps he wrote it to suggest jokingly that his adventure ideas and characters such as Tarzan could have been inspired from his vast "personal experience." Perhaps he was simply trying to fend off questions and have some fun.

Edgar Rice Burroughs, Fiction Writer:
AN AUTOBIOGRAPHICAL SKETCH*

I am sorry that I have not led a more exciting existence so that I might offer a more interesting biographical sketch, but I am one of those fellows who has few adventures and always gets to the fire after it is out.

I was born in Peking at the time that my father was military advisor to the Empress of China and lived there, in the Forbidden City, until I was ten years old. An intimate knowledge of the Chinese language acquired during these years has often stood me in good stead since, especially in prosecuting two of my favorite studies, Chinese philosophy and Chinese ceramics.

Shortly after the family returned to the United States, I was kidnapped by gypsies and held by them for almost three years. They were not unkind to me, and in many respects the life appealed to me, but eventually I escaped and returned to my parents.

Even today, after the lapse of many years, I distinctly recall the storm-torn night of my escape. Pedro, the king of the gypsies, always kept me in his tent at night where he and his wife could guard me. He was a very light sleeper, which had always presented a most effective obstacle to my eluding the clutches of my captors.

*Edgar Rice Burroughs, *An Autobiographical Sketch*, used by permission of Edgar Rice Burroughs, Inc. © 1975 Edgar Rice Burroughs, Inc.

This night the rain and the wind and thunder aided me. Waiting until Pedro and his wife were asleep, I started to crawl toward the tent flap. As I passed close beside the king, one of my hands fell upon a hard metal object lying beside him; it was Pedro's dagger. At the same instant, Pedro awoke. A vivid lightning flash illuminated the interior of the tent, and I saw Pedro's eyes fixed upon me.

Perhaps fright motivated me, or perhaps it was just anger against my abductors. My fingers closed upon the hilt of his dagger, and in the darkness that followed the lightning, I plunged the slim steel blade deep into his heart. He was the first man I had ever killed; he died without a sound.

My parents were rejoiced by my return, as they had long since abandoned all hope of ever seeing me again. For a year we traveled in Europe, where, under a tutor, I pursued my interrupted education to such good effect that I was able to enter Yale upon our return.

While at Yale I won a few athletic honors, annexing both the heavyweight boxing and wrestling championships, and in my senior year I captained the football team and the crew. Graduating summa cum laude, I spent two years at Oxford and then returned to the United States and enlisted in the army for a commission from the ranks.

At the end of two years, I received my appointment as a second lieutenant and was attached to the Seventh Cavalry. My first active service was with Custer at the battle of the Little Bighorn, of which I was the sole survivor.

My escape from death during the massacre was almost miraculous. My horse had been shot from under me, and I was fighting on foot with the remnant of my troop. I can only guess at what actually occurred, but I believe the bullet that struck me in the head must have passed through the head of a man in front of me and, with its force spent, merely stunned me.

I fell with my body between two small boulders. Later, a horse was shot above me, its body falling on top of mine and concealing me from the eyes of the enemy, the two boulders preventing its weight from crushing me. Gaining consciousness after dark, I crawled from beneath the horse and made my escape.

After wandering for six weeks in an effort to elude the Indians and rejoin my own people, I reached an army post, but when I attempted to rejoin my regiment, I was told that I was dead. Insistence upon my rights resulted in my being arrested for impersonating an officer.

Every member of the court knew me and deeply deplored the action they were compelled to take. But I was officially dead, and army regulations are army regulations. I took the matter to Congress but had no better success there. Finally, I was compelled to change my name, adopting that which I now use, and start life all over again.

For several years I fought Apaches in Arizona; but the monotony of it palled upon me, and I was overjoyed when I received a telegram from the late Henry M. Stanley inviting me to join his expedition to Africa in search of Dr. Livingstone.

I accepted immediately and also put $500,000 at his disposal, with the understanding that my name and my connection with the expedition was not to be divulged, as I have always shrunk from publicity.

Shortly after entering Africa, I became separated from the relief party and was captured by Tippoo Tib's Arabs. The night that they were going to put me to death

I escaped, but a week later I fell into the hands of a tribe of cannibals. My long golden hair and my flowing mustache and beard of the same hue filled them with such awe that they accorded me the fearful deference they reserved for their primitive gods and demons.

They offered me no harm but kept me a prisoner among them for three years. They also kept in captivity several large anthropoid apes of a species which I believe is entirely unknown to science. These animals were of huge size and of great intelligence. During my captivity I learned their language, which was to stand me in such good stead when I decided, many years later, to record some of my experiences in the form of fiction.

I finally escaped from the cannibal village and made my way to the coast, where, penniless and friendless, I shipped before the mast on a windjammer bound for China. Wrecked off the coast of Asia, I eventually made my way over-land to Russia, where I enlisted in the imperial cavalry. A year later it happened to be my good fortune to kill an anarchist as he was attempting the assassination of the czar; for this service I was made a captain and attached to the imperial bodyguard.

It was while in his majesty's service that I met my wife, a lady-in-waiting to the czarina. When, shortly after we were married, my grandfather died and left me eight million dollars, we decided to come to America to live.

With my wife's fortune and mine, it was unnecessary for me to work. But I could not be idle, so I took up writing, more as a pastime than as a vocation.

We lived in Chicago for some years and then came to Southern California, where we have lived for more than thirteen years at that now famous watering place, Tarzana.

We have eleven children, seventeen grandchildren, and three great-grandchildren.

I have tasted fame—it is nothing. I find my greatest happiness in being alone with my violin.

2. *Obvious Connections*

Why didn't someone think of that before? Perhaps, as in the case of George Bernard Shaw's great obsession, someone had, but the idea didn't work. Others did not have the genius to transform the mundane into a splendid epic, as did Dante. Buckminster Fuller saw the obvious advantages of a shape that every kindergartner knows, but his mind was original enough to put it to new uses.

Woody Guthrie directly translated his feelings about a terrifying phenomenon of nature into art, while Alfred Hitchcock's frightening childhood experience provided the impetus for his horror films. The inspiration for Robert Louis Stevenson's *Treasure Island* was what you might imagine it to be, and Lewis Carroll's inspiration for some of the fantastic experiences in *Alice in Wonderland* came from a far more literal event than you might expect. You never know, even when it stares you in the face . . .

Woody Guthrie Recalls the Wall of Dust

ONE hot Sunday afternoon in April 1935, a huge curtain of darkness, lit by weird specks of red, came sweeping toward the town of Pampas, Texas. A scourge of thousands of tons of dust, carried on high winds across immense prairies, sifted dust over everything—oil derricks and refineries, houses, people, and animals. It was so awesome that many people thought Judgment Day had come. Others, choking into wet washcloths, feared the devastation of their land—topsoil from northern fields, now became dust that lay on everything like a thick, murderous blanket. For forty-five minutes it was as dark as in an eclipse of the sun. The temperature fell fifty degrees. The humidity dropped below 10 percent. The "Great Dust Storm," as it came to be known, continued for another day before it abated and people could shovel out their houses. It was their worst experience with the Depression dust storms that were to destroy them.

Woody Guthrie, a twenty-three-year-old soda jerk, already trapped in marriage and Pampas, was astonished and angered at the devastation. He was so upset that he felt compelled to put his thoughts into song. "Dusty Old Dust" was one of his first folk ballads of protest. Using the melody from Carson Robinson's "Ballad of Billy the Kid," he composed new verses and added a chorus tune. The verses ridiculed the townspeople—the religious who awaited the end of the world, the shopkeepers who expected to make a profit on it, even Preacher MacKenzie who would "fold up his specs, put down his text, and take up a collection." The chorus was, "So long, it's been good to know you."

Woody later wrote in his autobiography, *Bound for Glory*, "And there on the Texas plains right in the dead center of the dust bowl, with the oil boom over and the wheat blowed out and the hard-working people just stumbling about, bothered with mortgages, debts, bills, sickness, worries of every blowing kind, I seen there was plenty to make up songs about . . . at first it was funny songs of what all's wrong, and how it turned out good or bad. Then I got a little braver and made up songs telling what I thought was wrong and how to make it right, songs that said what everybody in that country was thinking."

The last line of the chorus contained a central truth of his life: he was a drifter. He drifted in and out of Pampas for quite awhile. Often he would come home from a night of drinking, singing "Dusty Old Dust." He talked to people who left Highway 66, not far from town, looking for work or handouts. They told him of the promised land of the West and the jobs that waited there. In his guitar hole he kept matchbook covers from places that intrigued him. His curly hair grew longer and bushier, his baths were less frequent, and his relationship with his young wife grew more strained.

He did not have to move out of town in order to make a living. The Corncob Trio with which he continued to play was fairly successful; he made money as a soda jerk; and he had two good businesses on the side as a faith healer and a signpainter. His sign "He brought home the bacon, but the wrong kind" for the Cudahy Company even brought him a job offer, but he turned it down.

Finally, he decided he had had enough. Tucking his paint brushes into his back pocket, he took off for California, playing hobo on the freights and thumbing rides on the roads. It was worth it, he realized, when he came to California—"The world turned into such a thick garden of fruits and vegetables that I didn't know if I was dreaming or not. Coming out of the dustbowl, the colors so bright and smells so thick all around, that it seemed almost too good to be true."

Traveling over the country, hat on the back of his head, he sang to the sound of his guitar in the Hoovervilles to oilmen and migrant workers, to hoboes on the freights. As he later wrote, "Everywhere I went I throwed my hat down on the floor and sung for my tips." His fame began to grow. He sang for radio shows and counted among his friends Burl Ives, Pete Seeger, Will Geer, Leadbelly, and Stan Lomax.

But his early experiences never escaped him; they permeated all of his works. He wrote "Dust Bowl Refugees," "The Dust Pneumonia Blues," and "Dust Can't Kill Me."

They marked the beginning of a life of fame which saw him renowned for his protest songs and radical politics. His three marriages failed, and he suffered from the tragic disease of Huntington's chorea. Through it all, he never forgot that terrible curtain of dust.

The Writing of Treasure Island

A MASTER of the adventure story, Robert Louis Stevenson loved the world of make-believe and never outgrew his enthusiasm for toys and games. At seventeen the Scottish author still enjoyed building houses out of toy bricks. At thirty-one he invented an elaborate but excitingly addictive war game—complete with popguns (that shot printers' "ems") and a full array of toy soldiers.

On a rainy day in September 1881, Stevenson, in an attempt to entertain his thirteen-year-old stepson, painted a watercolor map of an imaginary island. Whimsically, it looked "like a fat dragon standing up," and the artist quickly played upon that idea by adding names such as "Spyeglass Hill," "Cape of Ye Woods," and "Houtbowline Head."

That map generated one of his most famous books. He later recalled: "It was elaborately and (I thought) beautifully colored: the shape of it took my fancy beyond expression; it contained harbors that pleased me like sonnets; and with the unconsciousness of the predestined, I ticketed my performance *Treasure Island*. . . . As I pored over my map of Treasure Island, the future characters of the book began to appear there visibly among imaginary woods; and their brown faces and bright weapons peeped out upon me from unexpected quarters, as they passed to and fro, fighting and hunting treasure. The next thing I knew I had some paper before me and was writing out a list of chapters."

Bucky and the Geodesic Dome

THE GEODESIC DOME had its beginnings in 1899 when inventor R. Buckminster Fuller was in kindergarten. The young boy was already far-sighted and cross-eyed, and according to Fuller's recollections:

One of my first days at kindergarten the teacher brought us some toothpicks and semidried peas and told us to make structures. The other children, who had good eyes, were familiar with houses and barns; with my bad sight, I was used to seeing only bulks—I had no feeling at all about structural lines. Because I couldn't see, I naturally had recourse to my other senses which were very sensitive. When the teacher told me to make structures, I tried to make something that would work.

Pushing and pulling, I found that a triangle held its shape when nothing else did. The other children made rectangular structures that seemed to stand up because the peas held them in shape. Meanwhile, after pushing and pulling, the triangle I made felt good.

The teacher called all the other teachers in the primary school as well as the kindergarten to look at this triangular structure. I remember being surprised that they were surprised. I began to feel then that all nature's structuring and patterning must be based on triangles.

Many years later his belief that the triangle was nature's most stable shape would manifest itself in the geodesic dome, a structure that has become Fuller's widely recognized trademark.

"Bucky" Fuller has been showered with a flattering assortment of titles: inventor, architect, author, mathematician, scientist, cartographer, engineer, environmentalist, philosopher, poet, educator, and world planner. One Fuller devotee states that Fuller is "as widely respected and loved internationally as Leonardo, Beethoven, or Santa Claus"; another calls him the Robin Hood of planetary planning"; and yet one more of his many disciples says conclusively that Fuller's very state of being was "a historical event." All this praise was bestowed upon a man who never even finished his freshman year of college (he was expelled twice from Harvard), but had thirty-nine honorary degrees behind his name and twenty books to his credit.

The title Fuller most preferred, "comprehensivist," is indicative of his philosophy as well as his accomplishments. While the geodesic dome was his most commercial success, he also invented Dymaxion House, a 4-D single-unit hexagonal dwelling hung from a central mast; Dymaxion Car, a three-wheeled streamlined vehicle steered from the rear wheel, which seated eleven people and got forty miles to a gallon of gasoline; and the Dymaxion Airocean World Map, a map that showed round earth as a flat surface with no negligible distortion. (Dymaxion comes from the words dynamic, maximum, and ions. It means "doing more with less.")

An optimist as well as a visionary, Fuller dedicated his life to the attainment of his basic goal/philosophy that human beings have the capability to live in total harmony, and that if all the nations of the world cooperated to use available technology, competition for survival of the fittest would be erased from the planet and war, starvation, and poverty would cease to exist. As he claimed, "Our only real problems are ignorance, fear, and greed. The rulers and the ruled are both largely unaware of the actual facts of our resources and our options."

While Fuller's philosophy is theoretically simple, its meaning is sometimes obscured by the new jargon ("Fullerese") that he invented. From "Dymaxion" to "tensegrity" (tensional integrity) to "chronofile" (Fuller's collective body of personal documents), Bucky's language amazed and intrigued his audiences, even though it also puzzled them. He lectured extensively, and before he died in July 1983, at age eighty-seven, his "toings and froings" added up to enough miles to cover the world forty-eight times. No matter where he traveled, the master designer was always asked about his geodesic dome—for there are more than 300,000 of them, on every continent on earth.

A spherical structure based on the triangle, the geodesic dome has no internal supports, can enclose unlimited spaces, and is incredibly stable. This simple, efficient, practical, economical, transportable dome is also graceful and beautiful. While Fuller had built some small domes in 1947–1948, his lucky break didn't occur until 1953 when the Ford Motor Company commissioned him to build a geodesic dome over its new rotunda office building at its plant in Dearborn, Michigan. Bucky accepted the challenge and constructed an 8½-ton aluminum dome (a conventional steel dome would have weighed 160 tons), 93 feet in diameter. Covered with a transparent fiberglass skin, the dome weighed 2½ pounds for each square foot of floor covered.

The Ford rotunda dome sparked a "dome boom" that was to last throughout the late 1950s and early 1960s. Bucky's domes became bigger and bigger as they sprouted up around the world. Four of the most notable:

Kabul, Afghanistan (1956)

Exactly 100 feet in diameter and 35 feet high, the aluminum dome covered the United States Pavilion at the International Trade Fair. Wrapped in white sailcloth, the structure was assembled by unskilled workers using a color-coding system in forty-eight hours. The Afghans were particularly enthusiastic about the dome since they regarded it as a modern-day adaptation of the Mongolian yurt (tent).

Honolulu, Hawaii (1957)

Henry J. Kaiser, owner of the Kaiser Aluminum Company, hired Fuller to build a concert auditorium at Hawaiian Village, his hotel complex in Honolulu. As soon as the parts were shipped in from Oakland, California, Bucky began to assemble the dome. Within a short twenty-two hours it was completed, and an audience of 1,800 persons (the hall's capacity was 2,000) was seated for a concert performed by the Hawaiian Symphony Orchestra. The dome, a 145-footer, had excellent acoustics. (As soon as Henry Kaiser heard that work on the dome was in progress, he quickly boarded a plane for Honolulu. By the time he arrived, the building was completed—even the concert was over.)

Moscow, U.S.S.R. (1959)

A 200-foot-diameter, gold anodized dome was erected by Kaiser Aluminum for the American Exchange Exhibition. It was in the dome's General Electric and Whirlpool kitchens that Vice-President Richard Nixon and Premier Nikita Khrushchev engaged in their famed "kitchen debate." Despite Soviet-American hostilities, Khrushchev was very impressed with the geodesic dome and supposedly said, "I want Mr. J. Buckingham [sic] Fuller to come to the Soviet Union to teach our engineers."

Montreal, Quebec, Canada (1967)

Built for Expo '67, this is the "Taj Mahal" of the geodesics. As tall as a twenty-story building, the American Pavilion was 250 feet across. A three-quarters steel sphere, designed by Fuller and Japanese architect Shoji Sodao, the dome did not have a whole plastic skin but was made up of thousands of individual plexiglass hexagons. Controlled by motors which were linked to a computer, the hexagons opened and closed to conform to weather conditions.

In addition to their exhibition popularity and recreational appeal (vacation homes, movie theaters, children's "playdomes"), Bucky's domes were in great demand by the United States Air Force. The 1950s Cold War and the fear of nuclear attack led to the building of geodesic radar stations along the Arctic Circle's Distant Early Warning Line. The "radomes," made of plastic and fiberglass, could withstand 150 mph winds and could be assembled in less than twenty-four hours. The success of the radomes paved the way for another large government order—this time from the Marine Corps. Lured by the dome's lightweight and transportable features, the Marines bought more than 300 domes. One colonel praised the structures as "the first major improvement in mobile military shelters in 2,600 years."

A Headache in Wonderland

MANY of Alice's adventures in Wonderland were the direct result of Lewis Carroll's migraine headaches. As all avid readers of the classic story will recall, Alice's body often grows larger or shrinks—after drinking a mysterious potion, eating a small cake, or nibbling on a fresh mushroom. Her first "size experience" occurs shortly after she falls into the rabbit hole, slips into Wonderland, and imbibes from a pretty bottle labeled "Drink Me":

"What a curious feeling!" said Alice. "I must be shutting up like a telescope!" And so it was indeed: she was now only ten inches high, and her face brightened up at the thought that she was now the right size for going through the little door into that lovely garden. First, however, she waited for a few minutes to see if she was going to shrink any further. . . .

A little later Alice finds a beautiful glass box which contains a cake with the words "Eat Me"—written in currants. She follows instructions, and soon her body again begins to change. Only this time she grows much larger:

"Curiouser and curiouser!" cried Alice. (She was so surprised that for the moment she quite forgot how to speak good English.) "Now I'm opening out like the largest telescope that ever was! Good-bye, feet!" (For when she looked down at her feet, they seemed to be almost out of sight, they were getting so far off.) "Oh, my poor little feet. I wonder who will put on your shoes and stockings for you now, dears? I'm sure I shan't be able! I shall be a great deal too far off to trouble myself about you." . . . Just at this moment her head struck against the roof of the hall; in fact, she was now rather more than nine feet high. . . . Poor Alice!

Lewis Carroll suffered from "classical" migraine headaches, the most complex and dramatic type of migraine. They usually occur in two stages: 1) the painless premonitory, or "aura," stage which manifests itself in hallucinations, and 2) the throbbing headache stage that can be accompanied by loss of appetite, dizziness, fever, nausea, and vomiting. It was the aura stage that suggested some of the bizarre incidents that appeared in *Alice's Adventures in Wonderland* and *Through the Looking-Glass*.

People or objects growing bigger or shrinking are just two of the many visual distortions that can occur in an aura migraine. Other fantastic sensory hallucinations include everything from flashing or whirling lights, shooting stars, and revolving multicolored circles to loss of hearing and strange tastes or smells. One common occurrence is a scintillating scotoma—a blind or blank spot in a person's visual field that is partly encased by a pattern of bright, moving (scintillating) lines. In *Through the Looking-Glass*, Alice undergoes this phenomenon:

> The shop seemed to be full of all manner of curious things—but the oddest part of it all was that whenever she looked hard at any shelf, to make out exactly what it had on it, that particular shelf was always quite empty, though the others around it were crowded as full as they could hold. "Things flow about so here!" she said at last in a plaintive tone, after she had spent a minute or so in vainly pursuing a large bright thing that looked sometimes like a doll and sometimes like a workbox, and was always in a shelf next above the one she was looking at.

Lewis Carroll was only one of many history makers who suffered from migraine headaches; some endured the less prevalent classical type while many more battled the "common" migraine. A few of the notables include Sir James Barrie, Alexander Graham Bell, Frederic Chopin, Charles Darwin, George Eliot, Sigmund Freud, Ulysses S. Grant, Thomas Jefferson, Immanuel Kant, Friedrich Nietzsche, Edgar Allan Poe, and Virginia Woolf. It is tempting to speculate what, if any, influence the migraines had on the achievements of this illustrious group.

Alfred Hitchcock: Fear Begets Fear

A REPORTER once queried Alfred Hitchcock: "You never watch your films with an audience. Don't you miss hearing them scream?" Hitchcock replied, "No. I can hear them when I'm making the picture."

For more the fifty years Hitchcock, the self-proclaimed "poet of civilized suspense," kept moviegoers bolted to their seats—eyes bulging, hands sweaty and trembling, hearts beating fast—as they waited, almost begging, to be scared. Who can forget the shower scene in *Psycho* in which Janet Leigh is repeatedly stabbed by a pyschopath? Or Cary Grant running for his life across an Illinois cornfield as a crop-dusting biplane dives down to kill him (*North by Northwest*)? Or Tippi Hedren in *The Birds*, trapped in an attic room, being attacked by hundreds of birds? (To achieve the desired effect, some seagulls were tied to Hedren's arms and legs. One almost clawed out her eye, and the actress ran screaming from the set.)

Alfred Hitchcock was a shy, very private family man who lived in the shadow of his own inescapable fears. Reporters and film critics fascinated by an anxiety-ridden genius making anxiety-producing films never ceased to probe for significant correlations. What did he fear and why? Did the fears stem from his childhood? Though he often tired of the endless attempts at analysis, Hitchcock always provided answers. Yes, he admitted, he was afraid of many things: heights, small children, closed spaces, open spaces, driving a car, and authority figures such as police, teachers, and church officials. When discussing his feelings about the police or his religious background, Hitchcock was particularly candid. Born the son of a London greengrocer, Hitchcock had a terrifying boyhood experience with the police when his father, for some inexplicable reason, gave him a note to deliver to the local police station. As Hitch told it: "I must have been five when I was sent along with a note to the chief of police, who read the note, promptly put me into a cell, and locked the door for five minutes. Then he let me out, saying, 'That's what we do to naughty little boys, you see.' "

The terror of being accused of wrongdoing, especially by police authorities, is why Hitchcock never got behind the wheel of an automobile. He said, "I won't drive a car for fear I will get a ticket. The thought that if I drove I would face that possibility day after day frightens me horribly, for I can't bear suspense." However, even the sanctuary of the back seat of a car did not free him from anxiety. On one occasion, while riding in a car en route to a business meeting in northern California, he threw a cigar butt out the window. A few seconds later he became highly agitated because he wasn't sure that the butt was fully extinguished. It took hours to convince him that his crime had gone undetected.

Hitch's police and incarceration paranoia are evident in many of his films, especially in *The Wrong Man*, starring Henry Fonda, in which a nightclub musician is falsely accused of robbery. It was one of his favorite films, and in an interview with fellow director Peter Bogdanovich, he explained why: "I enjoyed making this film because, after all, this is my greatest fear—fear of the police. And I had all of that going for me. I've often thought of a scene in which a man, being taken to jail in England in what they used to call the Black Maria, was able to see out the grille window at the back all the things people were doing. . . . And this man, on his way to jail for probably ten or fifteen years, got a kind of last glimpse of everyday life. . . . I liked the climax when the right man was discovered, while the wrong man was praying to the picture on the wall. I liked the ironic coincidence."

Any religious overtones in Hitchcock films were usually intentional and were linked to his very strict, very proper, Roman Catholic upbringing. Educated at Catholic schools, Hitchcock was a plump, lonely child, always more of an observer than a participant. Above all, he did his best to obey the rules no matter how unfair or distressing—such as drinking a laxative dissolved in tea every night to purge all physical and moral ills. His memories of one Jesuit boarding school, St. Ignatius in London, were particularly vivid. He once told French director François Truffaut, "It was probably during this period with the Jesuits that a strong sense of fear developed—moral fear—the fear of being involved in anything evil. I always tried to avoid it."

On vacation in Rome in the early 1970s, Hitchcock had the opportunity to schedule a special audience with the Pope. Even though he was still a churchgoing Catholic, he declined, confiding to a friend that he was not willing to take the chance that the pontiff might criticize the sex and violence in his films. Perhaps the most revealing picture of Hitchcock's religious attitudes is given by his official biographer John Russell Taylor. In *Hitch: The Life and Times of Alfred Hitchcock*, Taylor tells of the director and a friend driving through the streets of a city in Switzerland: "He [Hitchcock] surprised his companion in the car by suddenly saying, 'That is the most frightening sight I have ever seen,' and pointing to a little boy walking past with a priest who had his hand on his shoulder and was talking seriously to him. Hitch leaned out of the car and called, 'Run, little boy, run for your life.' "

Despite his acknowledged neurotic tendencies, Hitchcock was not an unhappy man. He took great pride in the fifty-three films to his credit and graciously accepted the many honors and awards which were heaped upon him. A man of refined tastes and good manners, he also possessed a robust—though sometimes bizarre—sense of humor. Married to the same woman, Alma Reville Hitchcock (a film editor and screenwriter) for fifty-three years, and the father of one daughter, Hitchcock had a home life that was secure, comfortable, and modest by Hollywood standards. By the time he died in 1980 at the age of eighty, his rotund profile (290 pounds in a five-foot five-inch frame) was as recognizable worldwide as were his films.

Shaw, Pygmalion, and the Alphabet

CAN a middle-aged phonetics professor transform a Cockney flower girl into a woman of refined manners and impeccable speech? George Bernard Shaw believed it could be done and stated his case—convincingly and humorously—in his 1913 play *Pygmalion*, the most successful of his fifty-two plays. Though now remembered most vividly in its reincarnation as the musical comedy *My Fair Lady*, the play *Pygmalion* was meant to be a didactic play about phonetics. Shaw didn't mind that audiences enjoyed the love triangle of Eliza Doolittle, Professor Henry Higgins, and Freddy Enysford Hill, but it was not the heart of his play and, in fact, had nothing to do with the way the play was conceived.

The inspiration for the play, Shaw's advocacy of a new phonetic alphabet, was not a mere passing interest. Since his early twenties Shaw had spoken out on the shortcomings of the English language: "The English have no respect for their language. . . . It is impossible for an Englishman to open his mouth without making some other Englishman hate or despise him. German and Spanish are accessible to foreigners. English is not accessible even to Englishmen. The reformer England needs today is an energetic phonetic enthusiast. That is why I have made such a one the hero of a popular play."

Shaw supported the "alphabet revolution" so passionately that he left the bulk of his million-dollar estate to any group that would devise a utilitarian alphabet—one that would save time, effort, and money. The bequest shocked and irritated some of his friends and contemporaries. Even if a suitable alphabet were devised, his critics insisted, persuading the English-speaking world to learn and use a new system of reading and writing was impossible.

The playwright's interest in alternative alphabets reached back to the

1870s. While living in Dublin, where he was born, a teenage Shaw mastered Pitman shorthand in six weeks. In subsequent years he reviewed several other shorthand systems, including Current shorthand, the brainchild of Oxford phonetician Henry Sweet (who may have been the model for Henry Higgins), but he always used Pitman's phonetic alphabet when writing his routine 1,500 words a day. He was also greatly impressed by "Visible Speech," a language devised by Alexander Melville Bell, the father of the telephone inventor. Bell's alphabet was based on a set of printed symbols that showed how to position the tongue and shape the lips to make various sounds. For example, the symbol for the sound *m* indicated "closed lips, voice passed through nose." (It was Visible Speech that Professor Higgins taught Eliza in *Pygmalion.*)

The English alphabet, said Shaw, is too terribly inefficient and inadequate. How ridiculous that a language with about forty phonemes (meaningful speech-sounds) has only twenty-six letters to express them—and some of those letters, like *x*, are greatly underworked compared to other overused letters. Why didn't letters with similar shapes, like *E* and *F*, represent similar instead of different sounds? And then there was the question of spelling; correctly pronouncing an English word doesn't necessarily lead to correctly spelling it. Shaw, a poor speller who hated to use a dictionary, was particularly bothered by the presence of silent letters. He vehemently complained: "As to spelling the very frequent word *though* with six letters instead of two, it is impossible to discuss it, as it is outside the range of common sanity."

While Shaw never had the time nor the inclination to develop an alphabet on his own, he made a determined effort to find a creator, or creators, before he died. In 1944, he wrote a lengthy, detailed letter to a number of government departments, colleges, trusts, and other private and public organizations, and offered to leave a large sum of money ("including certain copyrights, the value of which may run into six figures") to whichever group would develop what he called the "Proposed British Alphabet." When no one volunteered for the project, Shaw was discouraged, but nevertheless he made out a will that provided ample funds to any group that might later step forward and accept the challenge. However, the will did have some stipulations. Among them were: that the alphabet should have at least forty letters, sixteen of them vowels; that the language should be written without using groups of letters to indicate single sounds; that a phonetic expert use the Proposed British Alphabet to transliterate his play *Androcles and the Lion.*

Shaw died in 1950, and a seven-year fight over the will ensued. When the dust had cleared, Mr. Justice Harman of the chancery division of the High Court of Justice in England declared the alphabet bequest invalid, mostly due to the absence of a definite beneficiary. Since no predetermined group was named, the bequest had to qualify as a "charity" in order to be legal.

Shaw suspected that there might be trouble with his alphabet will, so he included a clause in the document which stated that if the trusts were not upheld, then the money should be equally divided among the National Gallery of Ireland, the British Museum, and the Royal Academy of Dramatic Art. Harman's decision was appealed, but before a decision was reached, the three institutions negotiated a compromise settlement of £8,300 (about $25,000) that was designated to carry out Shaw's wishes and at least begin the alphabet revolution.

Since $25,000 was hardly enough to finance a revolution, Shaw's alphabet supporters could do nothing more but sponsor a contest, offering a prize of £500 (about $1,400) for the development of a new alphabet. Of the 467 entries, none was singularly outstanding, but four contestants did invent praiseworthy systems. The prize money was therefore divided among those four contestants, and the Public Trustee of Shaw's will appointed a phonetics expert to take the best features of the four alphabets and reconstruct them into one that would fulfill Shaw's vision. In 1962, twelve years after Shaw's death, the task was finally accomplished with the publication of *Androcles and the Lion—Printed in the Shaw Alphabet with a Parallel Transcription in Traditional Orthography.*

In the preface of the special alphabet edition of the play, James Pitman of the House of Commons points out the advantages of the new alphabet. First of all, he claims, "the alphabet is both more legible and one-third more economical in space than traditional printing, and this should lead to a great increase in reading speed." Added to this, he promises an increase in writing speed. Shaw alphabet advocates claim that the average person using the system will read 50 to 75 percent faster and will write 80 to 100 percent faster.

George Bernard Shaw, true to his Socialist beliefs, hoped that his new alphabet would help to reduce the working hours of the laboring classes. In addition, he believed his plan was ecologically wise because a writing system that consumed less space would require less paper, which in turn would save millions of trees. Most important, he believed that the phonetic alphabet would help to eliminate "class distinction" in speech. As he said, "For the encouragement of people troubled with accents that cut them off from all high employment, I may add that the change wrought by Professor Higgins in the flowergirl is neither impossible nor uncommon."

Dante's Inspirations: It Wasn't All Beatrice

WHILE the works of the poet Dante are considered some of the most lyrical and imaginative writings in Western civilization, his sources for inspiration were often surprisingly commonplace. For example, consider these three inspirations for *The Divine Comedy*, which he completed in 1321.

When Dante visited Venice, he was not impressed with the town, for it was far cruder than his native Florence. The houses were huts and hovels made of wood, except for a few edifices like the half-finished palace of the doge and the campanile. The streets were swamps of mud and manure, and pigs rooted in the piazza.

One of the few sights that interested him was the Arsenal, the largest walled industrial complex in medieval Europe. It was a crowded, noisy workshop for ship building and repair, with dry docks, wet docks, rope and sail factories, all employing hundreds of workmen. A place of manufacture (which is what arsenal means in Arabic), the Arsenal was also a storage place for arms and ships. In one place all the parts of ships were manufactured, some of them standardized, a curiously modern arrangement centuries before the Industrial Revolution. Here Dante saw the tools to make sails, ropes, rigging, oars, spars—and vats of boiling pitch to caulk seams of damaged galleys.

Uninterested in the marvelous efficiency of this amazing place, Dante focused instead on the vats of steaming black pitch, which were eventually featured prominently in his poem, *The Divine Comedy*, at the entrance to the Inferno.

In the eighth circle of the Inferno, Dante and his guide, Virgil, move from bridge to bridge, through the darkening land. Then they come upon a lake of boiling pitch, which makes the bank sticky. There is nothing in it except slowly swelling and collapsing bubbles of tar. He describes it,

> As in the arsenal of the Venetians
> They boil in wintertime the sticky pitch
> Wherewith they do patch up their leaky vessels,
> For then they cannot sail and so instead

One builds a new ship while another caulks
The hull of one which has made many voyages;
One hammers at the prow, one at the stern;
One doth make oars, another splices rope;
One doth a foresail patch, the mainsail one,
So, not by fire, but by divine art,
A viscous tar did boil beneath me there.

Another inspiration stemmed from Dante's hometown of Florence. There housewives often had no place to cook, so they brought their meat and sausages to the public kitchens to be boiled in huge, steaming vats. Workers dripping with sweat, perhaps bare to the waist, used long iron hooks to push the pieces of meat under the infernally hot water when they bobbed up to the surface. This homely scene inspired the next lines of Dante's epic, in which a savage winged devil approaches Dante with a terrified sinner on his shoulder. As Virgil and Dante watch, the devil dumps the hapless creature into the boiling pitch. Demons refuse to let the sinner crawl out: "Then they bit into him with more than a hundred fleshhooks, saying, 'Here you have to dance under cover, to let you be secret, if you can, at your game of odd and even' . . . In just that way, cooks make their helpers push the meat down into the middle of the kettle with their hooks, to keep it from floating."

Florence also provides the source for another important scene. In the town, huge marble wells near the baptismal fonts at the Church of San Giovanni (John the Baptist) were once used by priests as places in which to stand while baptizing crowds. One day a child fell into one of the wells and could not escape. Dante, who was in the crowd near the church, took an ax and smashed the well to pieces, rescuing the poor child, Antonio di Baldinaccio de Caviccuili, who, ironically, was of a family which later persecuted Dante. And Dante was criticized for desecrating the "temple." Bitter, he got even in his poem. In Dante's Hell the punishment for simoniacs (those who buy or sell church office or privilege) is just such a marble well. He wrote,

I saw that on its sides and at the bottom
The ash-gray pit was filled of many a hole.
All of one size they were, and all were round,
Nor did they seem less wide to me, nor wider
Than those which in my beautiful San Giovanni
Fashioned had been to hold the baptizers.
And one of which not many years ago
I smashed to save one drowning in it.
That's the true story, let this clear all minds.

Moral: Great literature is often inspired by the mundane.

3. Visions and Voices

The stereotype of a visionary is a religious or spiritual leader transfixed, eyes heavenward, being visited by God or one of his emissaries. So it was with many in this chapter: Joseph Smith, Joan of Arc, Alfred Noyes, Wovoka, Billy Graham, Dorothy Day, Peter Maurin. Sometimes the visionary is an inventor such as King Gillette or a writer such as Harriet Beecher Stowe. But others far less saintly have also been so favored: Adolf Hitler and Nat Turner both had visions that inspired them to spill blood. Visitations come to the sane and insane, the good and the evil, the religious and profane.

Usually, visitations occur when the visited are alone. Billy Graham was on a solitary night walk on the golf course for both his revelations. Almost always, voices and visions come from above, not below.

Are visions and voices projections of the subconscious, a movie of the mind played out for an audience of one, its creator? Or are they "real," capable of being seen by anyone? These questions are in the laps of the psychologists. In any case, in some room of the mind or the real world, in a state of ecstasy, despair, or even lethargy, people experience visions. The visions can be startlingly graphic or simple. But the results are usually actions.

Visions of a Madman

ADOLF HITLER believed himself to be the savior of Germany, the man who would reshape Europe, and the architect of a new social order for the world. Guided by his unwavering belief in these missions, he was convinced that Providence had singled him out for greatness. Brought up a Catholic, he liked to refer to himself, in the words of Saint Matthew, "as a voice crying in the wilderness." His early years, in particular, were laced with out-of-this-world experiences—inner voices and inspirational visions which assured him that he was, indeed, a Chosen One.

Born in 1889 in Braunau, Austria, Hitler was the favorite child of his mother Klara, who showered him with praise and adoration. On the other hand, his father, Alois, a customs inspector, was a strict disciplinarian who beat young Adolf for even the smallest infraction of the rules. Except for his father's bursts of temper and the family's frequent uprooting to a new village, Adolf's early life was reasonably happy and similar to that of other Austrian farm boys. He spent the better part of the day in school, came home to a regular list of chores, and played at games of cowboys and Indians (he loved the works of James Fenimore Cooper).

In school at Lambach, the nine-year-old Adolf was a good student, a prankster, and often a leader. Endowed with an exceptional singing voice, he sang at the choir school of a nearby monastery. For a while the impressionable youngster dreamed of becoming a priest and liked to deliver sermons with a large kitchen apron draped around his shoulders. (At the monastery Adolf first saw a swastika, carved into a stone arch; it was part of the monastery's coat of arms.)

At age eleven Hitler entered a *Realschule* in Linz which was to prepare him for higher education. At first he had a difficult time: his grades, especially math and natural history, were failing; he was homesick; and his fellow classmates looked down on him because he was a country boy. However, the pale-faced, skinny lad soon pulled himself out of despair and once again became a masterful leader—though somewhat arrogant and tyrannical. As one of his classmates later recalled: "We all liked him, at desk and at play. He had guts. He wasn't a hothead but really more amenable than a good many. He exhibited two extremes of character which are not often seen in unison: He was a *quiet* fanatic."

Even though Adolf continued to have problems with most of his grades, he excelled in gymnastics and freehand drawing. Soon he became a music devotee (his mother bought him a grand piano) and a great fan of Wagner. He and his best friend, Gustl Kubizek, spent endless hours discussing their futures in the arts; Hitler wanted to be an artist while Gustl, already the master of four instruments, would be a musician.

The sixteen-year-old boys often attended the opera together and afterwards walked for miles, engaged in animated conversation. One evening in November 1906, Adolf and Gustl enjoyed Wagner's *Rienzi*, an opera about the rise and fall of a Roman tribune. After the performance Hitler was mysteriously silent and contemplative despite Gustl's efforts to engage him in a discussion of the opera. Climbing to the top of a steep hill,

Hitler grabbed his friend's hands and spoke in a hoarse, frenzied voice as he compared Rienzi's ambitions to his own. Gustl, somewhat frightened by his companion's rapturous state, said later that Hitler raved about "a special mission which one day would be entrusted to him."

In 1907, Hitler set out for Vienna, determined to study at the Academy of Fine Arts. But his talent did not equal his desire, and he failed the entrance exams. His devastation was compounded by an urgent letter asking him to return home—his mother was dying of cancer. For two months he remained at Klara's bedside, her constant companion. Her death almost destroyed him. As the attending Jewish doctor said, "In all my career I never saw anyone so prostrate with grief as Adolf Hitler."

Back in Vienna, Hitler tried to make a living as an artist but met with little financial reward. He worked diligently to build up a portfolio of his work, and once again, in 1908, he tried to gain admittance to the Academy of Fine Arts. This time he was met with a staggering rejection: his drawings were judged to be of such a low caliber that he was not even permitted to take the entrance tests. Since his money was running out, Hitler gave up his apartment and soon was reduced to sleeping on park benches and standing in soup lines for the destitute.

For a while he lived at the Mannerheim, a residence for the homeless, and spent most of his time in the writing room where he painted postcards of Viennese buildings (his architectural paintings were much better than his renderings of human forms). Of his bohemian days in Vienna, Hitler later wrote: "I was a young, inexperienced person, without financial help and also too proud to seek assistance from anyone or beg. Without any support, depending only on myself, the kronen and heller received for my work were often only enough to provide a place to sleep. For two years my only girlfriend was Sorrow and Need, and I had no other companion except constant unsatisfied hunger. I never learned to know the beautiful word 'youth.' "

On June 28, 1914, Austria's Archduke Franz Ferdinand was assassinated, Germany prepared for war, and Adolf Hitler joined the army. Long an admirer of the German national spirit, Hitler was a first-rate soldier. One comrade remarked that Hitler looked at his first rifle "with the delight that a woman looks at her jewelry." His devotion to duty was obsessive, and he often volunteered for dangerous assignments. To many of his fellow soldiers, Hitler seemed to be enjoying a somewhat calculated game with death. It was in the trenches that Hitler once again was overcome—this time by a voice that saved his life.

He later gave an account of this experience to a British journalist. As the Führer recalled:

I was eating my dinner in a trench with several comrades. Suddenly a voice seemed to be saying to me "Get up and go over there." It was so clear and insistent that I obeyed automatically, as if it had been a military order. I rose at once to my feet and walked twenty yards along the trench carrying my dinner in its tin can with me. Then I sat down to go on eating, my mind being once more at rest. Hardly had I done so when a flash and deafening report came from the part of the trench I had just left. A stray shell had burst over the group in which I had been sitting, and every member of it was killed.

By the end of 1918, Germany was losing the war. Soldiers were deserting the army, civilians were plagued with food shortages, and work strikes called for a peace settlement. Surrender seemed imminent, and the thought of it devastated Adolf Hitler. Fighting near the village of Werwick in Belgium, his Sixteenth Bavarian Reserve Infantry Regiment was attacked with mustard gas on October 14. Hitler, along with many others, was temporarily blinded and taken to a hospital in Pasewalk, Germany. What subsequently happened is reported in the definitive biography of the dictator, *Adolf Hitler*, by John Toland: After two weeks he regained his sight, but on November 9 he suffered a severe setback when he heard the official news that the war was almost over and Germany was going down in defeat. Seized by hysterical blindness, Hitler sobbed uncontrollably over " 'the misfortune of the Fatherland.' " For several days he remained in bed, convinced that he was permanently blind. Later he stated that the experience was the turning point in his career, " 'The great vacillation of my life, whether I should enter politics . . . came to an end. . . . I resolved that if I recovered my sight, I *would* enter politics.' " On November 11 or 12 Hitler had "a supernatural vision" accompanied by voices that instructed him to save Germany. The rest of the story is history.

Joan of Arc's Voices

"EVERYTHING that I have done that was good I did by command of my voices," proclaimed Joan of Arc, the young peasant girl who, in May 1429, led French armies in a stunning victory against the English at Orléans. Joan believed that, through her voices, God had directed her to become an ally of the dauphin Charles, son and heir of Charles VI, who was trying to regain the French throne from the English. After Orléans, Joan continued into enemy territory, taking towns along the Loire, routing the English at Patay, and pushing into Rheims where Charles's coronation finally took place on July 17 . Ten months later Joan was captured during a battle at Compiègne.

Brought before a French ecclesiastic court in Rouen, Joan faced seventy charges, including heresy, witchcraft, predicting the future, and immodesty (because she dressed in men's clothing). However, since many of the charges overlapped each other and many were minor—like running away from home to join the French army—the seventy charges were reduced to a more manageable twelve.

Joan's voices and visions became a focal point for the interrogators who tried to discredit and ridicule her. The voices had called her to save France, had led her into battle, and were still with her, telling her how to act at the trial. She was reluctant to talk about her revelations; they were a gift from God. When she was sworn in at the opening session of the trial, the nineteen-year-old woman boldly asserted: "Of my father, of my mother, and of all that I have done since I came to France I will willingly swear, but of the revelations which have been made to me by God's means, never have I said or revealed anything to anyone whatsoever, excepting it be to Charles only, my King, and I will not reveal them though it cost me my head. I have orders from my visions and my secret counsel to reveal them to nobody."

But the inquisitors did not relent. Slowly, but with great hesitation, Joan revealed some information about the voices and visions that she had experienced hundreds of times over a period of seven years. There were three saints who visited Joan: St. Michael, St. Catherine, and St. Margaret. It was St. Michael who first came to Joan. According to her testimony:

> I was in my thirteenth year when God sent a voice to guide me. At first I was very much frightened. The voice came toward the hour of noon, in summer, in my father's garden. I had fasted the preceding day. I heard the voice on my right hand, in the direction of the church. I seldom hear it without [seeing] a light. That light always appears on the side from which I hear the voice.

As the trial progressed, Joan revealed much more, usually in simple, direct replies. But she told them only what she felt she could, refusing some questions with a pre-emptory "Pass over that." Some of Joan's testimony:

QUESTION: Do you see Saint Michael and the angels corporeally and really?

JOAN: I see them with my corporeal eyes as well as I see you, and when they withdrew from me I wept, and I should have liked them to take me with them.

QUESTION: Do you always see them in the same clothes?

JOAN: I always see them in the same shape, their heads very richly crowned. I am allowed by our Lord to say this. I know nothing of their robes.

QUESTION: Have your saints hair?

JOAN: It is a comfort to know that they have!

QUESTION: Have they arms and other limbs and organs?

JOAN: I do not know.

QUESTION: How do they speak?

JOAN: Very beautifully. I understand them well.

QUESTION: How can they speak, since they have no organs?

JOAN: I leave that to God.

QUESTION: What is the character of the voice?

JOAN: This voice is beautiful, sweet and humble, and it speaks the French language.

QUESTION: Does not Saint Margaret speak the English tongue?

JOAN: How should she speak English since she is not on the side of the English?

QUESTION: What did Saint Michael look like when he appeared to you?

JOAN: I did not see any crown, and I know nothing about his garments.

QUESTION: Was he naked?

JOAN: Do you think our Lord has nothing to dress him in?

QUESTION: Had he any hair?

JOAN: Why should it have been cut off?

QUESTION: Did you kiss or embrace Saints Catherine and Margaret?

JOAN: I embraced both of them.

QUESTION: Had they a pleasant odor?

JOAN: It is good to know that they had a pleasant odor.

QUESTION: When embracing them, did you feel any warmth or any other thing?

JOAN: I could not embrace them without feeling and touching them.

QUESTION: In what part did you embrace them, the upper part or the lower?

JOAN: It is more fitting to embrace them by the lower part than the higher.

QUESTION: Do Saints Catherine and Margaret hate the English?

JOAN: They love those whom Our Lord loves, and hate those whom He hates.

QUESTION: Does God hate the English?

JOAN: Whether He loves them or hates them, and what He proposes to do with their souls I know not; but this I know for certain, that all of them will be thrown out of France, except those who perish there.

On Thursday, May 24, Joan was taken to the cemetery of the Abbey of Saint Ouen where a large outdoor platform had been erected to accommodate the judges who had reached a verdict. As Joan listened to them pronounce her guilty, the red-clothed executioner stood by to take her away. There was only one way to save her life—to sign a six-line abjuration statement in which she disavowed her voices and visions, renounced her male dress, and agreed to submit to the authority of the Church. In a moment of weakness her spirit broke, and she signed the recantation. While this act released her from excommunication and death, it did not free her from prison. She was sentenced to "perpetual imprisonment." Immediately thereafter she returned to jail where she agreed to put on women's clothing and was forced to have her hair (worn in a masculine pudding-basin style) completely shaved off. Her change of mind and dress were short-lived.

Two days later Joan was once again wearing men's clothes. The ecclesiastic judges rushed to the prison as soon as they were informed of Joan's relapse and demanded to know the meaning of her actions. Once again she was subjected to an intense interrogation as a recording clerk carefully wrote down all that she said. In the margin of his book, beside one of Joan's replies, the clerk wrote "fatal answer." That particular statement reaffirmed her belief in her voices and ultimately sealed her fate: "They [Saints Catherine and Margaret] told me that, through them, God declared His grief that I behaved like a traitor by consenting to recant in order to save my life; by saving my life I was damning myself. . . . Ever since Thursday my voices have told me that I had behaved very wickedly in saying that what I did was wrong. What I said last Thursday I said only because I was frightened of the stake. Now I would rather die than stay in this prison. If you want me to, I will put on women's clothes, but I will do nothing else."

On Wednesday, May 30, 1431, wearing a long black robe and a kerchief on her head, Joan was taken to the Old Market Place in Rouen where thousands of people had gathered. As the Church authorities turned her over to secular authorities, she dropped to her knees, begged the crowd to forgive her for any harm she had done them, and for a half hour prayed to God and called out for her three saints. Many spectators, including a few of her judges, wept openly at the sight of the girl whose youth and innocence were a stark contrast to the large plaster stake which loomed behind her. The sentiment of the crowd had little effect on the chief magistrate who elected to forgo a formal execution statement and simply waved his hand, saying, "Take her."

As she was chained to the post, a soldier placed a paper miter on her head that read: "Heretic, Relapsed Sinner, Apostate, Idolater." The executioner lit the faggots piled high around the base of the stake, and flames began to shoot out. As the fire engulfed her, Joan continued to appeal to God and her saints. As one monk described her final moments: "We could hear her in the fire, invoking her saints, her archangel; she kept repeating the name of our Savior. . . . Finally, her head dropped, and she uttered a great cry—'Jesus.' "

Afterwards the executioner pushed aside the burned wood to allow onlookers to see the charred body. In the ashes he found her heart. It had not burned. The haunting execution scene was to plague the minds of many witnesses for years to come, including one secretary to the king of England who said, "We are all lost, for we have burned a saint."

Nat Turner's Rebellion

NAT TURNER, thirty-one-year-old leader of the only effective slave insurrection in America, was convinced early in his life that he was singled out for a special purpose. Growing up in Southampton County, Virginia, the boy was a healthy adolescent who displayed extraordinary intelligence and skill. He was able to read and fascinated his friends with scientific experiments. At the age of three or four, Nat stunned his parents by recalling, in detail, an event that happened before he was born. Believing that the boy was gifted with special powers, his parents told everyone that Nat was destined to be the leader of men, that God had singled him out for some special mission.

Nat Turner had his first prophetic vision while he was plowing in the fields. A voice said to him: "Seek ye the kingdom of Heaven and all things shall be added unto you." While Nat did not fully understand this occurrence, it strengthened his religious convictions. Refusing the temptations of drinking, smoking, and gambling, he studied the Bible and spent much time memorizing the chapters of the Old Testament. Several years after the first religious revelation, Turner ran away from his master but returned when "the Spirit" ordered him back.

In 1825, Turner had one of his most apocalyptic experiences. As he recalled:

I saw white spirits and black spirits engaged in battle, and the sun was darkened—the thunder rolled in the Heavens, and blood flowed in streams—and I heard a voice saying, "Such is your luck, such you are called to see, and let it come rough or smooth, you must surely bear it."

Convinced that the day of judgment was imminent, Turner began to spread the word to his people. He held audiences spellbound as he re-enacted his moments of divine inspiration and told of the miracles he had seen, like drops of blood on corn in the fields and hieroglyphic characters on leaves in the woods.

Turner soon felt compelled to conduct his own Sunday prayer meetings throughout the county. Few whites were worried, for Turner had never been known as a troublemaker. On the contrary, he was praised as a hardworking, polite, intelligent slave. His appearance, though somewhat striking, was hardly threatening: medium height, a little overweight, knock-kneed, and thinning hair on his head. As "the Prophet" continued to preside over his scattered congregation, he awaited further instructions on his earthly mission.

The revelation came to him on May 12, 1828. As he put it:

I heard a loud noise in the heavens, and the Spirit instantly appeared to me and said the Serpent was loosened, and Christ had laid down the yoke he had borne for the sins of men, and that I should take it on and fight against the Serpent, for the time was fast approaching when the first should be last and the last should be first. . . . And by signs in the heavens that it would make known to me when I should commence the great work—and until the first sign appeared, I should conceal it from the knowledge of men—And on the appearance of the sign, I should arise and prepare myself, and slay my enemies with their own weapons.

With his four most trusted followers, Turner plotted the rebellion as he awaited the sign for him to begin. The sign—a solar eclipse—came in February 1831, and Turner scheduled Judgment Day for July 4. On the appointed day, however, he became ill and the plans were called off until August 21. On that Sunday he met with six of his disciples in the woods near Cabin Pond (not far from the Travis home where Turner lived and worked). The plan was horrifyingly simple: Kill all white men, women, and children.

Late that evening the seven men, armed with one hatchet, one broadax, and the vengeance of an entire race, arrived at their first stop, the home of Joseph Travis. After quietly breaking into the house, Turner entered his master's dark bedroom and swung the hatchet at Travis's head. The hatchet came close but missed, and Turner's aide, Will the Executioner, stepped in and killed Travis with one blow. The raiding party then axed Mrs. Travis, her twelve-year-old son, and a fourteen-year-old boy who worked for the Travis family. After stealing some guns, muskets, and gunpowder, the rebels set out for their next destination, the farmhouse of Salathiel Francis. But before they reached their second target, Turner remembered the Travis baby and promptly ordered two men to return and kill the infant who peacefully slept in its cradle.

After clubbing Francis to death, the insurgents moved to another farm, and then another. Since the farmhouses were relatively close to each other, the conspirators did not want to warn the whites by using their guns and instead continued to use axes, clubs, and hatchets, sometimes decapitating the victims. The slaughter continued through the night; white after white was mercilessly chopped down. By dawn on Monday morning Turner's forces had doubled, and the army split into two divisions in order to cover more territory.

By now, however, word of the massacre was spreading throughout the countryside. Turner found some farms deserted as alerted residents fled into the nearby town of Jerusalem. But Turner pressed on, gathering more troops and weapons as he hit homestead after homestead. At one boarding school ten children were killed and decapitated (one girl survived unharmed by crawling up a dirt chimney).

By noon on Monday, Turner, accompanied by an army of seventy men, planned to storm Jerusalem. But before he could enter the town, he was stopped by a band of white soldiers. A battle ensued, and Turner's troops retreated and scattered in many directions. After a few small skirmishes on Tuesday, the rebellion—less than two days old—was crushed. In all, the insurgents raided fifteen farms. Nearly sixty whites were dead, more than half of them women and children.

Widespread panic among the whites had caused three thousand soldiers to pour into Southampton—many from surrounding Virginia counties, some from neighboring North Carolina, and even some federal troops. White retaliation was swift. Vigilante groups comprised of local citizens did most of the killing, as they roamed the county searching for any black who even looked suspicious. Some soldiers also participated in the carnage; one militia unit from North Carolina beheaded fifteen prisoners and put their heads on poles where they remained for two weeks. The black community reeled in shock as innocent slaves and free men were shot, hanged, and butchered. At least 120 blacks died. As one newspaper reported: "Some of the scenes are hardly inferior in barbarity to the atrocities of the insurgents."

Nat Turner was not captured until eight weeks later. When brought to trial, he pleaded not guilty, but was convicted and sentenced to hang (of the fifty insurgents tried, twenty-one were executed). On November 11, Turner went to the gallows. His body was given to surgeons to dissect, and according to one report, "They skinned it and made grease of the flesh."

Mephitic Ecstasy and the Delphic Oracle

LEGENDS say that thousands of years ago, in ancient Greece, a herdsman named Koretas led his flock of goats into a gorge between the two peaks of the Phaeidriades, under the brooding, lightning-struck face of majestic Mount Parnassus. As a goat approached the gorge, it began to bleat and gambol as if it were mad. And each goat, as in its turn it came too close to the chasm, also leapt aside and cried. Curious, Koretas was drawn to the cleft and, overcome by the same vapor, went into a frenzy and began to prophesy about the future.

Over a period of time, the gorge became a shrine, visited by those eager to know the future and experience the euphoria from the vapor. It was rumored that the fumes came from the rotting body of a python, the dragon protector of the shrine. Apollo had killed it and thrown it into the gorge when he took the holy place from Thetis, daughter of Ge, goddess of earth. It was said, too, that Ge, avenging her daughter, sent up dreams, dangerously ambiguous, that revealed the future.

In their frenzy, goats and humans jumped ecstatically into the chasm, never to be seen again. So it was decided that one person, the Pythia, be chosen to inhale the marvelous and perilous fumes. The Pythia was, except possibly in one case, a woman. She sat on a tripod over the gorge and told of what would come. She was the first oracle of Delphi.

All of this is probably legend, going back at least to the sixth century B.C., originating in layers of early religions. But hazy as the beginnings are, a Delphic oracle, of supreme power in the ancient world, did in actuality exist. At first virgins were enthroned as the Pythia, but when one was raped by an importunate visitor, older women, usually over fifty and married, were chosen, though they dressed as maidens. In later times virgins again reigned. In the heyday of Delphi, sometimes two Pythias officiated, with a third as assistant. All remained pure during their tenure.

The complicated, symbolic ritual for worshipping the oracle began with fasting and bathing in the Castilian spring nearby. Attendants poured cold water on a goat to see whether the omens were favorable for prophecy—if the goat shuddered, all was well. Accounts differ on what the Pythia did next. She may have chewed sacred laurel leaves, drunk from the sacred spring Cassotis, worshipped at the egg-shaped rock *omphalos* (navel of the world), and burned barley meal, laurel, or myrrh on Apollo's altar. Wearing a laurel crown and holding a sprig of bay in her hand, she mounted the tripod and began her utterances. Some said she raved, wild-eyed, shouting so incoherently that only her *hosioi* (holy ones) could understand her. But that seems unlikely, though once, when the goat failed to shudder and the attendants, to please important visitors, kept pouring water on it until it did, the Pythia turned rough-voiced and hysterical, "raised an unintelligible and fearful shout and rushed for the door," and, unconscious, died a few days later.

The Pythia's prophecies were placed in a sealed envelope and given to the envoys who had brought questions to pose to her. At one time she was known throughout the world, and many consulted her, paying great prices to do so. It was said that in 550 B.C. Croesus sacrificed two hundred cattle and sent her jewels, statues, and 117 silver and gold bowls, one weighing one-and-a-half tons. What he asked in exchange was the answer to the question of whether he should invade the territory of Persian emperor Cyrus. The oracle told him simply that "Croesus by crossing the Halys would destroy a mighty kingdom." Croesus assumed that Persia was the kingdom to be destroyed. Delighted, Croesus made war—and lost. The kingdom he destroyed was his own. Held captive by the Persians, he sent the Pythia his chains, asking why she had led him astray, and she explained the answer to him. But she kept the treasure.

With Delphi in full flower, there were marble temples and huge treasuries to hold the gifts brought to propitiate the oracle. It had been a long time since the first temples had been raised—simple wooden structures and, in myth, the first three made of bay, beeswax, feathers, and bronze. But then, as Greece lost power, so did the oracle, and in the end, only one Pythia answered the trickle of questions that came to her.

What were the gases that rose from the cleft? Perhaps they were volcanic, but such gases, as far as we know, do not induce trances. And perhaps there was no cleft, and no vapor. Perhaps it is all a myth. Starting in 1892, a team of French archaeologists excavated at Delphi in the foundations of the fourth-century temple, but could find no cleft and no sign of one. This is not conclusive proof, for chasms can be closed by earthquakes, shutting the door on emanations from underground and underworld. The truth, like the Pythia's prophecies, will remain forever ambiguous.

The Little Lady, the Book, and the Big War

THIRTY-NINE-YEAR-OLD Harriet Beecher Stowe, author and mother of six, walked into the sitting room of her home in Brunswick, Maine, and tore open a letter from Boston. It came from "Sister Katey," wife of Harriet's brother, Edward. Like most of her sister-in-law's recent letters, this one, dated late September 1850, was filled with news of the Fugitive Slave Act. In vivid detail Katey told of federal troops sent to Boston to squelch antislavery demonstrations. Despite the cool tranquility of that New England afternoon, Harriet felt her pulse quicken as she gathered together her children to share the letter with them. Many years later even the younger children remembered their mother's fevered expression as she read aloud, "Now, Hattie, if I could use a pen as you can, I would write something that would make this whole nation feel what an accursed thing slavery is." The slender, impassioned daughter of a strict Calvinist preacher rose to her feet, and in a voice filled with religious indignation, she exclaimed, "God helping me, I will write something."

A veteran magazine writer, Harriet searched her mind for months, but the great antislavery idea eluded her. The quest finally ended one wintry Sunday in February as Harriet sat at a communion table in church. Suddenly she fell into a trance. Her son, Charles Edward, later reported: "Like the unrolling of a picture, the scene of the death of Uncle Tom passed before her mind. So strongly was she affected that only with difficulty could she keep from weeping aloud. Immediately on returning home she took pen and paper and wrote out the vision which had been, as it were, blown into her mind as by the rushing of a mighty wind."

Harriet's entire life was steeped in religion. She was born in Litchfield, Connecticut, and her father, Lyman Beecher, was a celebrated New

England clergyman who was never at a loss for religious conviction or enthusiasm (to work off excess energy, he would shovel gravel from one pile to another in the basement of his home). Married three times, Beecher fathered thirteen children; six of the boys became ministers. Ruled by her devotion to Christ, Harriet once wrote: "He has been the Inspirer, Consoler, and Strength of my life, and to read of those who struggle for goodness without knowing *Him* is as painful to me as to read of those who die of hunger when there is bread enough and to spare. Christ is my Life."

Destined to be a writer, Harriet was reading adult books by the age of eight. At eleven she won a school contest with a twenty-five-hundred-word essay, "Can the Immortality of the Soul be Proved by the Light of Nature?" After completing her education at a girls' school in Hartford, she became a teacher. In 1832, the Beecher clan moved to Cincinnati where Lyman Beecher became president of Lane Theological Seminary. It was here that Harriet began writing in earnest. Soon her articles, mostly character sketches, began to appear in such publications as *Western Monthly Magazine* and *The Mayflower*.

For eighteen years Harriet remained in Cincinnati. Across the Ohio River in Kentucky was a slave-holding community which she visited in 1833. It was one of her few direct contacts with slaves (a fact that later became a rallying point for her critics). While she witnessed no atrocities, Harriet was sickened to see human beings treated as pieces of property. However limited her personal experiences, Harriet was living in a city that hosted the largest Underground Railway in the United States; newspapers were filled daily with stories of abolitionist activities and runaway slaves. The omnipresent issue was slavery, and there was hardly a neutral American citizen to be found.

In 1836, Harriet married Calvin Ellis Stowe, a professor of Biblical literature, and in 1850, the couple left Cincinnati for Brunswick, Maine, home of Bowdoin College, where Calvin had accepted a teaching position. On June 5, 1851, the first installment of *Uncle Tom's Cabin, or Life Among the Lowly* appeared in the *National Era*, an antislavery paper based in Washington, D.C. Harriet had previously queried the paper about her story—"a series of sketches which give the lights and shadows of the patriarchal institution"—and sent along the opening chapters. The editors had agreed to a three-or four-part serialization and paid her $300.

Night after night Harriet, after putting her children to bed, wrote at the kitchen table. The characters of Uncle Tom, Eliza, St. Clare, and Simon Legree came to life on pages sometimes saturated with the author's uncontrollable tears. (After writing the scene where Little Eva died, Harriet was so distraught that she needed two full days in bed to recover.) The original three or four weekly installments grew to forty, and the story did not reach its conclusion until April 1, 1852.

In the meantime, Calvin and Harriet worked to get the serial into book form. The two-volume *Uncle Tom's Cabin*, bound in black cloth with a woodcut of a Negro cabin on the cover, was published on March 20, 1852 (just before serialization ended) and sold for $1.20. The first printing was five thousand copies; more than three thousand copies were sold on the first day. On the second day the remaining copies were snatched from bookstore shelves.

Reaction to the book was swift. Congratulatory messages poured in from across the country and around the world, but protest from the South was vicious. One noted journal called the book mere propaganda and "a criminal prostitution of the high functions of the imagination." Proslavery advocates attacked the book's accuracy. Mrs. Stowe, they cried, was completely ignorant of social customs in the South. Furthermore, they insisted, she knew nothing of the laws that governed the treatment of slaves. The outrage shocked Harriet, who believed all along that she had written a fair and balanced book that would help to resolve the slavery controversy. She had naively believed that if she faced criticism, it would come from the abolitionists who would say her book was too mild. That presumption was quickly destroyed as thousands of angry letters arrived at her Brunswick home. One package, fortunately opened by Calvin, contained the ear of a slave—a warning of what would happen to those who meddled in other people's affairs.

Within a year more than 350,000 copies of *Uncle Tom's Cabin* were sold in the United States alone. Success abroad was even more spectacular. Great Britain brought out forty different editions, and the book soon appeared in seventeen languages, including Serbian, Armenian, and Siamese. Eventually the book was translated into more than forty languages, the hero known by many names: Wuya Tomasza, Tio Tomas, 'Ewyrth Twm, to name a few. Best estimates of worldwide sales, in the fifty-eight years that the Stowe family held copyrights, approach 9.5 million copies.

Before *Uncle Tom's Cabin*, Harriet's total earnings from magazine and journal articles were minimal (at best she earned $2.00 a page). The success of her first book spurred her on to a great literary outpouring which included regular contributions to such prestigious publications as *The Atlantic Monthly* and the *New York Independent*. In addition she continued to write books—about one a year for the next thirty years.

While none of her other books enjoyed the same spotlight as *Uncle Tom's Cabin*, most of them sold reasonably well. She wrote only one more slavery novel, turning instead to more autobiographical stories filled with the rich, full-bodied flavor of New England. (From 1856 to 1860, she averaged $6,000 a month or $72,000 a year—quite a sum in the days when bread sold for a penny a loaf and a year's tuition at Harvard cost $50.)

Harriet's religious armor, however, did show a few scratches. She loved being recognized and thoroughly enjoyed the wealth that accompanied fame. While she did give generously to charitable causes, Harriet also hired a number of servants, sent her daughters to expensive schools, and built an extravagant Gothic-style home in Hartford. She loved to travel to Europe, and among her friends she numbered Elizabeth Barrett Browning, Robert Browning, John Ruskin, and George Eliot. Acting as her own agent, the New Englander was hard-nosed in the financial arena. She fought for top pay for her writing (sometimes insisting on a cost-of-living increase), kept careful records of her book royalties, and chastised publishers if her books were not properly marketed and advertised. Harriet's financial obsessiveness reached its peak in 1866, following the death of her husband. Asked by one magazine to write an obituary of Calvin, Harriet immediately contacted the *Atlantic*, since she preferred to have Calvin's obituary appear in that magazine. Her letter insisted that if a deal was to be made, she would have to be paid according to her customary rate.

In public, Harriet was a teetotaler. However, in 1856 while visiting the offices of her Boston publisher, Harriet almost fainted and was given two glasses of champagne to help revive her. Shortly thereafter, she ordered six bottles of the beverage sent to her home "to support the hot weather and the *long pull*." For an undetermined period of time, imbibing alcohol was a part of her daily routine. According to Harriet, "*The stimulus* will be used up in active out-of-door exercise which will strengthen my general health." This justification bewildered some of Harriet's friends, especially since she sometimes had a drink at six o'clock in the morning!

Through her eighty-five years of life Harriet Beecher Stowe was called many names—from saint, genius, and humanitarian, to hack writer, liar, and rabble-rouser. She gained yet another label in November 1862, when she met Abraham Lincoln. The White House meeting, initiated by Harriet, took place in the President's study. Accompanied by her twelve-year-old son Charlie, Harriet entered the room to find Lincoln seated before a fireplace. He stood up, and his six-foot, four-inch frame towered over her as he took her small hand in his. The President's opening remark, as aptly remembered by Charlie: "So this is the little lady who wrote the book that made this big war."

Look Sharp, Feel Sharp, Be Sharp

FOR MILLIONS of Americans, "Look sharp, feel sharp, be sharp" evokes an image of only one product—the Gillette safety razor.

The revolutionary shaving device was the brainchild of King C. Gillette, who in 1895 was a traveling salesman and frustrated inventor. Employed by the Crown Cork & Seal Company, Gillette was envious of the firm's president, William Painter, who had invented the company's best-selling product—a bottle stopper consisting of a tin cap with a cork lining. Painter, an amicable boss, encouraged Gillette (who had patented a handful of inventions, none of them noteworthy) to cultivate his inventive talents.

One day Painter gave Gillette an invaluable piece of advice. He said: "King, you are always thinking and inventing something. Why don't you try to think of something like the Crown Cork which, when once used, is thrown away, and the customer keeps coming back for more? And with every additional customer you get, you are building a foundation of profit." Gillette never forgot those words. For years he tried in vain to think of a product to fit Painter's qualifications for success. Sometimes he mentally raced through the alphabet, A to Z, trying to conjure up a product that would be useful, salable, and disposable.

One day in the spring of 1895, the idea he had been waiting for finally surfaced. Gillette's account of his initial vision of the safety razor with disposable blades:

> It was born as naturally as though its embryonic form had matured in thought and only waited its appropriate time of birth. One morning when I started to shave, I found my razor dull, and it was not only dull but it was beyond the point of successful stropping. It needed honing, which meant it would have to be taken to a barber or cutler. "A razor is only a sharp edge," I said to myself, "and all back of it is just support. Why do they go to all the expense and trouble of fashioning a backing that has nothing to do with shaving? And why do they forge a great piece of steel and then spend so much labor in hollow grinding it when they could get the same result by putting an edge on a piece of steel only thick enough to hold an edge?"

As I stood there with the razor in my hand, my eyes resting on it as lightly as a bird settling down on its nest, the Gillette razor was born—more with the rapidity of a dream than by a process of reasoning. In that moment I saw it all: the way the blade could be held in a holder; the idea of sharpening the two opposite edges on the thin piece of steel; the clamping plates for the blade, with a handle halfway between the two edges of the blade.

All this came more in pictures than in conscious thought, as though the razor were already a finished thing and held before my eyes. I stood there before that mirror in a trance of joy. My wife was visiting in Ohio, and I hurriedly wrote to her: "I've got it! Our fortune is made!" Fool that I was, I knew little about razors and nothing about steel, and I could not foresee the trials and tribulations I was to pass through before the razor was a success. But I believed in it with my whole heart.

"If Any Man Espouse a Virgin and Desires to Espouse Another . . ."

JOSEPH SMITH, leader and "Prophet" of Mormonism, claimed to have experienced many visions during his short thirty-eight years—visions that led to the founding and doctrines of his church, the Church of Jesus Christ of Latter-Day Saints. One of those revelations instructed him to adopt polygamy, a practice which became immersed in controversy and was a contributing factor to his murder in 1844.

One of the most colorful and enigmatic of religious leaders, Smith was a poor backwoods farmer and necromancer, born in Vermont, who refused to fall victim to poverty and obscurity. At fourteen, while living in Palmyra, New York, he had his first revelation, in which both God and Jesus Christ appeared to him. At eighteen he was visited by a messenger from God, the angel Moroni, who told him of a new Gospel written on gold plates, buried nearby, which gave "an account of the former inhabitants of this continent." At twenty-five, after he had dug up the plates and translated the "reformed Egyptian" hieroglyphics into the *Book of Mormon*, Smith established the Church of Jesus Christ of Latter-Day Saints. His career was unusually swift, especially for a semiliterate man who had once been arrested on charges of disorderly conduct and who was characterized by his father-in-law as "a careless young man . . . very saucy and insolent to his father."

But Joseph Smith was far from an ordinary man. Physically appealing—six feet tall with an athletic physique, brilliant blue eyes, and thick, light brown hair—he oozed charm and possessed an imagination that seemed to have no limits. As one of his most devoted followers, Brigham Young, once said of him: "That the Prophet was of mean birth, that he was wild, intemperate, even dishonest and tricky in his youth, is nothing against his mission. God can, and does, make use of the vilest instruments. If he acts like a devil, Joseph has brought forth a doctrine that will save us, if we abide by it. He may get drunk every day of his life, sleep with his neighbor's wife every night, run horses and gamble . . . but the doctrine he has produced will save you and me and the whole world."

Smith's first thoughts about polygamy probably surfaced when he was translating the gold plates in 1829 while living in Harmony, Pennsylvania. Although the finished manuscript of *The Book of Mormon* was over 275,000 words, about ten percent of it was taken verbatim from the Bible. Particularly interested in the Old Testament, Smith was fascinated by the polygamous marriages of Jacob, Abraham, Isaac, and David. According to Brigham Young, it was during this period when the book was being written that Smith had a revelation about polygamy. While the exact year of the revelation is still in question, Smith's accounts of it to various friends generally contained the same basic facts.

Dramatic, definitive, and awe-inspiring—that's how Smith explained the vision. An angel with a drawn sword appeared to him and instructed him to go forth on the direct orders of God to establish the practice of plural marriage. Careful to point out that he was at first cautious and dubious, Smith made sure that those he took into his confidence were convinced of one fact: If the Prophet did not obey God's commands regarding polygamy, he would be destroyed.

Though he was discussing the possibility of polygamy with his closest friends as early as 1831, the Prophet did not turn his revelation into an official edict until twelve years later. He did, however, begin to practice polygamy as early as 1836 when he was "sealed" to Frannie Alger, a seventeen-year-old orphan girl who was living with Joseph and his wife Emma in Kirtland, Ohio. Soon afterward the attractive teenage girl, unable to keep the knowledge of the affair to herself, inadvertently started rumors which quickly reached Emma. The first wife promptly drove the second wife out of the house.

During his lifetime Joseph Smith may have taken as many as forty-nine wives, thirty-one of them *before* the polygamous revelation was written into Mormon law on July 12, 1843. The decision to record the revelation came at a very convenient time. Not only had charges of adultery followed Smith from Kirtland to Nauvoo, Illinois, where the Mormons had relocated in 1839, but Emma was becoming more and more vocal in her opposition to the new marital arrangements. Even after the revelation had been written down, it was disclosed only to a selective group within the church hierarchy. (A public statement concerning polygamy was not made until August 29, 1852, eight years after the death of Joseph Smith.)

The document was long, wordy, at times confusing, but the essential law was concisely laid out in section 24: "If any man espouse a virgin and desires to espouse another, and the first give her consent, and if he espouse the second, and they are virgins, and have vowed to no other man, then he is justified; he cannot commit adultery . . . for they belong to him. . . ."

Anticipating Emma's reactions, the Prophet wrote into the doctrine a special section—addressed specifically to Emma Smith. In it God told Emma that she would be destroyed if she did not obey the new law. In addition, Smith feared that Emma might ask for the same connubial privileges as he would have—that she might demand a plurality of husbands. But God, via Smith, halted that possibility: "Verily, I say unto you, a commandment I give unto mine handmaid, Emma Smith, your wife, whom I have given unto you, that she stay herself, and partake not of that which I commanded you to offer unto her . . ."

Smith's brother Hyrum volunteered to show the revelation to Emma, confident that he could persuade her to accept it. But Emma flew into a rage and, after lecturing him on the evils of polygamy, she ordered him out of her home. The failed diplomat promptly returned to Smith and complained, "In all my life, I have never been so abused by a woman." Nonetheless, because Emma loved her husband and feared the wrath of God, she had no other alternative but to accept the practice of polygamy.

A husband was supposed to seek the consent of his first wife before marrying another, but if the consent was refused, the husband was still free to do as he pleased. It is certain that Emma Smith did not know how many women her husband had married. From 1843, when the revelation was recorded, until his death eleven months later, Smith added another eighteen women to his family. In Fawn M. Brodie's award-winning biography of Smith, *No Man Knows My History*, the author lists all of the Prophet's wives and uncovers some fascinating statistics regarding the forty-nine women: their ages ranged from fifteen to fifty-nine; all except four or five were of childbearing age; there were at least twelve married women; six women at various times lived as wards in the Smith house; included among his wives were five sets of sisters and one mother/daughter pair.

While the great majority of the twenty thousand Mormons in and around Nauvoo were totally oblivious to the multitudinous marriages taking place in their community, the two or three dozen men who were involved often helped each other to arrange the secret marriages. Some women, upon first hearing of the practice, required a lot of convincing. Smith's approach, though at times romantic, was usually direct, like this proposal to seventeen-year-old Lucy Walker: "I have no flattering words to offer. It is a command of God to you. I will give you until tomorrow to decide this matter. If you reject this message, the gate [to heaven] will be closed forever against you."

Most of the Mormon women approached by Smith and his small group of associates consented to the secret marriages, but there were some who stubbornly refused—and a few who dared to expose what was going on in Nauvoo. One such woman was eighteen-year-old Martha Brotherton who, on a summer day in 1842, was coaxed into a meeting with Brigham Young in a room on the second floor of Smith's grocery store. After explaining plural marriage to her, Young proposed. Stunned and confused, the young woman asked for time to think the matter over. Whereupon, an impatient Young asked her if she would discuss the matter with Smith. Even though she agreed, Young locked her in the room while he left to locate Smith. When the two men returned, the Prophet confidently stated to Martha: "Just go ahead and do as Brigham wants you to. He is the best man in the world except me. . . . If there is any sin in it, I will answer for it before God; and I have the keys of the kingdom . . . for I know Brigham will take care of you, and if he don't do his duty to you, come to me and I will make him—and if you do not like it in a month or two, come to me and I will make you free again; and if he turns you off, I will take you on." But Martha begged for time, was allowed to leave, and in a few days went to St. Louis where she made a sworn statement before a justice of the peace detailing the three-way conversation. The story was printed in a St. Louis newspaper and gossip ensued, but both Smith and Young denied the incident.

On June 7, 1844, the *Nauvoo Expositor*, operated by former members of the Mormon church, published its first issue which was a scathing indictment of Smith and his "vicious principles"—including polygamy. Smith immediately ordered that the newspaper's printing press be destroyed. Arrested and imprisoned in Carthage, twenty miles from Nauvoo, Smith was shot and killed on June 27 when a mob stormed the jail. He was thirty-eight years old.

Polygamy gained acceptance among the Mormons after Brigham Young led them to the Great Salt Lake basin in Utah in 1846–1847. The practice came out from under its clandestine cloak and became a respectable, accepted way of life. On August 29, 1852, the Mormons made a public statement that acknowledged to the world that they did indeed practice polygamy and explained why they had adopted it. However, an indignant American public would not tolerate the "lurid" practice, and the federal government confiscated church property, refused Mormons the right to vote, and even put some polygamists in prison. Almost four decades later, in 1890, Wilford Woodruff, president of the church, officially renounced polygamy.

A Vision Turned Inside Out: The Ghost Dance and the Massacre at Wounded Knee

WOVOKA, a fat-faced thirty-five-year-old Paiute with heavy eyebrows, was high with fever on "the day the sun died" (was eclipsed) in 1889. As the sky went dark, something lifted him up, and he felt himself ascend into the spirit world, where he saw Indians long dead now alive and young at work and play as in the old days. The Great Spirit, disheartened with what was going on in his world below since the coming of the whites, gave Wovoka instructions to bring back to his people. They were to be good, love one another, work, refrain from lying and stealing, "live in peace with the white," and "put away the old practices that savored of war." If they did these things, the Great Spirit promised, the Indians would soon be in heaven and free forever of the ills of mankind. The Great Spirit also taught Wovoka a dance—the Ghost Dance—which, if performed as he requested, would bring closer the day when heaven came. Wovoka was given control over the weather and Western affairs, while President Benjamin Harrison was in charge of the East, and the Great Spirit, of course, would continue to rule the "world above."

It was not the first Second Coming message to arise from anxious Indians' visions. Great waves of whites were pushing west, killing off the Indians' buffalo, covering the Great Plains with wagon tracks, threatening the sacred Black Hills of the Sioux in the Dakotas, penning the tribes up in reservations. Helpless in the face of this, Indians turned to visions. Involved in wishful thinking of the most serious kind, the visionaries adopted the idea of the Christian messiah, while trying to call back the old days before they had ever heard of the white man's God. As the terrestrial world failed the Indians, they desperately attempted to merge heavens. Some twenty years before Wovoka's encounter with the Great Spirit, the Paiute prophet Tavibo envisioned an earthquake which swallowed up all people except Indians, leaving behind an earthly paradise, its plains alive with buffalo and thick with grass. Waugh-zee-waugh-ber, also a Paiute, not long after the Southern Pacific's first transcontinental run, went into a trance in which he saw a large railroad train bring back the dead. By singing and dancing, he said, the Paiutes could speed up the train's arrival time. No such train came.

But it was Wovoka who inflamed the Western tribes. The son of an assistant of Tavibo, he knew both Indian and white culture. As a child he was taken into the family of a white farmer, David Wilson, who renamed him Jack. On the day of the eclipse Wovoka/Jack Wilson took a third name—that of his grandfather, Kwohitsauk (Great Rumbling Belly).

In the year of the eclipse, the United States government, in an open land grab, had seized a large part of the Great Reservation of the Sioux and reassigned its Indians to smaller tracts of land. Everywhere, Indians were losing their lands. They objected but could do little. And because of that, facing impotence, they grabbed onto the Ghost Dance, which would bring back power. Wovoka, messenger of the Great Spirit, became Wovoka, son of the Great Spirit, the new messiah, who would save the Indians. It was not Wovoka's idea to be a messiah; he was dragooned into the role by the great need of the Indians. Word traveled from tribe to tribe—the Utes, the Shoshoni, the Kiowa, the Sioux—through the Oklahoma and Dakota reservations.

In 1890, the Ghost Dance was brought back to the Sioux by Kicking Bear, a Minneconjou Sioux. Kicking Bear had heard a voice telling him to go meet the ghosts of Indians who were to come back to earth. With his brother-in-law Short Bull and other Indians, he traveled west by railroad for five days. Indians met them when they debarked from the train and gave them food and horses. After riding another four days, they came to the Paiute camp near Pyramid Lake in Nevada, then went on two days more to Walker Lake, where Indians from many tribes had gathered to see Wovoka. Porcupine, a Cheyenne who made a similar journey, reported that in a space cleared out like a circus ring, huge crowds of Indians waited until, in the flickering light of an immense fire, Wovoka appeared in a striped white man's coat and moccasins.

Wovoka said, "I will teach you to dance a dance, and I want you to dance it. Get ready for your dance, and when the dance is over, I will talk to you."

After they had danced, Wovoka spoke to them. He said that the Great Spirit would come and create a new world through earthquake and flood, a new world with grass, water, and trees, rich with game, a new world in which the blind would see, the old grow young, the dead arise. As the catastrophic earthquake and flood began, the Indians would be lifted above it into the air, while the new earth passed below them in a wave. The whites and the Indians who did not dance would all die. Wovoka said, "Then medicine man tell Indians to send word to all Indians to keep up dancing and the good time will come. Indians who don't dance, who don't believe in this word, will grow little, just about a foot high, and stay that way. Some of them will be turned into wood and be burned in fire."

According to Wovoka's orders, the dance continued for four days, with a final full night of dancing. The dancers, in eccentric and hypnotic movements, circled around a fire, worked themselves into an ecstatic trance, then fell from fatigue, to arise as if from the dead. On sunup of the fifth day, the dance ended and the participants bathed in the river. Every six weeks the dance was to begin again.

The day after Wovoka told them this, the Indians looked at his body for stigmata like Christ's. They saw a scar on his wrist and one on his face, but that was all.

Kicking Bear later said that Wovoka flew above, teaching them songs for the new dance, as they rode homeward toward the railroad. It was Kicking Bear who started the Ghost Dance at the Cheyenne River agency in the Great Reservation. It was he, too, who created the idea of ghost shirts which, decorated with symbols from dreams (stars, moons, suns, arrows), supposedly acquired the magical property of repelling white men's bullets.

Sitting Bull, the intransigent Hunkpapa Sioux, long back from his exile in Canada and retired from his starring role in Buffalo Bill's Wild West Show, was living at Standing Rock agency, unwilling to give in to the white takeover. Kicking Bear visited him and told him about the Ghost Dance, now a religion. Sitting Bull, though not converted to the faith, saw the value of the Ghost Dance in promoting Indian solidarity. He asked Kicking Bear to teach it to his tribesmen.

A week after Kicking Bear approached Sitting Bull, Indian agent James "White Hair" McLaughlin had Kicking Bear arrested. On October 16, McLaughlin said to the commissioner of Indian affairs that Sitting Bull, too, was dangerous—that he was the power behind the rabble-rousing Ghost Dance—and suggested that he be imprisoned. His superiors disagreed.

Two weeks later, at Red Leaf camp at the Pine Ridge agency in the Great Reservation, Short Bull gave a speech in which he said, "We must continue this dance. If the soldiers surround you four deep, three of you, on whom I have put holy shirts, will sing a song, which I have taught you, around them, when some of them will drop dead. Then the rest will start to run, but their horses will sink into the earth. The riders will jump from their horses, but they will sink into the earth also. Then you can do as you desire with them." He then told the tribesmen to gather naked at Pass Creek, where they would meet the dead.

Sitting Bear and Short Bull decided to take their people in a Ghost Dance march to the Badlands in South Dakota, those fantastic fossil beds with their natural castles of eroded stone on the edge of the Great Reservation. Agents told the government that at least half the Indians were dancing and that they, the agents, were losing control.

By mid-November, the Ghost Dancers were in a state of frenzy. Children stopped going to school, farmers neglected their work, stores were empty. At Pine Ridge, the agent, D. C. Roper, sent an hysterical telegram to Washington, D.C.: "Indians are dancing in the snow and are wild and crazy. . . . We need protection and we need it now. The leaders should be arrested and confined at some military post until the matter is quieted, and this should be done at once." Three thousand soldiers were stationed at Pine Ridge and Rosebud agencies in the Reservation.

Not all the whites agreed that the Ghost Dance was a forerunner to Indian violence. A former agent, Valentine McGillycuddy, said, "I should let the dance continue. The coming of the troops has frightened the Indians. If the Seventh Day Adventists prepare their ascension robes for the Second Coming of the Savior, the United States Army is not put in motion to prevent them. . . . Why should not the Indians have the same privilege? If the troops remain, trouble is sure to come."

The Indians kept dancing.

On December 15, McLaughlin sent Indian police ("Metal Breasts") led by Lieutenant Bull Head to arrest Sitting Bull. In a melée involving 150 of Sitting Bull's men and 40 Indian police, Sitting Bull and eight of his followers as well as 16 Indian police were killed. According to eyewitnesses, Sitting Bull's show horse, given him by Buffalo Bill Cody, then performed a bizarre requiem, a circus trick in which he raised one hoof as if in farewell.

Word of Sitting Bull's murder spread. The Ghost Dances became even more intense.

The War Department ordered the arrest of Big Foot, a sixty-year-old Minneconjou chief whose tribe was dancing; Colonel E. V. Sumner, of the Eighth Cavalry guarding the old Indian, refused. Big Foot, ill with what turned out to be pneumonia, moved on with his people, then set up camp near the Cheyenne River, where he took in dozens of Sitting Bull's followers. Sumner followed him and said he would have to take Big Foot in on the next day.

That night, Big Foot and his people sneaked out of camp and headed south for the Badlands through the notch that became known as Big Foot Pass. Three thousand army men were then moving in on the fringes of the Badlands, trying to force the Indians in that territory east and north. Big Foot bumped into a squadron of Seventh Cavalry led by Major S. M. Whitside. By then Big Foot was so sick he was riding on a travois. He put up a white flag and asked to talk. Whitside persuaded him to surrender. As the medicine man Yellow Bird played on an eagle-bone whistle and Indians joked with the soldiers, the captive group was marched to a spot in the trail called Wounded Knee. Colonel George A. Forsyth arrived with more Seventh Cavalry troops to take over the command. He gave Big Foot a tent and a stove, and sent the regimental surgeon to take care of him. He also had four Hotchkiss guns arranged on a hill. Then his men searched the Indians for weapons and found forty.

Yellow Bird danced, telling the warriors, "You wear ghost shirts, and the bullets will not go toward you. The prairie is large, and the bullets will not go toward you." When a soldier looked under the blanket of a brave named Black Fox, he found a hidden Winchester. Black Fox said the gun cost too much for him to willingly surrender it. What followed is unclear. Who fired first? Some say the Indians, others the whites. But a fight began, which turned into a massacre of the Indians. The Hotchkiss guns fired at a deadly speed of a round per second, killing Indian men, women, and children, as well as some Army men. When the Indians took to the hills, the soldiers chased and killed them. When it was over, the dead, frozen into grotesque shapes and their ghost shirts stained with blood, were buried in a common grave, Big Foot among them. Less than half the band remained alive. They were herded back to the reservation. It was the end of Ghost Dancing.

After the massacre, Wovoka said, "Hoo-oo! My children, my children. . . . Now [the hunting trail and the war trail] are choked with sand; they are covered with grass, the young men cannot find them. My children, today I call upon you to travel a new trail, the only trail now open—the White Man's Road." He swore he had never claimed to be a messiah, had not created the ghost shirt idea, had never incited the Indians to war. His peaceful vision had been turned inside out. Most people considered him an old bore.

The Hobo and the Bohemian:
The Founding of the
Catholic Worker Movement

AN UNLIKELY PAIR—a French hobo of peasant stock in dirty clothes and a fierce, beautiful American journalist—met by a peculiar set of circumstances in a New York apartment in 1933. Both were at a crossroads reached through a series of inspirational crises in their lives. The meeting marked the beginning of the Catholic Worker movement.

Peter Maurin was one of twenty-two children of a peasant family that had owned land for fifteen hundred years. "I am neither a bourgeois nor a proletarian," he once said. "I am a peasant. I have roots!" Nonetheless, as a young man he uprooted himself to search for meaning. After time spent as a novice with the Christian Brothers and as a member of religious youth movements, he became a believer in the ideas of the Christian personalists.

In his early thirties Maurin went to Canada as a homesteader, then migrated to the United States to become a vagabond. His life was a grind of hard labor and the open road. He worked as a miner, a janitor, and as a laborer on a railroad gang. His trousers were his pillow, and he wrapped his coat around his feet as he slept so it would not be stolen. Only rarely did he bathe.

In 1925, he underwent a religious experience. Though he always refused to talk about it, it changed his life. He argued with radicals in New York's Union Square, talking of his ambition to be a "troubadour of Christ," to create a new world, to "build the new within the shell of the old," "a society in which it is easier for people to be good." To do so, he needed a partner. Both *Commonweal* editor George Schuster and a "redheaded Irish Communist in Union Square" suggested he call on Dorothy Day.

As a child, Dorothy Day played with religion as if it were fire. To her, God was "a great noise that became louder and louder." After reading

Upton Sinclair's novel *The Jungle*, she wheeled her baby brother around the Chicago slums to see for herself the scenes Sinclair wrote about. But, as she wrote in adolescence, "I did not have the spiritual happiness that I crave, only a wicked, thrilling feeling at my heart. . . . All the old love comes back to me. It is a lust of the flesh."

In 1915, at the University of Illinois, one of her professors suggested that religion was a crutch for the weak, and she gave up her flirtations with God. She wrote, "For me Christ no longer walked the streets of this world. He was two thousand years dead, and new prophets had risen up in His place." Those prophets were Darwin, Marx, and Kropotkin, and their words were of class war. Day joined the Socialist Party.

At eighteen, she took a lover—a Marxist. For the next twelve years she lived the life of a young radical bohemian newspaper woman. She interviewed Leon Trotsky for *The Call*, wrote for *The Masses*, and went to jail as a suffragette. Her friends were New York political literati: John Reed, Hart Crane, Max Eastman, Peggy and Malcolm Cowley, Eugene O'Neill. To avoid being alone, they "sat on the ends of piers singing revolutionary songs into the starlit night, dallied on park benches, never wanting to go home to sleep but only to savor . . . youth." Sometimes in the mornings, after a night in taverns or at balls at Webster Hall, Day, the woman who had given up religion, went to mass and knelt in the back of the church, not to pray but for some nameless comfort. The "lust of the flesh" she had rejected as an adolescent assailed her: she took lovers, had an abortion at twenty-two, married, and quickly divorced.

The change in her life, a culmination of peripheral yearnings, came during her common-law marriage to a loner anarchist, Forster Battingham, with whom she lived in an old house on Staten Island, a short ferry ride from New York City. She loved "his lean, cold body as he got into bed smelling of the sea, and . . . his integrity and pride." Then she became pregnant. She did not want her child to be like her—"doubting, undisciplined, and amoral"—so she prayed for her faith. The baby, Tamar, was born March 3, 1927, when Dorothy was almost thirty. In that year, Dorothy had Tamar baptized, broke off with Forster, and was baptized herself. Doubts still plagued her. She saw the church as too luxurious and the priests as overconcerned with the mundane rather than social justice. "Grimly, coldly," she made acts of faith and hoped for a miracle.

In December 1932, on an assignment in Washington, D. C., she witnessed a hunger march, a "ragged horde" of three thousand parading with flying banners and placards through the streets. She watched them with "joy and pride in the courage of this band of men and women mounting in my heart, and with it a sense of bitterness, too."

After she completed writing her assignment, she went to the un-finished Shrine of the Immaculate Conception at Catholic University. She later wrote, "There I offered up a special prayer, a prayer which came with tears and with anguish, that some way would open up for me to use what talents I possessed for my fellow workers, for the poor." The prayer, inspired by a "ragged horde," was answered shortly after.

When Dorothy Day returned home to her New York apartment, she found waiting for her a short man in a tie, dirty shirt, and suit he had slept in, whom she described as a "broad-shouldered workingman with a high, broad head covered with graying hair, gray-eyed, with a wide mouth." It was Maurin.

Together, the two became "fools for Christ," espousing voluntary poverty and "active love." Dorothy Day ran their newspaper, *The Catholic Worker*. The first issue went on sale May Day, 1933, at Union Square, where leftists had gathered in great crowds to celebrate the Russian revolution. It sold for a penny. It still does.

Their houses of hospitality, manned by live-in workers, fed, clothed, and housed the down-and-out. Maurin brought home bums, whom he called "ambassadors of God." Without trying to rehabilitate their clients, the Catholic Workers, then as now, cared for people who stank, weren't grateful, and were sometimes violent.

Maurin remained a saintly bum, no matter how famous he became. Ill for the last five years of his life, and silent (perhaps from a stroke), he lay in bed and picked the plaster off the walls. He died in 1949. He was laid out in a suit donated for the poor. Crowds attended his simple funeral.

Dorothy Day continued in the work, a leading force in the civil rights and antiwar movements of the 1960s. She demonstrated against H-bombs and was jailed four times between 1956 and 1960. With her noble face, slanting eyes, disciplined long mouth, and elegant bone struc-ture, she was beautiful, even as an old woman, but unconscious of it. In 1980, in a residence for the poor on the Lower East Side of New York, in a room next to a shopping bag lady, she died. Her funeral, attended by hundreds, including Cesar Chavez and I. F. Stone, was held in the Church of the Nativity, a simple place with a linoleum floor. When it was requested that only the family follow her coffin, three hundred people got in line.

The Perfect Man: John Humphrey Noyes

DURING his life John Humphrey Noyes experienced a series of difficult conversions. In a sense, the first occurred before he was born. Walking in the garden while pregnant with him, his mother experienced "a baptism that was indescribable." The baby must have been included.

Later, in 1831 as Noyes, a young man just out of Dartmouth, was contemplating entering his uncle's law firm, he was consciously converted. He was drawn to religion, but reluctant—he didn't want to give up law for the ministry and believed that for him, if he converted, the ministry would be a requirement. With a feeling of "dread at being present at it," he dragged himself to a revival meeting, bearing with him the judgment that religion was a "sort of frenzy" and an intense desire not to make of fool of himself. The revival did not convert him. The day after, he felt "calm as a soldier in the day of battle" and caught a cold. The cold was a catalyst: "The severity of my cold suggested to me the idea of the uncertainty of life, and also seemed to be sent for the purpose of keeping me at home for a few days until I could humble myself." With his mother, he read the New Testament until he broke out in a sweat—and experienced successive waves of rapture: "Light gleamed upon my soul in a different way from what I had expected. It was dim and imperceptible at first, but in the course of the day it attained meridian splendor. Ere the day was done I had concluded to devote myself to the service and ministry of God."

The following winter, studying for the ministry at Andover, he engaged in a battle between God and Satan. His studies seemed too intellectual, without heart. He returned to his Bible for illumination and received it in a passage from Matthew: "Fear not ye! For I know that ye seek Jesus which was crucified. HE IS NOT HERE." It was a clear message—he decided to transfer to Yale.

In 1833, his greatest revelation came. He was enmeshed in consideration of Christ's intimation that the Apostle John would live until Christ came again. Yet almost every Christian of Noyes's time believed that the Second Coming would occur in the future. "With much zeal and under severe pressure of spirit," he read through the New Testament to find all the passages which referred to the Second Coming and reached the conclusion that it had already happened, within John's lifetime. Now he "no longer *conjectured* or *believed*, in the inferior sense of the word," he *knew* that it had occurred in A.D. 70.

Attacks against him for this unorthodox view led him to doubt established religion. He became a Perfectionist, a believer in the perfectability of man—for if the Second Coming had already been and gone, then man was living in a time when perfectability was possible. His motto: Perfection, Prayer, and Preaching. His regimen: "systematic temperance, fasting, exercise, and prayer" to conquer his "morbidly excitable" nervous system. For fourteen to sixteen hours a day he studied the Bible, and often prayed for three hours, yet sin, a remorseless pursuer, chased him until again the Bible spoke, in *Luke* 1:35: "The Holy Ghost shall come upon thee, and the power of the Highest shall overshadow thee; therefore also that holy thing which shall be born of thee shall be called the Son of God." Lighting up the page, it promised Noyes a second birth and confirmed his conviction of the Second Coming.

In 1833, he had started preaching in North Salem, New York. On February 24, 1834, in church, he confessed to the congregation his Perfectionist beliefs. That night, back in his room, "Three times in quick succession a stream of eternal love gushed through my heart." His claim of perfection naturally elicited ridicule and worse. Maybe his doubts were gone, but others' doubts weren't. When a theological student asked if Noyes himself ever sinned, Noyes answered no. The student was dumbfounded. Another student fainted at the news. Noyes lost his preaching license. "What does John mean?" his mother asked in unhappy perplexity. His friends fought him, and he felt like an outcast.

In 1834, Noyes went to New York City, "a vast accumulation of diabolical influences," where he experienced another deep depression. He felt like someone dragged down a street, pelted with brickbats and rotten eggs. The spiritual atmosphere was lurid, and the Devil stood in the wings ready to attack. All was "crawling in the dark, nauseous spirit of Satan." Only two outcomes were possible, he felt—rebirth or death. He lay in his bed and experienced a recurrent vision: he was in a net on the way to hell, to burst out of it, reborn, just before entering the flames. He felt Christ's crucifixion as if it were happening to him, and the love of Christ flooded through him like a river emptying into a huge sea where he was united with God. But the rebirth fell into chaos and doubt—a radical turning of the tides. The Bible no longer nurtured him. Even his lost love, Abigail Merwin, seemed to be the Devil in disguise. He turned atheist, felt eternally damned, and wandered the seamy side of the city, sitting on park benches to nod off only to awaken in startled fear. He could not sleep. For three weeks this went on. He made friends with lowlifes and bums to whom he preached salvation. Finally a friend rescued him and took him to New Haven.

Three years went by. Abigail reviled and finally completely rejected him by marrying someone else. He then wrote his famous Battleaxe Letter proclaiming the "marriage supper of the lamb" where "every dish is free to every guest"—open marriage, nineteenth-century-style. Moral outrage ensued. But he turned his beliefs into reality in the Oneida Community, a utopia first based in Putney, Vermont, then in Oneida, New York. Married to Harriet Holton, a homely follower three years his senior, he fathered five children in six years, all but one stillborn. These tragedies inspired one more precept—male continence, a method of intercourse without ejaculation. He said, "to be ashamed of the sexual organs is to be ashamed of God's workmanship . . . of the most perfect instruments of love and unity." In 1845, he put into practice his complex marriage plan, through which many men married many women.

The Oneida Community flourished until, in 1884, it became a joint stock company in the business of making mousetraps and silverplated cutlery. But in its heyday it was a great experiment—in sexual freedom, birth control, eugenics (planned matching of parents), and communal ownership of property. Its membership once reached nearly three hundred. And, according to Noyes, it all flowed from God and His word in the Bible.

Billy Graham Talks with God on the Eighteenth Hole

IN his seventeenth year, Billy Graham, who loved sports and girls and good times, was converted to Fundamentalism by an evangelist at a tent show. His friends started calling him preacher, even though he was considering being a dairy farmer like his father or playing pro baseball.

Still, he went to a religious college, at first Bob Jones College, then Florida Bible Institute (now Trinity College). He earned his own way by washing dishes, shining shoes, and caddying at the local golf course. In his spare time he taught himself to play golf there, and the course became one of his favorite haunts.

On a spring night in his first year at the Bible Institute, uncertain about his future, he paced the golf course. At the eighteenth hole he asked the Lord whether he should be an evangelist. He heard a voice saying: "I can use you. I need you. You make the choice; I will find the way."

He replied, "All right, Lord, if you want me, you've got me."

The following year he met a girl, Emily Cavanaugh. It was love at first sight. He was impressed with her spirituality, her gospel singing, and her intelligence. She was impressed with the way he prayed at student meetings.

That summer he proposed, and after some months of thought, she agreed. As part of a tradition at the Institute, he sent her a bunch of flowers; if she wore them in a corsage, she agreed to be engaged. Billy bought a fifty-cent bouquet—twice the usual price—but to his chagrin, she refused it. She was worried that he did not have a clear enough Christian purpose. Besides, she admitted she was in love with another man at school.

Disconsolate, he went back to wandering. One night, on the golf course, he walked along thinking of the evening of his conversion when he came to a realization. He thought, "What a fool I've been! What a hypocrite! Here I've pledged my life to Christ, and now I am about to walk out on Him just because some girl doesn't love me! The Lord is all that matters!"

He changed completely. On his lonely walks he practiced preaching to a cypress stump by the river. He went to Emily's wedding.

A few years later, when he was a sophomore at Wheaton College, he met another girl, Ruth Bell, daughter of missionaries. In 1943 they married.

And Billy went on to great personal and public success. At a Los Angeles tent crusade he caught the attention of William Randolph Hearst, who told his papers to promote the young preacher. Soon he was running Decision for Christ crusades on television, going on world tours where he preached to thousands at a time, and hobnobbing with U.S. presidents. Since 1951, Gallup has ranked him as one of the ten most admired men in the world. In 1980, he was awarded the Templeton Prize for Progress in Religion from Great Britain as one of the most influential religious leaders in the twentieth century. He and Ruth have five children. And he still plays golf.

4. Dreams and Drugs

There are those who will soberly tell you that a dream reflects the work of a mind digging within itself for hidden truth. They are probably right. But still dreams seem miraculous, for even when answering prosaic puzzles, they can come in such fantastic guises: spear-carrying savages demonstrating the key to an invention, a snake biting its tail to represent the solution to a knotty dilemma of science, the Devil playing a new sonata on a violin, Brownies acting out stories on a dream stage. Sometimes, true, they are more literal, like Loewi's dream about frog hearts. And Mary Shelley's great dream novel was conceived when she was daydreaming.

Literal or fanciful, dreams often solve things. The same is sometimes true of drug-induced trances. Drugs can give trance for the sake of trance. A great poem, supposedly drug-inspired, turned out to be no such thing. Castaneda, inspired (or maybe not) by native drugs, wrote a dissertation that turned into a best-seller. And Jack Kerouac's picaresque stream-of-consciousness novels may have been partly inspired by drugs, but he paid a huge price—his "liquid suit of armor" helped bring about his early death.

Frankenstein: *Mary Shelley's Waking Dream*

MARY SHELLEY'S CLASSIC, *Frankenstein*, was born over a series of evenings that began on the rainy night of June 16, 1816, at the Villa Diodati on the south shore of Lake Leman near Geneva, Switzerland. Gathered around the fireplace inside the main living room of the grand resort home was an illustrious group of five men and women whose arrival in May had caused quite a sensation among local gossips. Anyone eavesdropping on the group that night would have seen and heard:

LORD GEORGE GORDON BYRON, twenty-eight years old. The outrageously handsome English poet was hailed for his literary genius and scorned for his shocking personal life. Rumored to have committed many crimes—including the murder of his Turkish mistress and incest with his half-sister—the magnetic poet drew a crowd wherever he traveled. Women found him utterly irresistible; one of his lovers called him "mad, bad, and dangerous to know."

DR. JOHN WILLIAM POLIDORI, twenty-three years old. A frustrated writer, Polidori was Byron's personal physician and traveling companion. Though Polidori was a sophisticated, intelligent man with a respectable family background, Byron delighted in insulting and unnerving him. Polidori, said Byron, was "exactly the kind of person to whom, if he fell overboard, one would hold out a straw to know if the adage be true that drowning men catch at straws."

PERCY BYSSHE SHELLEY, twenty-four years old. Expelled from Oxford in 1811 because of his pamphlet *The Necessity of Atheism*, he was a commanding personality who promoted many radical views, including free love and the emancipation of women. Tall, with a fair complexion, blue eyes, and curly brown hair, Shelley, like Byron, was a brilliant conversationalist. Though married, he had won the heart of Mary Godwin, daughter of his friend William Godwin, and the two had been living and traveling together since 1814.

MARY WOLLSTONECRAFT GODWIN, nineteen years old. The daughter of two famous writers—feminist Mary Wollstonecraft and the political philosopher William Godwin—she was a petite, graceful woman with long golden hair, hazel eyes, and a placid manner. While Mary never knew her mother, who died shortly after giving birth to her, she followed in her mother's footsteps, determined to become a recognized writer. Incurring the wrath of her father by running away with Shelley (whom she later married), Mary Wollstonecraft Godwin was, behind her icy, indifferent exterior, a strong, independent, free-spirited woman. As one friend commented: "From her father she had inherited clearness and precision of intellect, firmness of will, and a certain quietude of manner, which sometimes gave way before an outbreak of strong feeling; for under this quiet bearing lay her mother's sensibility and ardor, with an imaginative power which quickened and widened her sympathies."

CLAIRE CLAREMONT, eighteen years old. Mary's stepsister was an attractive, scheming, bold young woman who for some time had been offering herself to Lord Byron. Had it not been for Claire, the group of five would never had been in Geneva at the same time. Claire, who recently had had an affair with Byron in England and was pregnant with his child (facts unknown to Shelley and Mary), was desperate over Byron's loss of interest in her. Since Shelley and Byron, each an admirer of the other's talent, had never before met, she skillfully played the role of go-between and brought them together, while at the same time she tried to maneuver herself permanently into Byron's life.

On that wet evening of June 16, the group entertained themselves by reading a French translation of a collection of German ghost stories, *Fantasmagoriana, ou Recueil d'Histoires d'Apparitions*. With the wind howling amid the thunder-and-lightning storm, they filled up their minds with tales of horror and adventure. The emotion-charged atmosphere prompted Byron to suggest that each of them write an original ghost story. All agreed.

For the next few days the writers revealed their stories. Claire, who had no interest in the game at the start, wrote nothing. Shelley, much better at poetry than at ghost stories, began a tale about a grandmother and a ghost made of ashes. Byron composed a partial tale called "The Vampyre" which years later became part of his poem "Mazeppa." Polidori, who was eager to impress the literary demigods, threw himself into the competition with great gusto but succeeded only in coming up with a terrible plot about a skull-headed lady who was punished for peeping through a keyhole. Mary Wollstonecraft Godwin, anxious to establish her literary merit, struggled to conceive an idea "to make the reader dread to look around, to curdle the blood and quicken the beatings of the heart." Hard as she tried, her efforts proved fruitless.

Her inspiration came quite unexpectedly one evening, probably June 18, as she listened to Shelley and Byron discuss the nature of the principle of life and whether it would ever be discovered. They spoke at length of Dr. Erasmus Darwin and his scientific experiments. Then they considered the possibility of reanimating a corpse. Could the parts of a creature be manufactured, put together, then given a "vital warmth"? Mary remained silent during the illuminating conversation, but her mind was spinning with images conjured up by the daring suppositions. When the discussion concluded late in the evening, Shelley and Mary returned to their nearby cottage, Villa Chapuis, but the nineteen-year-old woman was transfixed in thought, unable to sleep. Years later she vividly recalled the incident in the introduction to the 1831 edition of *Frankenstein*:

My imagination, unbidden, possessed and guided me, gifting the successive images that arose in my mind with a vividness far beyond the usual bounds of reverie. I saw—with shut eyes but acute mental vision—the pale student of unhallowed arts kneeling beside the thing he had put together. I saw the hideous phantasm of a man stretched out, and then, on the working of some powerful engine, show signs of life and stir with an uneasy, half-vital motion. Frightful must it be, for supremely frightful would be the effect of any human endeavor to mock the stupendous mechanism of the Creator of the world. His success would terrify the artist; he would rush away from his odious handiwork, horror-stricken. He would hope that, left to itself, the slight spark of life which he had communicated would fade; that this thing which had received such imperfect animation would subside into dead matter, and he might sleep in the belief that the silence of the grave would quench forever the transient existence of the hideous corpse which he had looked upon as the cradle of life. He sleeps, but he is awakened; he opens his eyes; behold, the horrid thing stands at his bedside, opening his curtains and looking on him with yellow, watery, but speculative eyes. . . .

Swift as light and as cheering was the idea that broke in upon me. "I have found it. What terrified me will terrify others; and I need only describe the specter which had haunted my midnight pillow." On the morrow I announced that I had thought of a story. I began the day with the words, "It was on a dreary night of November," making only a transcript of the grim terrors of my waking dream.

Frankenstein was born.

Eye of the Needle: Elias Howe and the Iron Seamstress

ELIAS HOWE was a desperate man. Born into a poor family, he was still poor at age twenty after years of hard work, and the future looked even bleaker. With a wife and three children to support, Howe—a machinist by trade—needed more than a lucky break. One day in 1839, while working at his job in a Boston machine shop, he overheard his boss telling a customer that fortune was assured to anyone who could invent a sewing machine. That became his goal.

At first, Howe carefully observed his wife's hand sewing and tried to make his machine duplicate her motions. When that failed, he decided to devise a new kind of stitch—one that was just as sturdy but that a machine could make. Once he changed courses, his work started to progress. But he had a problem with placement of the eye in the machine's needle. Initially, he pierced an eye in the middle of the needle, only to find that his stitches were irregular and imperfect. However, he was discouraged for only a short time. The answer came to him in a nightmare.

After falling into a sound sleep, Howe dreamed that he was kidnapped by a band of savages who threatened to kill him if he did not invent a sewing machine in twenty-four hours. Unable to meet the deadline, the machinist was led to his execution. As the spears of the savages descended on him, Howe noticed that they had eye-shaped holes close to the tips. At that moment he shook off the nightmare, woke up, and knew exactly where to place the eye in his sewing machine needle.

Howe completed his working model in April 1845, secured a patent on September 10, 1846, and began to demonstrate his sewing marvel. There were some shortcomings: it could only sew a straight line a short distance before the cloth had to be repositioned; the thread kept breaking; and the feeding mechanism was faulty. However, the machine made a good lock-stich—250 a minute—and easily outdistanced any seamstress. Impressed as they were with the machine, American manufacturers did not want it. They believed it would put American laborers out of work. And the cost of the machine—$300—was too high.

Discouraged but not defeated, Howe and his family sailed to England to offer his machine there. He sold the rights to the machine to corset-maker William Thomas and for eight months worked in London adapting the machine to sewing corsets. When Howe finished, Thomas demoted him to general repairman and errand runner. Howe protested and was promptly fired. Once again in dire financial straits, Howe borrowed money to send his family back to America. When he followed months later, arriving in New York in April 1849, he learned that his wife was dying of consumption and that all of their household goods, homeward-bound from England, had been destroyed in a shipwreck.

After his wife died, Howe lost interest in promoting his sewing machine—until he learned that during his trip abroad several American manufacturers had started to market sewing machines based on his original model. Determined to protect his interests, Howe confronted each manufacturer, demanding financial compensation for patent infringement. Some companies, afraid of court battles, readily agreed, paying Howe a handsome sum for manufacturing under his patent and then promising to pay him a specified sum per machine sold. Elias Howe, without producing any machines of his own, was beginning to reap big profits. Some manufacturers, most notably I. M. Singer & Co., were not so easily maneuvered.

While Howe had patented a working model of the sewing machine, Isaac Singer, also a former machinist, turned it into a "practical" machine in 1851. Singer's machine was undeniably better than Howe's with these major improvements: a straight needle that moved up and down (Howe's needle was curved and moved horizontally); an adjustable presser-foot that held the fabric in place and enabled the machine to sew a long, continuous seam or a curved seam (instead of Howe's baster plate that only permitted short, straight seams); and a foot-treadle (to replace Howe's hand-driven crank wheel). But Singer's machine did have an eye-pointed needle and made a lockstitch formed with a second thread from a shuttle—all features patented by Howe. Nevertheless, Singer, a flamboyant, ambitious businessman ("I don't give a damn for the invention; the dimes are what I'm after"), refused to make any kind of a deal with Howe.

When Howe first made a personal visit to Singer's machine shop in 1851, the two men got into a quarrel. Unable to meet Howe's demand of $2,000 for the rights to manufacture under his patent, Singer lost his temper and threatened to throw Howe down the steps of the shop. A year later Howe returned to ask Singer for an even larger sum—$25,000. For a second time Howe was asked to leave the shop. Singer's business partner Edward Clark said, "Howe is a perfect humbug. He knows quite well he never invented anything of value. We have sued him for saying that he is entitled exclusively to use of the combination of needle and shuttle. . . ." The "Sewing Machine War" was on.

Singer and Clark set out to prove that Elias Howe was not the first man to invent a sewing machine—a fact that was certainly true. In 1790, an English cabinetmaker, Thomas Saint, took out a sewing machine patent in London. After him came Barthélemy Thimmonier, a French tailor, who constructed his machine as early as 1829. But American courts did not care about foreign machines that were never sold in America. Singer and Clark were on the verge of defeat when they learned of an American inventor, Walter Hunt, who had invented a sewing machine in 1834, eleven years ahead of Howe.

The prolific Walter Hunt was a genius with a wide assortment of inventions to his credit, among them a paper collar for men's shirts, an ice plow, a repeating rifle, and the safety pin which he devised in three hours. His brilliance, sad to say, did not extend to the financial arena: He sold the full rights to the safety pin for $400 in order to repay a $15 debt. In addition, he never applied for a patent for his sewing machine, because he feared that his invention would take jobs away from the laboring classes.

By 1853, Hunt's machine was a rusty piece of disassembled junk. Yet it was clear that the sewing apparatus had an eye-pointed needle and turned out a lockstitch by use of a shuttle. Singer convinced Hunt to apply for a belated patent and to bring suit against Howe. The case was decided on May 24, 1854, in favor of Elias Howe. The ruling, in part: "When the first inventor allows his discovery to slumber for eighteen years, with no probability of its ever being brought into useful activity . . . all reasonable presumption should be in favor of the inventor who has been the means of conferring the real benefit upon the world." Following that decision was one against Singer, who subsequently paid $15,000 to Howe plus a royalty on every machine he sold.

Before long Howe was receiving more than $4,000 a week in royalties and was well on his way to becoming a millionaire.

Frogs' Hearts in a Physiologist's Dream

IN 1936, German physiologist Otto Loewi won the Nobel Prize for his study of the chemical transmission of nerve impulses. Loewi first conceived his transmission theory in 1903, but he was not able to prove it until 1920. The blueprints for the experiment that won his prize came to him in a dream. He recalled this remarkable vision:

The night before Easter Sunday of that year [1920] I awoke, turned on the light, and jotted down a few notes on a tiny slip of thin paper. Then I fell asleep again. It occurred to me at six o'clock in the morning that during the night I had written down something most important, but I was unable to decipher the scrawl. The next night, at three o'clock, the idea returned. It was the design of an experiment to determine whether or not the hypothesis of chemical transmission that I had uttered seventeen years ago was correct. I got up immediately, went to the laboratory, and performed a simple experiment on a frog heart according to the nocturnal design. Its results became the foundation of the theory of the chemical transmission of the nervous impulse.

The hearts of two frogs were isolated, the first with its nerves, the second without. Both hearts were attached to Straub canulas filled with a little Ringer solution. The vagus nerve of the first heart was stimulated for a few minutes. Then the Ringer solution that had been in the first heart during the stimulation of the vagus was transfered to the second heart. [This second heart] slowed, and its beats diminished just as if its vagus had been stimulated. Similarly, when the accelerator nerve was stimulated and the Ringer from this period transferred, the second heart speeded up and its beats increased. These results unequivocally proved that the nerves do not influence the heart directly but liberate from their terminals specific chemical substances which cause the well-known modifications of the function of the heart characteristic of the stimulation of its nerves.

The Snake Biting Its Tail

GERMAN CHEMIST Friedrich August Kekulé had planned to be an architect. After studying architecture for only one semester in 1847, however, he took a chemistry class that changed the course of his career. Nonetheless, he still relied on his drawing and building talents when working out structural theories of the carbon atom and its compounds.

The formula for the structure of benzene had puzzled him for years until one night in an armchair in front of his fireplace, he fell asleep. The formula for benzene—a closed chain of six carbon atoms—came to him in a dream. Later he recollected the dream: "I dozed off. . . . The atoms danced before my eyes. . . . The smaller groups remained in the background. My inner eye . . . now distinguished bigger forms of manifold configurations . . . long rows, more densely joined, everything in motion, contorting and turning like snakes. . . . One of the snakes took hold of its own tail and whirled derisively before my eyes. I woke up as though I had been struck by lightning. . . . I spent the rest of the night working out the consequences."

Robert Louis Stevenson and His Brownies

AS A CHILD, author Robert Louis Stevenson experienced nightmares that caused him to wake up screaming, his body contracted in distortion. When he grew older the dreams lost some of their terrifying intensity but still left him with "a flying heart, a freezing scalp, cold sweats, and the speechless midnight fear." While a student at Edinburgh College in Scotland, the dreams continued to hound him to such an extent that he sought treatment from a doctor. The medical aid, whatever it was, seemed to cure his physical reactions, and though he still had frequent dreams, he found a creative and profitable outlet for them.

In his essay, "A Chapter on Dreams," Stevenson, writing in the third person, described in great detail how his dreams became a stage upon which he conceived some of his best story ideas. That stage was filled with little people called Brownies, who night after night conjured up an assortment of entertaining tales. Sleep was no longer a prison, it was a ticket to a box seat at the theater. While Stevenson admitted that he had to pull the stories together and tighten up the plots, the Brownies could be trusted to produce entertaining, intriguing dramas. Occasionally, he conceded, they turned in a less than adequate performance, usually when he had fallen into a very deep sleep. When that happened, he stated, drowsiness overcame them, and they went "stumbling and maundering through their parts, and the play, to the awakened mind, is seen to be a tissue of absurdities." At the end of the dreams essay, Stevenson lavished praise upon his nocturnal friends: "And for the Little People, what shall I say they are but just my Brownies, God bless them! who do one-half my work for me while I am fast asleep. . . . I am an excellent adviser, something like Molière's servant; I pull back and I cut down; and I dress the whole in the best words and sentences that I can find and make. I hold the pen, too; and I do the sitting at the table, which is about the worst of it. . . . On the whole, I have some claim to share, though not so largely as I do, in the profits of our common enterprise."

One of the stories which the Brownies coauthored was a "fine bogey-tale," *The Strange Case of Dr. Jekyll and Mr. Hyde.* In Stevenson's words: "I had long been trying to write a story on this subject, to find a body, a vehicle, for that strong sense of man's double being, which must at times come in upon and overwhelm the mind of every thinking creature. . . . For two days I went about racking my brains for a plot of any sort; and on the second night I dreamed the scene at the window, and a scene afterward split in two, in which Hyde, pursued for some crime, took the powder and underwent the change in the presence of his pursuers. All the rest was made awake and consciously, although I think I can trace in much of it the manner of my Brownies."

Jack Kerouac: The Recording Angel
Inspired by Dope and Booze

BOOZING, doped up, sometimes down-and-out, Jack Kerouac, father/ brother of the Beats, rocketed with his hipster friends across the America they hated and loved, seekers after nirvana, seekers after truth. Ideas flashed across the big screen of Kerouac's jazzed-up mind, like reflections of rainwet, neon-splashed maws of the Main Streets they sped through, inspired by the goddesses of dope, alcohol, and car lot–smokestack cities. He seemed to be a beatific drunk zonked on stream-of-consciousness, an ecstatic desperado always, in bed or scribbling or watching life flash by, searching for the unnameable grail.

Even as a child he was prone to visions. Born of French Catholic parents, brought up in the ordinary town of Lowell, Massachusetts, as a little boy he saw Christ or the Virgin Mary pushing the foot of his bed— after which a Santa Claus elf slammed the door.

He entered Columbia University on a football scholarship in 1941, but his college life lasted only a little more than a year. Soon his New York apartment became home to a number of New York intellectuals, including Allen Ginsberg (beat poet, skinny, with horn-rimmed glasses) and William S. Burroughs (author of *Naked Lunch*, a love song to dope), who cut off his little finger on what he called a "Van Gogh kick." In 1944, Kerouac and Burroughs shared an apartment. Reading decadent French authors Céline and Rimbaud, they experimented with amphetamines, which they obtained by disassembling a nasal inhaler, removing the amphetamine-soaked pads, and swallowing them with coffee. Jack was so pale from speed that he had to wear pancake makeup to look human in the subway.

In 1946, he met Neal Cassady, an ex-jailbird who stole five hundred cars by the time he was twenty-one. Super-athletic and sexual, Cassady became Kerouac's foster brother.

Meanwhile, carefully and thoroughly, Kerouac was writing his first book, *The Town and the City*. To inspire himself, he once tried to have intercourse with a hole he dug in the backyard of his parents' house in Ozone Park, Queens, where they had moved. And by then he often went on the road, sometimes with Cassady and sometimes alone, traveling to North Carolina, San Francisco, Mexico. After his father died, his mother often accompanied him, and her home was his home base.

By 1949, he had started a new book, the embryo of *On the Road*. On the summer nights of 1950, he smoked grass with his friends in Elitch Gardens, a deserted public park in Denver, a custom they called "Elitching." That year he went to Mexico, where he and Neal, stoned, orgied to a mambo in a whorehouse. After Neal went back home to his wife Carolyn, Kerouac settled down in Mexico City, living on cheeseburgers, mangoes, and fifteen joints a day.

In the fall, back home with his mother, whom he called Mémère, he lived a more ordinary life—on the surface. After eating dinner with her, he smoked two or three joints in the bathroom, then began writing at the kitchen table.

In April 1951, by then married to Joan Haverty, he began the final version of *On the Road*, "bop prosody," feeding two-foot rolls of glued-together Chinese art paper into his typewriter in a continuous scroll and typing at a hundred words a minute, throwing the last seven years of his life, starring Neal, down on the paper, a picaresque tale of wanderers on the move. The writing rules he had learned at school did not apply. They had nothing to do with the wild, unfettered, speedy life he was trying to impose on the paper. In "Essentials of Spontaneous Prose," he wrote: "Write excitedly, with writing-or-typing cramp." He said, "Once God moves the hand, you go back and revise it's a sin."

Joan threw him out. He ended up at a friend's house, typing, now on a roll of teletype paper, a revision of the book he had written in only twenty days. It took him six years to sell it.

Meanwhile, in Neal Cassady's attic, he wrote *Visions of Cody*, "tranced fixation dreaming," a process he described as beginning "not from preconceived idea of what to say about image but from jewel center of interest in subject of image at *moment* of writing," in which he wrote "outwards swimming in seas of language." In the book itself, he said: ". . . let us ascertain, in the morning, if there is a way of abstracting the interesting paragraphs of material in all this running consciousness stream that can be used as the progressing lightning chapters of a great essay about the wonders of the world as it continually flashes up in retrospect; as, for example, this night I ran cold water into a glass at the sink while everybody was high and immediately was reminded completely and perfectly of the cool exact waters of Pine Brook on a summer afternoon."

He revised *Visions of Cody* while stoned in Mexico, eating peyote, listening to jazz, and having sex with a Mexican whore and an American tourist. In a nickel notebook, sitting on the toilet, he wrote *Dr. Sax*, commemorating an imaginary childhood friend, who sought to kill the World Snake.

In 1955, again in Mexico, he wrote spontaneous poems, "jazz poet blowing long blues in an afternoon jazz session on Sunday"—poems of his dead brother, maps, rivers, doves—zonked on Buddhist meditation, marijuana, and sometimes morphine. While living in a hut on the roof of a house, following that, he started a novel, *Tristessa*, about his inamorata, a hooker-addict.

By the 1960s, his muse had changed from dope to booze; though he had always been a drinker, he now became a bona fide alcoholic, loving his "liquid suit of armor, the shield which not even Flash Gordon's super ray gun could penetrate." While it protected him from outside, it killed him inside. He saw snakes coming out of his vomit, sperm in mineral baths ready to attack him, and poison in his food. He dreamed of devils, trolls, the Cross, God Monster Machine, copulating vultures, and slime.

Timothy Leary, guru of the 1960s dopers, gave him psilocybin. Under its influence Jack remarked, "Walking on water wasn't built in a day" and "I think I'll take a shit out the window at the moon." But the 1960s were not his time. When he saw an American flag draped over a hippie couch, he asked if those who had put it there were Communists. He disapproved of dopers and all the young who, taking up the love crusade, copied his pilgrimages.

In 1966, long divorced from Joan, he married the sister of a childhood friend. Working for $1.70 an hour as a seamstress, she helped him take care of his mother, paralyzed by a stroke "except for her asshole and her mouth." He drank. One day, drinking, watching "The Galloping Gourmet" on television, eating a can of tuna, he began to bleed internally. He was dead by the next morning.

A Dream of the Devil

THE DEVIL and his works seemed bent on becoming part of the brilliant eighteenth-century Italian violinist Giuseppe Tartini's life. Though his father wanted him to become a priest, he abandoned his religious studies and went to Padua, where he studied law and led a wild life. He also fell in love with his pupil, who was the daughter of a cardinal. To make her entirely his own, or so he thought, he kidnapped and married her. This was a crime, particularly in view of the eminence of the woman's family, and he had to run away to avoid jail. He hid in a Franciscan monastery in Assisi, where he studied violin under the monastery organist.

After he returned to Padua, he became an expert violinist. He eventually opened a violin school and was solo violinist and leader of the Basilica di Sant' Antonio. Known for his brilliant technical skill and ability to innovate, Tartini introduced new methods of bowing and discovered new violin tones. He wrote 150 sonatas, 140 concertos, and 50 trios, but of all the compositions he wrote he is probably most famous for the work that came to him in a dream: the "Devil's Trill Sonata." One night the devil came to Tartini in his sleep, seeking to buy his soul. To tempt him, the devil picked up a violin and started playing a beguiling, difficult sonata with double stopping and intricate, breathtaking trill passages.

Tartini was overwhelmed by its beauty. As he later said, "I felt enraptured, transported, enchanted; my breath was taken away, and I awoke. Seizing my violin I tried to retain the sounds I had heard. But it was in vain. The piece I then composed, the Devil's Sonata, was the best I ever wrote, but how far below the one I had heard in my dream!"

Whether he had to sell his soul to capture even a shadow of the sonata on paper, he would not say.

Castaneda: The Anthropologist Who Passed Through the Door to Another Reality—and Became a Best-selling Author

ON AUGUST 4, 1961, Carlos Castaneda, a young anthropology graduate student at the University of California, Los Angeles, bumped down an Arizona road in an old pickup truck. It was the beginning of a trip into another reality—an Indian world that he would later describe, to controversy and acclaim, in best-selling books. With him were six Indians. One was Don Juan (Juan Matus), an old Yaqui Indian *bruyo* (sorcerer) whom the student had met in a Greyhound bus depot because of a mutual interest in the Indian use of drugs. When they arrived at a small house, the student, in a dimly lit room, experienced the first of twenty-two drug trips. He chewed six peyote buttons, following each with a swig of tequila and a little water and food. Then, after a time, his vision narrowed to a pinpoint, and he saw a transparent dog drink from a water bowl. After that he crawled out of a hard metal tunnel to see the dog again, now iridescent, as he himself became. Both had long glowing manes. The two played together, then the student ran toward a yellow place, looked through a tank of water, and returned to consciousness. One of the Indians told him that during this time he had vomited thirty times, had convulsions, and barked like a dog. He had also, he was told, pissed on the dog and endured the dog pissing on him. The dog was Mescalito, the spirit of peyote.

From then on, for ten years, the young man, Carlos Castaneda, was the disciple of Don Juan, who taught him to be a sorcerer. One avenue of learning was drugs: peyote—serious and philosophical; jimson weed—like an unpredictable woman; hallucinogenic mushrooms, with all their spiritual power.

Under peyote, he saw Mescalito again—as a creature with a cricket body, green, warty skin, and a pointed head. He saw in the dark, watched things be transformed, learned peyote songs, and went from intense joy to total terror.

Under jimson weed, which he smeared on his body, he divined the truth by observing lizards, their mouths and eyes stitched shut by Don Juan. He flew naked to a half mile from the house, then walked back home. He asked Don Juan if he had really flown: "Did my body fly like a bird?" Don Juan replied that he had flown like a man who had taken jimson, the Devil's weed. Castaneda then said: "If I had tied myself to a rock with a heavy chain, I would have flown just the same, because my body had nothing to do with my flying."

Don Juan was incredulous. "If you tie yourself to a rock, I am afraid you will have to fly holding the rock with its heavy chain."

Under mushrooms, he felt his flesh melt, flowed through walls, and traveled inside Don Juan's chest. He turned into a crow and flew; saw a giant gnat, guardian of other worlds, which was 100 feet tall, and thought he overpowered it; rode in a bubble image in green fog.

It was not just raw experience. The plants provided the door to power;

through intricate Indian ritual he entered into an Indian view of reality, a place where he could "see" the essence of the world, not through intellect but direct bodily experience, in a direct flow of uncensored images. And if he wrestled with other world figures, he would, if victorious, gain super-human powers. But in the end, fear of losing himself and an experience in which Don Juan made his car disappear, then reappear under a sombrero, made him decide to give up drugs.

He turned his field notes into a master's thesis, dedicated to Don Juan. In 1973, U.C.L.A. awarded him a Ph.D., based on a dissertation consisting of his notes about Don Juan and his third volume of field reports. That dissertation became a book: *Conversations with Don Juan*. It was followed by *A Separate Reality*, on the same theme, and many others. Castaneda became rich, for the counterculture, wanting a legitimization of their drug scene, took up his works. Later, when those of the "new age consciousness" turned from drugs, so did Castaneda and Don Juan—they had their mystical experiences without the help of plants.

Scholars picked over the books looking for flaws in logic, playing with the ideas of separate realities, trying to prove Castaneda holy man or hoaxer. Anthropologists, who reviewed his first book mostly with favor, raised general questions: Was it art or science? Fake or real? What does *fake* mean? Isn't raising these questions at all as ridiculous as Carlos asking if he really flew? Is the self a dream? Is there a non-ordinary reality which one can enter?

Others pointed out inconsistencies; for example, the Yaquis do not have drug cults, but Don Juan was supposedly a Yaqui. (Castaneda said that Don Juan, born of Yaqui parents, became a wanderer after his parents were killed.) Weston La Barre, author of *The Peyote Cult*, called *Conversations* "tiresomely dull, posturing pseudo-ethnography, and, intellectually, kitsch." And Jacques Meunier, an anthropologist, described Castaneda as a "marvelous cheater."

The object of this fierce scholarly debate is short, with black curly hair and a loquacious manner. His story of his life does not gibe with the documented facts. He claims, for example, to have been born in Brazil in 1935, but his birth certificate places him in Peru in 1925. He says his father was a professor of literature, but in truth, though his father passed a liberal arts course, he was an intellectual artisan-shopkeeper who read philosophy and played chess.

In 1948, Carlos went to Lima where he finished high school and attended the Bellas Artes school. He was a gambler—his schoolmates called him Smile of Gold. In 1951, he married a Chinese-Peruvian girl by whom he had a child, Esperanza, who was raised in a convent. By 1955, he was in Los Angeles and entered U.C.L.A. In that year, too, he became an American citizen.

He has told Gwyneth Cravens, in an interview published in the February 1973 issue of *Harper's* magazine, how he "dreams" his books:

> Don Juan taught me to control my dreaming as a way of gaining power. First, you establish a familiar reference point, like your hands, and as you dream, you keep returning to that image. You *will* yourself to do it. From there you can go on to analyze particular details in a given dream or choose what you want to dream about. In the afternoon I go through the notebooks with all my field notes in them and translate them into English. Then I sleep in the early evening and dream what I write.
>
> When I wake up, I can work all night. Everything has arranged itself smoothly in my head, and I don't need to rewrite. My regular writing is actually very dry and labored.

As for what he writes: Is it true? What is truth? Is it real? What is reality? And does it matter?

"Kubla Khan": Composed in a Dream?

IN THE PREFACE to "Kubla Khan" (subtitled "A Vision in a Dream"), British poet Samuel Taylor Coleridge gave a very precise accounting of how he had come to write the highly acclaimed, magical, musical poem. That explanation, one of literature's most enthralling and often-repeated stories, is one that is also riddled with gaping holes. To repeat Coleridge's claims:

> The following fragment is here published at the request of a poet of great and deserved celebrity [Lord Byron], and, as far as the author's own opinions are concerned, rather as a psychological curiosity, than on the ground of any supposed *poetic* merits.
>
> In the summer of the year 1797, the author, then in ill health, had retired to a lonely farmhouse between Porlock and Linton, on the Exmoor confines of Somerset and Devonshire. In consequence of a slight indisposition, an anodyne had been prescribed, from the effects of which he fell asleep in his chair at the moment that he was reading the following sentence, or words of the same substance, in *Purchas's Pilgrimage*: "Here the Khan Kubla commanded a palace to be built, and a stately garden thereunto. And thus ten miles of fertile ground were enclosed with a wall." The author continued for about three hours in a profound sleep, at least of the external senses, during which time he has the most vivid confidence that he could not have composed less than from two to three hundred

lines, if that indeed can be called composition in which all the images rose up before him as *things*, with a parallel production of the correspondent expressions, without any sensation or consciousness of effort. On awakening he appeared to himself to have distant recollection of the whole, and taking his pen, ink, and paper, instantly and eagerly wrote down the lines that are here preserved. At this moment he was unfortunately called out by a person on business from Porlock, and detained by him above an hour, and on his return to his room found, to his no small surprise and mortification, that though he still retained some vague and dim recollection of the general purport of the vision, yet, with the exception of some eight or ten scattered lines and images, all the rest had passed away like images on the surface of a stream into which a stone has been cast, but alas! without the after restoration of the latter!

The "anodyne" referred to in the preface was two grains of opium. An admitted opium addict, Coleridge spent two-thirds of his life tormented by a habit he despised but could not kick. Suffering from ailments that resulted from a bout of rheumatic fever when he was eighteen, the poet insisted that he took the drug only to ease his constant, dreadful pains. However, he also consumed opium to relieve his ever-present mental stress and, at least in the beginning, to give himself pleasurable, sensual experiences.

The drug, which Coleridge took orally in the form of laudanum (a tincture of opium), caused the poet to develop chronic physical problems. Among his numerous complaints were indigestion, constipation, nausea, sleeplessness, dizziness, sweating, loss of appetite, and loss of weight. His life was a continuous struggle to support his wife and family—and his addiction. Opium eventually tore apart his home life and cost him the valued friendships of several of his closest and most trusted colleagues. A slave to opium, he would commit almost any sin to get it.

Even before opium became his earthly god, Coleridge was quite adept at lying. It was a vice that most of his friends tried to overlook. For, despite his shortcoming, he was a charming, kind, gentle man whose engaging conversation and superior intellect captured for him many devoted and loyal friends. Yet it was his habitual lying that has led a number of the poet's biographers to investigate the facts concerning the composition of "Kubla Khan." Most of the skeptics agree that the following questions have never been adequately answered:

1. If "Kubla Khan" was written in 1797, why wasn't it published until 1816? Why did Coleridge, who was always worried about money, hold on to the poem for almost twenty years?
2. Coleridge was a prolific letter writer and also kept extensive diaries/notebooks. Yet nowhere in his correspondence or records is there a

mention of the incredible opium- and dream-inspired poem. This is very out of character for Coleridge, who usually kept his friends well informed of the progress of his work. But even if he chose, for whatever reason, not to tell anyone about the poem, why is there no trace of it in his notebooks which were only for his personal use?

3. "Kubla Khan" is carefully and methodically constructed. It is the work of a man who labored over his poems. Yet the preface claims that in his dream "all the images rose up before him as *things*, with a parallel production of the corresponding expressions, without any sensation or consciousness of effort." Was the poem delivered to him in mint condition? He didn't have to change a word? No, say several of his biographers. One author, Molly Lefebure, author of *Samuel Taylor Coleridge: A Bondage of Opium*, notes that some of Coleridge's poems, or poem fragments, written while he was drugged, do appear in his notebooks, but Lefebure calls them nothing more than "poor doggerel." As an example she cites the following, written on a trip to Malta aboard the *Speedwell*, a British merchant vessel:

> A Health to Captain Findlay!
> Bravo! Captain Findlay!
> When we made but ill Speed with the Speedwell,
> Neither Poet, nor Sheep could feed well
> The Poet ate Muffin, the Sheep eat its Hay
> And Poet & Pig how [grief?] rotted Liver
> And yet Malta, dear Malta as far off as ever
> Bravo! Captain Findlay—
> Foretold to a fair wind
> Of a constant mind,
> For he knew which way the Wind lay.

Another of Coleridge's biographers, Norman Fruman, author of *Coleridge, the Damaged Archangel*, points out that an autographed manuscript of "Kubla Khan," predating the 1816 published version, shows many alterations in the text of the poem. These changes show a conscious reworking of the lines, a direct contradiction to the assertions found in the preface.

4. Before falling into the opium-induced sleep, Coleridge was reading Purchas. The book, *Purchas, His Pilgrimage*, was not only a rare book, but also a huge folio, approximately one thousand pages long. It is very unlikely that the poet would have taken such a massive book along on a short visit to a lonely farmhouse. And it is even more

unlikely that the farmhouse had a library which contained such a unique book.

Conclusion? It is possible, even probable, that in 1797 at the farmhouse Coleridge had a dream or reverie in which the major components of "Kubla Khan" were revealed to him. These images stayed with him, until at a later date he took the time to write down the verses and polish them into a beautifully crafted poem, published as a "fragment" in 1816.

Although he had made several attempts to rid himself of the opium addiction, Coleridge met with repeated failure until he agreed to live with a surgeon, James Gillman, who resided at Highgate, a suburb of London. When he arrived at the Gillman home on April 16, 1816, he needed a dose of opium at least every sixty hours. In a relatively short time he learned to trust and confide in the doctor. The two men became close friends, and Coleridge remained with Gillman and his family for the next eighteen years, until the poet's death in 1834. While Coleridge was unable to totally divorce himself from drug dependence, he did cut down considerably on the amounts of opium he consumed. Under Gillman's strict medical supervision, he was able to pull himself up out of his self-imposed hell. Still, the opium had destroyed much of his personal happiness and professional satisfaction. As Molly Lefebure concludes: "Opium was an essential part of Samuel Taylor Coleridge. He and opium traveled literally as blood-brothers for close on forty years of his entire sixty-two. The central action of the greater part of these forty years was almost unremitting struggle against a devastating tyranny and an even more devastating burden of guilt arising from his obsessive self-reproach for wasted gifts and ingratitude to the Maker who had so liberally endowed him, all to such abortive purpose."

5. *On Death*

In contemplating the waste of death, creators are overwhelmed, like most of us, with huge, towering emotions, rage and sorrow, unutterable regret. The death can be personal—that of a friend or members of the family. It can be impersonal—the wanton destruction of strangers.

Lives have been irrevocably altered by the premature deaths of loved ones. The death of a sibling affected Selman Waksman, discoverer of streptomycin, and James Barrie, author of *Peter Pan*, to such an extent that the course of their lives was set. Tennyson wrote "In Memoriam" to immortalize a friend who died young. The angry young playwright John Osborne never got over the horror of his father's death and the tawdriness of his funeral: the themes keep cropping up in his plays.

Movers, doers, and great artists can be profoundly moved by the idea of death: strangers killed in holocausts, executed for their political beliefs, dying from malnutrition, obliterated by the pointless destruction of a small village. From those deaths have come a philosophy of death and dying, a life passionately dedicated to politics, and the great painting *Guernica*.

Guernica: *Picasso's Indictment of War*

GUERNICA, a farming village in Vizcaya, one of the three Basque provinces in northern Spain, has always been the cultural and religious capital of the Basques and has always been politically autonomous. When civil war broke out in Spain in July 1936, the Basques supported the Republican government against the rebel military forces of General Francisco Franco, who was backed by the fascist governments of Germany and Italy. So, on April 26, 1937, when seven thousand citizens of Guernica heard gunfire in the distance, they did not panic; for their town was not a military base, it was an undefended village, an historic and revered site.

The first German bomber arrived over the village at about 4:30 P.M. After making one cursory pass, Lieutenant Rudolf von Moreau of the Condor Legion dropped six bombs in the center of town, near the railway station plaza. Since Monday was market day in Guernica, the streets were filled with people. About 350 of them were in the plaza area when the bombs exploded. One eyewitness who saw the first group of people killed said: "They were lifted high into the air, maybe twenty feet or so, and they started to break up, legs, arms, heads, and bits and pieces flying everywhere."

The single plane disappeared, but within a half hour three bombers, flying abreast, swept down on the town, dropping high-explosive, antipersonnel, and incendiary bombs (which could reach five thousand degrees Fahrenheit when ignited). Soon those planes were joined by additional air squadrons; altogether there were forty-three German fighters and bombers. Wave after wave of planes descended on Guernica. A newspaperman from the *Times* of London reported: "The tactics of the bombers . . . were as follows. First, small parties of airplanes threw heavy bombs and hand grenades all over the town, choosing area after area in orderly fashion. Next came fighting machines, which swooped low to machine-gun those who ran in panic from dugouts, some of which had already been penetrated by 1,000-pound bombs, which make a hole twenty-five feet deep. . . . The rhythm of this bombing of an open town was, therefore, a logical one: first, hand grenades and heavy bombs to stampede the population, then machine-gunning to drive them below, next heavy and incendiary bombs to wreck the houses and burn them on top of the victims."

Primarily a town of wood-frame buildings, Guernica was soon ablaze. The town's narrow streets acted as wind tunnels, fanning the fires and spreading the flames. Since one of the first structures destroyed was the fire station, citizens resorted to bucket brigades in a feeble attempt to put out the fires. The smell of scorched wood, plaster, and human flesh was everywhere.

By the time the three-hour attack was over, the valley town was covered by a thick blanket of smoke. According to Gordon Thomas and Max Morgan Witts, authors of *Guernica: The Crucible of World War II*, more than ten thousand pounds of explosives were dropped on the village. Approximately three-fourths of all buildings were destroyed; more than eight hundred people were dead. Within three days Franco's forces moved in and took over.

As soon as news of the civilian massacre leaked to the outside world, Franco issued an immediate denial of the bombing. A member of his staff claimed the Basques themselves had gutted the town in order to blame it on Franco and use that propaganda to their political advantage. Subsequent investigations clearly showed that Franco's closest advisers had conspired with the German high command, but neither had anticipated the worldwide outrage that followed the holocaust.

When Guernica was bombed, Pablo Picasso was in Paris trying to come up with an idea for a mural for the Spanish pavilion at the upcoming International Exhibit in Paris. Commissioned by the Republican government of Spain, Picasso searched for a theme that would rally support against the Franco regime. A Spaniard, Picasso had strong political convictions but was having a difficult time putting his thoughts to canvas—until Guernica.

When he read the reports and saw the gruesome photographs of dead women and children in the Paris newspapers, Picasso was enraged. He knew he had found the theme for his mural, and by May 1 he had already completed a number of sketches. By May 11 the sketches were transferred to a huge sheet of unbleached muslin measuring 25 feet 5¾ inches by 11 feet 5 inches. In six weeks *Guernica* was finished.

Picasso considered color for the painting but ultimately did the work in black, white, and gray. The absence of color only intensified the starkness of the figures: a horse transfixed with a spear, a dismembered soldier, a bull with human eyes, a woman screaming in agony as she holds her dead child. In May 1937, the artist issued a statement. In part he said, "The Spanish struggle is the fight of reaction against the people, against freedom. My whole life as an artist has been nothing more than a continuous struggle against reaction and the death of art. . . . In the panel on which I am working and which I shall call *Guernica*, and in all my recent works of art, I clearly express my abhorrence of the military caste which has sunk Spain in an ocean of pain and death."

In 1939 (the year that Franco won the civil war in Spain), *Guernica* went on exhibit in major cites of the United States. When World War II broke out, Picasso agreed to safeguard the masterpiece in New York City's Museum of Modern Art. Except for a handful of times when it was loaned out to various American museums and a tour of European museums in 1955–1956, *Guernica* remained in New York until 1981.

Picasso stipulated in writing that *Guernica* belonged to the Spanish people and that the painting be returned to Spain only "after the complete reestablishment of individual liberties." (He never returned to Spain after Franco's takeover and died in France in 1973.) After ruling as dictator for thirty-six years, Franco died in 1975. His death combined with free elections in 1977 and a new democratic constitution fulfilled Picasso's conditions. In September 1981, *Guernica*, exiled from Spain for forty-four years, was flown to Madrid where it is currently on display in the Prado Museum.

The Boy Who Never Grew Up

THE SCOTTISH AUTHOR J. M. Barrie claimed that his immortal character Peter Pan sprang from the antics and personalities of the five young sons of his friends Sylvia and Arthur Llewelyn Davies. In the dedication to *Peter Pan*, he wrote: "I made Peter by rubbing the five of you violently together, as savages with two sticks produce a flame."

Barrie first became acquainted with the Davies boys in 1898 as he strolled through London's Kensington Gardens. Barrie had been married for three years but had no children, and he was immediately attracted to the energetic boys in their bright clothes and red tam-o'-shanters. The attraction was mutual. The boys were magnetically drawn to the skinny, five-foot, round-shouldered man with deep-set, almost brooding eyes and a thick, drooping mustache. Accompanied by his large black-and-white St. Bernard named Porthos, Barrie was an instant hit with the boys. He was quite adept at sports and games, but best of all he had an endless supply of adventure stories. Never had the boys heard such tales of pirates, thieves, fairies, and desert islands.

The friendship between Barrie and the Davies boys lasted for many years. When the boys' father died in 1907, Barrie did his best to substitute for him. When Sylvia Davies died three years later, Barrie assumed guardianship of the five boys. Still, the Davies boys provided only part of the raw material for *Peter Pan*. The theme of "the boy who wouldn't grow up," which was at the heart of the tale, had its origins in a tragedy in Scotland that occurred when James Matthew Barrie was only six years old.

Born in Kirriemuir, a Scottish weaving town, Barrie was one of eight children, three boys and five girls. Of all the children, David, the second oldest boy, was the obvious favorite of Barrie's mother Margaret. David was intelligent, studious, good-looking—and destined to be a minister. She lavished attention on him. When he died in an ice-skating accident in 1867, on the day before his fourteenth birthday, Barrie's mother suffered a crippling blow.

After David's death, Margaret Ogilvy (in Scotland women kept their maiden names after marriage) took to her bed, prostrate with grief, and her six-year-old son James ("Jamie") took it upon himself to make her well. Convinced that laughter was a sure remedy, Jamie told jokes, stood on his head, acted out incidents that he had seen in the streets—anything to brighten his mother's face. The boy kept a record of how many times his mother laughed and proudly presented his score card to the village doctor on the physician's daily visits.

Many years later, in 1896, when Barrie was thirty-six and his mother was dead, he wrote a biographical tribute. In *Margaret Ogilvy* he recalled those desperate days following the death of David:

It was doubtless . . . [my] sister who told me not to sulk when my mother lay thinking of him [David], but to try instead to get her to talk about him. I did not see how this could make her the merry mother she used to be, but I was told that if I could not do it nobody could, and this made me eager to begin. At first, they say, I was often jealous, stopping her fond memories with the cry, "Do you mind nothing about me?" but that did not last; its place was taken by an intense desire (again, I think, my sister must have breathed it into life) to become so like him that even my mother should not see the difference, and many and artful were the questions I put to that end. Then I practiced in secret, but after a whole week had passed I was still rather like myself. He had such a cheery way of whistling, she had told me, it had always brightened her at work to hear him whistling, and when he whistled he stood with his legs apart and his hands in the pockets of his knickerbockers. I decided to trust to this, so one day after I had learned his whistle (every boy of enterprise invents a whistle of his own) from boys who had been his comrades, I secretly put on a suit of his clothes; dark grey, they were, with little spots, and they fitted me many years afterwards, and thus disguised I slipped, unknown to the others, into my mother's room. Quaking, I doubt not, yet so pleased, I stood still until she saw me, and then—how it must have hurt her! "Listen!" I cried in a glow of triumph, and I stretched my legs wide apart and plunged my hands into the pockets of my knickerbockers, and began to whistle.

She lived twenty-nine years after his death, such active years until toward the end, that you never knew where she was unless you took hold of her, and though she was frail henceforth and ever growing frailer, her housekeeping again became famous, so that brides called as a matter of course to watch her ca'ming and sanding and stitching. . . . But I had not made her forget the bit of her that was dead; in those nine and twenty years he was not removed one day farther from her. Many a time she fell asleep speaking to him, and even while she slept her lips moved and she smiled as if he had come back to her, and when she woke he might vanish so suddenly that she started up bewildered and looked about her, and then said slowly, "My David's dead!" Or perhaps he remained long enough to whisper why he must leave her now, and then she lay silent with filmy eyes. When I became a man . . . he was still a boy of thirteen.

While he remained devoted to his mother until the day she died, Barrie was never able to take the place of his brother. Despite enormous success as a writer, Barrie could not compete with David, the boy who would never grow up, the son who would forever remain perfect.

In one of the opening scenes of *Peter Pan*, Wendy asks Peter his age. He replies, "I don't know, but I am quite young. Wendy, I ran away the day I was born. It was because I heard father and mother talking about what I was to be when I became a man. I don't want ever to be a man. I want always to be a little boy and to have fun."

Emma Goldman: Death and Anarchy

Dateline Chicago: May 4, 1887. BOMB THROWN AT RALLY, KILLING 7, WOUNDING 70.

The meeting of anarchists and Communists was held in Haymarket Square to protest police brutality at a McCormick-Harvester strike for an eight-hour day. It was raining, just a light mist. The crowd of three hundred listened quietly to the speakers who, it was later said, were not particularly inflammatory. The mayor of Chicago, Carter Harrison, described the meeting as "tame." But Captain John ("Black Jack") Bonfield of the Chicago police, virulently antilabor, marched his men in threatening ranks into the crowd and began to club heads. Someone in the crowd threw something. It exploded, killing seven police and wounding seventy other people, both police and audience. The identity of the bomb thrower was never determined. Pistols were fired on both sides.

Eight leading anarchists were arrested and tried for the crime. They were charged with conspiracy and other offenses.

During the trial a young Russian immigrant woman went with her sister to a Sunday meeting of the German Socialists in Rochester, New York. The walls of the meeting room were lined with police. The speaker, Johanna Greie, inveighed passionately against the system that had brought eight anarchists to trial on trumped-up charges. After the meeting she called up the young immigrant woman, Emma Goldman, to speak with her. She had noticed the intense expressions of emotion on Emma's face during the speech and wondered if Emma knew the men on trial. Emma replied that she did not know them. "I have a feeling that you will know them better as you learn about their ideal, and that will make their cause your own," Greie said. It was a prophetic statement.

Dateline Black Friday, November 11, 1887: FOUR HAYMARKET ANARCHISTS HANGED IN CHICAGO.

Their names were Albert Parsons, August Spies, Adolf Fischer, and George Engel. The others who had been on trial met various fates; some received jail sentences, one hanged himself in his cell.

That evening Emma and Helena, her sister, went to their parents' house. Helena was in tears, but Emma was dry-eyed—it was, she later wrote, "too horrible even for tears." Everyone was talking about the hangings. Emma heard a woman laugh derisively and say, "What's all this lament about? The men were murderers. It is well they were hanged." Emma leapt for the woman's throat. Someone grabbed her and held her back. Had she gone crazy? someone else asked. Emma then reached for a pitcher of water, which she dashed in the woman's face. "Out, out, or I will kill you!" she shouted. Then she fell to the floor.

Shortly after, she went to bed and slept well. When she awoke the next morning, she felt as if she had just recovered from a serious illness. She later wrote, "I had the distinct sensation that something new and wonderful had been born in my soul. A great ideal, a burning faith, a determination to dedicate myself to the memory of my martyred comrades, to make their cause my own, to make known to the world their beautiful lives and heroic deaths." That sensation inspired her the rest of her life.

But she was unable to just take off and begin spreading the word. For one thing, she was married. For another, she had almost no money. Her marriage, only a few months old, was already in trouble. Jacob Kersner had turned out to be a big disappointment—impotent, jealous, and intellectually lightweight (his professed love for reading soon degenerated into card-playing). Emma, passionate and energetic, divorced him. She then decided to go to New York to meet Johann Most, editor of the anarchist journal *Freiheit*. Her first stop was a job in a New Haven corset factory, but poor health brought her back to Rochester and an importunate Kersner. Threatening suicide and waving the poison bottle in front of her to convince her of the seriousness of his intentions, he persuaded her to remarry him. She agreed, but took a secret course in dressmaking, so that when the marriage again foundered in three months, she was able to go directly to New York, arriving with five dollars and her sewing machine.

At Sach's, a radical-literary café on the Lower East Side, she met anarchist Alexander Berkman, who was also distressed by the Haymarket hangings. He became her lover and friend for the rest of his life. They formed a ménage à trois with Fedya, an artist. Berkman introduced her to Most, who became her teacher. Under his tutelage, she developed into a fiery, hypnotic speaker, a phrase-maker (for example, describing marriage as a "poor little State-and-begotten weed") who roused audiences to a fever pitch of rage at injustice and made the authorities of the established order extremely nervous.

During the rest of her life—she lived to be seventy-one—she was committed to the cause of anarchism. She was loved for her maternal concern for the sick and miserable, and hated by right and left (the former for her anarchism and the latter for her disillusioned repudiation of revolutionary Russia). Her behavior was shocking to bluenoses: she smoked, advocated free love and birth control, and engaged in outrageous behavior which got her thrown out of restaurants. At the tenth anniversary party for the radical magazine *Mother Earth*, which she founded, she came dressed in a nun's habit and did a dance called "anarchist's slide." Her nickname was Red Emma.

Rarely did she fail in what she set out to do to fulfill her goal. However, she once did fail—miserably. It was when Berkman and she planned to assassinate Henry Clay Frick, chairman of Carnegie Steel Company, which had staged an anti-union lockout. Berkman made a bomb, using instructions from a subversive pamphlet. It would not go off. Instead, he said, he would use a gun, but unfortunately he did not have one or the money to buy one. He and Emma had only enough to send him to Pittsburgh, where the steel company was, and buy some necessary items. Emma stayed home to raise more, so that he could buy the gun and clothes that would make him look respectable enough to gain admittance to Frick's office.

Inspired by Sonya, the young prostitute in Dostoyevsky's *Crime and Punishment*, she determined to make the money by selling her short, stocky body, which, she admitted on gazing in the mirror, was too large in the hips. But she had other attributes, she told herself—blue eyes and blonde hair. Wearing a corset and high heels (unfamiliar to her), she nervously tottered down Fourteenth Street in the company of the other hookers, but when a man approached her, she could not help but walk faster to avoid him. Finally she resolved to stand her ground. A white-haired man offered her a beer; then, at the table in the bar, he told her she didn't have the aptitude for prostitution, and gave her ten dollars. She was off the hook. Helena, her sister, loaned her the rest of the money she needed.

Berkman's attempt to kill Frick also failed. He succeeded only in wounding the businessman and was sentenced to twenty-two years in jail. Emma, locked out of her apartment, probably for nonpayment of rent, rode streetcars all night and finally, ironically, found a room in a whorehouse.

Goldman's beliefs changed somewhat when she was deported to Russia after two years in jail for organizing World War I antidraft Conscription Leagues. Appalled at the excesses of the revolutionary government, she said, "My dreams crushed, my faith broken, my heart like a stone. Mother Russia bleeding from a thousand wounds, her soil strewn with the dead." From them on she was against violence, even in the cause of justice.

After leaving Russia she found herself stateless, as did Berkman, who had joined her after getting out of jail. She married a sixty-five-year-old English miner to obtain a passport, then went off to Spain to fight Franco.

The chain of events that began with the Haymarket hangings came full circle many times. She, once inspired by injustice, in her turn inspired many others. One was Roger Baldwin, founder of the American Civil Liberties Union, who said: "She was a great speaker—passionate, intellectual, and witty. I'd never heard such a direct attack on the foundations of society. I became a revolutionist, though I continued to work at practicing reforms."

All her life she strove for her causes: to stop czarist and Communist persecution, to promote birth control, to gain power for unions, to eliminate private property, and to advance feminism. She had more success than she knew, for much of what she wanted came to pass after she died in 1940. Her body was buried in Waldheim Cemetery near the graves of the Haymarket martyrs, whose deaths and one woman's careless remarks about them set off a lifetime of passionate commitment.

"In Memoriam"

POET Alfred Lord Tennyson was stunned when he heard of the death of his closest friend, Arthur Hallam, on September 15, 1833. Hallam was a talented poet and child prodigy whose career had promised to be one of meteoric success. More than that, he was the "prime passion" of Tennyson's life, a man whose death "blotted out all joy" from Tennyson's life, and left him longing for death. To reconcile himself and to preserve the memory of his friend, Tennyson wrote a series of elegies. In June 1850, those verses were connected into a whole and published in a slim purple volume titled *In Memoriam*. It became one of Tennyson's most acclaimed works, and its overwhelming popularity, with critics and the public alike, led to his appointment as Poet Laureate of England.

"He was as near perfection as mortal man could be," said Tennyson of Hallam. The two first met in 1828 while both were attending Trinity College in Cambridge. A passion for poetry undoubtedly brought them together, and both were members of the Apostles, a literary and debating group at Trinity. Hallam—witty, gregarious, charming, optimistic—was an ideal friend for the shy, unsophisticated Tennyson.

During their five-year friendship Hallam offered Tennyson affectionate support. He encouraged Tennyson to write, helped him find a publisher, read and reread pages of Tennyson's 1832 *Poems* before it went to press, and wrote glowing reviews of Tennyson's work, which were published in literary magazines. In addition, Hallam spent much time at the Tennyson family home in Somersby, where he fell in love with Tennyson's sister Emily. The two were soon to be married when the twenty-two-year-old Hallam died of apoplexy in a hotel room in Vienna.

Within several months after *In Memoriam* was published, 60,000 copies were sold. One reviewer called it "the noblest English Christian poem which several centuries have seen." Tennyson summed up the essence of its widespread appeal: "It is rather a cry of the whole human race than mine. In the poem altogether private grief swells out into thought of, and hope for, the whole world. It begins with a funeral and ends with a marriage—begins with death and ends in a promise of new life. . . ."

Dirt and Death: The Discovery of Streptomycin

LONG BEFORE he had even thought of medicine, much less developing antibiotics such as streptomycin, Selman Waksman watched his young sister lie gasping for breath, suffocating from diphtheria. It was 1897, and Waksman was nine years old. Years later, long after he had won the Nobel Prize for the discovery of streptomycin, which saved millions, he wrote, "As I watched her die, my childish and observant mind may have speculated upon the disease and the potential salvation of her life. Here, for the first time, I was brought in contact with a type of problem that was later to receive much of my attention. I was worried and I cried. I loved my little sister!"

Although his sister's early death made a great impression on Selman, it was not the only inspiration for his lifelong devotion to fighting disease. He was also inspired by something far more commonplace—the soil.

Selman's hometown in Russia, Novaya Priluki, was set in the flat plains of the Ukraine, with its rich, black earth called *tchernozem*. When the peasants' plows tore furrows in that earth, laying it bare to the sun, Selman became excited. "The smell of the open fields early in the spring, when being plowed, and late in fall when the crops were harvested! That odor of the black soil so filled my lungs that I was never able to forget it." He followed the plowmen to pick up handfuls of freshly turned earth and smell it. It made him, he later wrote, decide to study the processes of life. He would find out later that the smell was not of the earth itself but of the exudations of microorganisms that lived in it—the actinomycetes, neither molds nor bacteria, but something in between. One of them is *streptomyces griseus*. He would identify it years later.

Selman's father Jacob spent a good deal of time twenty miles away in Vinnitsa, where he made copper pots. His mother Fradia, who ran a dry goods business, exerted a greater influence on his life than his father did. After the death of Miriam, her only other child, she concentrated on Selman and the development of his mind. She even hired tutors for him. He won by correspondence a diploma from Odessa's Fifth Gymnasium— he could not attend in person because he was a Jew.

In 1910, Fradia suddenly became ill. Selman took her in a wagon to Vinnitsa, then by train to Kiev, but she was too far gone for an operation and was dead in two weeks, probably of some intestinal condition. Shortly after, Jacob Waksman married again. Because little was left for Selman in Russia, he decided to emigrate to the United States. With four friends and forty dollars, he arrived in America and went to live with his cousins, Molki and Mendel Kornblatt, on their five-acre farm in Metuchen, New Jersey. For a while, he helped with farm chores and learned English from the Kornblatt children.

Determined to study microbiology, but really too poor to afford medical school, Waksman visited Jacob Lipman, a fellow Russian who was head of the Rutgers College of Agriculture. Lipman, who had been a census taker of soil microbes for nearly a decade, convinced him to attend the agricultural school and study soil science.

As an undergraduate, Selman dug ditches thirty inches deep in clay, loam, and sand, then took samples from each at various layers to be analyzed in the laboratory. His purpose was to determine the effects of fungi and bacteria on soil fertility. In 1915, he found and named *streptomyces griseus* (white-twisted fungus), but he did not test it as a bacteria fighter. He paid little attention to it for the next twenty or so years.

In 1916, he married someone from his hometown and received his Master of Science degree from Rutgers; then he attended the University of California at Berkeley, where he earned a Ph.D. in biochemistry. Always he carried with him his precious soil cultures.

Waksman once said, "I can truthfully say that I owe much to my professors, that I owe more to my colleagues, but that I owe most to my students, of whom I had a brilliant array." One of the most brilliant was René Dubos. In 1938, Dubos fed pneumonia microbes to other microorganisms, which promptly killed them. The active killer ingredient in the microorganisms was not usable on human beings, but Dubos knew he had discovered a major principle of disease fighting—there were warrior organisms with secret chemical weapons that could wipe out microscopic invaders. Dubos persuaded Waksman to look for such warriors in the soil. It was a propitious time for such a study. Scientists were searching for useful strains of penicillin, the disease-fighting mold discovered by Alexander Fleming in 1928.

Waksman, a methodical worker, began a painstaking search for microbe-killers in the dirt, at first with seven assistants, later with fifty. Several of their discoveries proved to be too poisonous for human beings. He coined the term *anti-biotic* ("against life") to describe what he was looking for.

In 1942, he almost lost his job because Rutgers was cutting back on expenses, but Lipman intervened, and the search went on. It finally paid off, not through a stroke of luck, but from hard work and long hours of sifting and discarding and starting over. As he described it later: "It was the story of the ten thousand microbes. We isolated ten thousand microbes and tested them for ability to inhibit the growth of pathogenic bacteria. We found that ten percent had that quality. We tried to grow that thousand microbes in cultures and found that ten percent lent themselves to the process. From that one hundred we tried to extract the active substances, and we ended with ten chemical compounds. We tested them in animals, and one is the antibiotic known as streptomycin." The culture was found in the gizzard of a sick chicken—a bit of dirt there had a strange mold on it that killed tubercle bacilli. The mold was also found on a manure pile. But it was an old acquaintance to Waksman—*streptomyces griseus* which he smelled in Ukranian soil and named in 1915 after finding it in an American ditch.

Streptomycin, the effective ingredient extracted from the mold, cured, among other things, tuberculosis, tubercular meningitis, typhoid fever, brucellosis, tuleremia, Klebsiella, bubonic plague, syphilis, and gonorrhea—a whole panoply of human ailments—and a couple of plant diseases besides. With royalties from streptomycin, Rutgers built its Institute of Microbiology, which Waksman headed from 1949 to 1958. In 1952, he won the Nobel Prize in medicine. His laboratory discovered several other antibiotics. But none, including streptomycin, was effective against diphtheria, the disease that killed his sister.

The Rattling of the Rails

AS A SMALL CHILD, English playwright John Osborne observed the body of his great-grandmother lying luxuriously in state in a grand coffin in the front parlor. During his childhood, his sister Faye also died—of meningitis at the age of two. He remembers seeing his parents walk down the steps of the hospital where she died as London's Big Ben chimed.

Neither death affected him as much as that of his father and the long agonizing apprehension that led to it. In the summer of 1938, when John was eight, his father left his job as advertising copywriter, so ill with tuberculosis he could no longer work.

In his autobiograpy, *A Better Class of Person*, Osborne remembers his father as white-haired, with transparent skin and pale hands with nicotine-stained fingers. Once a week, in his younger days, his father would bring home comic books for John, and he would sing and play on the piano "Red Sails in the Sunset," "On the Isle of Capri," and music hall songs. When John's mother threatened to publicize the boy's habit of bedwetting, his father—much more sympathetic—took him to a doctor for help. His pessimistic mother would say, "Can't expect too much, go too far, only get disappointed." She had such a fetish about cleanliness that she boiled the boy's pocket money to kill the germs.

His father's illness made John into a quiet, orderly boy, anxious not to disturb the invalid when he was sleeping. For at the end, the man spent most of the day in bed. As he grew weaker, the two—father and son—read aloud to each other from the newspapers.

Finally, in the winter of 1938, the doctors told John's mother that her husband had only six weeks to live. That Christmas, when asked what he wanted, the sick man suggested three books, expecting John to buy one. The boy bought all three. "But I didn't mean you to get all three of them, Skipper, I only meant you to get me one," he said. On Christmas day he ate almost nothing and toasted the King sitting down. Trying to eat, John, then eleven, was overcome with loneliness and burst into tears. He left the rest of his food uneaten. His mother complained about all the trouble she had gone to, cooking a meal that no one ate.

One day two weeks later, John heard his mother scream. He ran to see his father standing naked on a stair landing. "Look at him! Oh, my God, he's gone blind!" shouted John's mother. Losing his balance, the man fell down the stairs on top of them.

When John's father died, the boy was staying with friends. His mother took him in to see the corpse in the coffin. "Of course, this room's got to be frumigated [sic]," she said. Sitting by the coffin, she read *News of the World*. "For the first time I felt the fatality of hatred," Osborne later wrote.

In his diary he recorded his impression of the funeral, of the coffin rattling on rails past a purple curtain into the crematorium.

The rest of his childhood was plagued with illness (rheumatic fever), bad times at school, and fear of World War II bombing raids. While playing games at school, he later said, "I still found my heart pounding unexpectedly, immediately summoning up the image of the purple curtain swallowing up a rattling coffin." But he was determined to live, to make his mark, to rise above the mediocrity to which his life seemed to have destined him.

In 1956 his famous play *Look Back in Anger* was staged to enormous success. It revolutionized the theater. The story of a bitter middle-class misfit, Jimmy Porter, rebelling against the class system and the trashiness of his life, made the English stage seethe with a wit and rage it had never seen before. Kenneth Tynan of the *Observer*, a sympathetic critic, described Jimmy as "all scum and a mile wide," a man with the "determination that no one who dies shall go unmourned." In the play, Jimmy tells of the death of his father, the only person who cared, and sitting with him, as a "lonely, bewildered little boy" who "learnt at an early age what it was to be angry—angry and helpless." And later, at the deathbed of a friend's mother, Jimmy talks of watching "someone I love very much going through the sordid process of dying."

The public loved the play, but some of the critics did not. Ironically, they criticized Osborne for the same character trait the playwright despised in his mother—negativity. Milton Schulman of the *Evening Standard* said, "Underneath the rasping negative whine of this play one can distinguish the considerable promise of its author."

The tall, long-faced playwright was championed by Tynan, who described him as "wearing his shoulders in a defensive bunch around his neck . . . sharp-toothed, yet a convinced vegetarian. He looks wan and driven, and is nervously prone to indulge in sudden, wolfish, silly-ass grins."

Osborne's plays deal with emotion: "I want to make people feel, to give them lessons in feeling"; with class struggle: to Osborne, royalty is the "gold filling in a mouthful of decay"; and with death.

In a later play, *Inadmissible Evidence*, Bill Maitland envisions his cremation, bringing back a haunting image: ". . . all that G-plan light-oak and electrical department brass fittings and spanking new magenta hassocks. And the pink curate sending you off at thirty bob a head as I go rattling on little rails behind him and disappear, like a ghost train at Dreamland, in the amusement park, behind the black curtains, and all that noise."

Butterflies on a Death-Camp Wall:
The Visions of Elisabeth Kübler-Ross

IN 1947, Elisabeth Kübler, a twenty-one-year-old Swiss, visited Maidanek, a Polish concentration camp, with its sinister crematorium chimney, barbed wire fences, and watchtowers. Near the tracks she found two railroad cars—one filled with moldy shoes (men's, women's, and children's), the other laden with human hair. It was a horrible place, and her imagination could easily create feelings of the misery felt by its inhabitants, most doomed to die. If any place should be without hope, this should. Inside the barracks she found rows of bunks, five abreast, where the prisoners slept. And there, amid the graffiti on the wall, she saw something that never entirely left her mind—butterflies, symbols of hope, scratched into the wood by children. She always remembered those butterflies; they were associated with her long study of death and dying.

This was not her first experience with death. Born the first of triplets, she developed pneumonia at the age of five, was taken to the hospital where she was treated with chilly impersonality, then put into an isolation room with another child, who died in her presence. And later came others—the deaths of her beloved brother-in-law and patients she treated as a medical intern in Maidanek.

Back in Switzerland, she qualified as a doctor and married another physician, Immanuel Ross. The two came to the United States, at first New York, then Colorado. The night before they arrived, she dreamed of herself in Indian costume riding a horse through an unfamiliar desert. Traveling through the Monument Valley, months later, she saw the place she had dreamed of—red earth, fantastically shaped rocks, blue sky, a pueblo in the distance—and knew she had been there before. She wrote in her journal:

I know very little about the philosophy of reincarnation. I've always tended to associate reincarnation with way-out people debating their former lives in incense-filled rooms. That's not been my kind of upbringing. I'm at home in laboratories. But I know now there are mysteries of the mind, the psyche, the spirit that cannot be probed by microscopes nor proved by chemical reactions. In time I'll know more. In time I'll understand.

Later, in a trance as part of psychophysiological research in Denver, she "lived" a life as a southwestern Indian who experienced near-drowning at the hands of an enemy Indian but escaped by climbing up a riverbank to safety. When the recording on tape of her experience was played, a man who was hypnotized in another building cried out that he had "lived" as the one who tried to drown her.

Death, she thought was not total annihilation. Something remained after the body died—to live again in another body. Knowing that, who could fear death? But Americans, in particular, turned their minds away from it. As a physician, she began to develop a particular interest in dying patients, so often neglected by medical personnel.

Shortly before leaving Denver, she gave her first lecture on death. Before an audience of medical students, she talked of dying patients, then had the students question such a patient. It was highly unorthodox, but it accomplished what she wanted—it made the students aware of their own avoidance of death.

With their two children, the couple moved to Chicago. At Billings Hospital on the campus of the University of Chicago, she continued to give seminars on death and dying with dying patients interviewed in a screening room. She noted that people who were terminally ill usually went through five psychological stages, not necessarily in order, from the moment they learned of impending death until they made their peace with it: denial, anger, bargaining, depression, and acceptance.

Meanwhile, she was developing a growing belief in life after death, which was supported by patients who described out-of-the-body experiences while deathly ill or clinically dead. Dying but lucid people talked to invisible companions. A housewife told of how she had "died" and watched, out of her body, as doctors worked on her. She could repeat jokes she heard an attendant tell when she was without vital signs. Three hours after, she returned to her body and lived another eighteen months.

Kübler-Ross's book, *On Death and Dying*, became a best-seller in 1969, and later that year (November 21) a photographic essay by Loudon Wainwright on her interview with Eve, a beautiful twenty-one-year-old dying of leukemia, appeared in *Life Magazine*. Suddenly she was famous. In the hospital, she was notorious. She was told: "We have tried for years to make this hospital famous for our excellent cancer care. Now this woman comes along and makes us famous for our dying patients!" The hospital stopped her seminars. But by then she was receiving invitations to lecture all over the United States.

Her faith in life after death grew—she believed in it "beyond the shadow of a doubt." Those who had experienced it described it to her as ecstatic. They felt peace and relief, often traveled through a dark tunnel to light, felt themselves to be in spiritual bodies, were quite often accompanied by incorporeal guides.

She never forgot the butterflies in the concentration camp. As a doctor, she once told a five-year-old girl that her dying mother was in a cocoon but would eventually emerge as a butterfly. In the late 1970s, she stopped to pick wild flowers at a field in Escondido, California. A butterfly flew on her hand. At that spot she later built Shanti Nilaya (Sanskrit for "Home of Peace"), a workshop center and hospice for the dying.

Once she wrote:

Watching the peaceful death of a human being reminds me of a falling star— one of the million lights in a vast sky that flares up for a brief moment only to disappear into the endless night. To be with a dying patient makes us conscious of the uniqueness of the individual in this vast sea of humanity, aware of our finiteness, our limited lifespan. Few of us live beyond our three score years and ten, yet in this brief time most of us create and live a unique biography, and weave ourselves into the fabric of history.

It is true—and beautifully exemplified in the very brief lives of those anonymous concentration camp victims who, lying in bed waiting for death imposed by the hands of monsters, etched on the wall the butterflies that inspired Elisabeth Kübler-Ross, who has profoundly changed the experience of dying in the Western world.

A Cow in a Can

FOOD INVENTOR Gail Borden was always interested in the idea of condensing food. So obsessed was he that he wanted to "put a potato in a pillbox, a pumpkin into a tablespoon, the biggest sort of watermelon into a saucer." Once he even told a minister: "Condense your sermons. The world is changing. Even lovers write no poetry, nor any other stuff and nonsense now. They condense all they have to say, I suppose, into a kiss."

His early efforts were imperfect at best. At the London Exhibition of 1851, Borden presented a "meat biscuit," made for Texans going to the 1850s Gold Rush. Consisting of the extract from eleven pounds of meat mixed with flour and baked into a two-pound loaf, it was supposed to be perfect for those wanting to travel light. The only problem was the terrible taste.

After the exhibition was over, Borden sailed back to the United States. He was appalled that the children on his ship were so pale and sick. He thought that milk would have brought them back to health, but most of the cows on board were too seasick to produce healthy milk. Four children had died from drinking contaminated milk. This tragedy gave Borden an idea—he would condense milk so that it would be safe and readily available.

He had taken on a tough project. First he tried boiling the milk, but it burned and tasted bad. Then, on a visit to the Shaker community in New Lebanon, New York, he was struck by their method of condensing fruit juice and sugar in vacuum pans. He borrowed a pan to experiment with. Finally he was able to devise a vacuum process that removed the water from milk and made it safe.

He applied for a patent. At first the Patent Office refused him, saying that he hadn't invented anything new, but two scientists—Robert Mac-Farlane and John Currie—interceded for him. He obtained his patent three years later, in 1856.

The following year he started manufacturing condensed milk. The enterprise was financially shaky until he obtained the backing of financier-grocer Jeremiah Milkbank. Circumstances helped to make condensed milk a success. One contributing factor was the abysmally poor control of the quality of fresh milk. Sometimes "swill milk" (thin blue milk from cows fed on leftovers from distilleries) was sold as whole milk. Often milk was dirty. To combat this problem, Borden set rigid sanitation standards. During the Civil War condensed milk demonstrated its convenience convincingly and made Borden a fortune.

True to his bold nature, Borden had his tomb built in the shape of a condensed milk can. His epitaph: "I tried and failed; I tried again and again, and succeeded."

6. Love and Romance

Love, that insanity that can attach itself to the most unlikely objects, is an obvious source of inspiration. Consistently, creators glorify their love objects, transmuting quite ordinary people into divine muses.

Some are deeply intimate with the objects; others worship from afar. Elizabeth Barrett Browning's *Sonnets to the Portuguese* symbolizes a long, enduring love. The Taj Mahal is a magnificent memorial to a beloved wife. Salvador Dali's wife Gala was the centerpiece of many of his paintings, though he represented her in many strange ways.

Yet the passion can be felt from afar. A. E. Housman's secret beloved may never have known of the poet's feelings, and Simonetta, seductress madonna model for Botticelli, was married to someone else. Author Alexandre Dumas faced rejection from the woman he adored, and he later neglected her when she needed him; yet he immortalized her in his play *Camille*. Emily Dickinson's "master letters" hint at a mysterious love affair, inspiring some of her greatest poems, but with whom?

The object of a creator's love also can be totally unworthy. The Queen of the Badger Game, who inspired a sentimental song, is but one of countless examples. In the end, the object doesn't matter, for the work of art does not reflect the object's worth—only that of the artist.

How Do I Love Thee?

ON JANUARY 10, 1845, Robert Browning, a gifted poet but a man who shunned social correspondence, took pen in hand and composed a letter to Elizabeth Barrett, whose two-volume *Poems* he had just read. He wrote, "I love your verses with all my heart, dear Miss Barrett. . . . Into me has it gone, and part of me has it become, this great living poetry of yours . . . the fresh strange music, the affluent language, the exquisite pathos and true new brave thought. . . . I do, as I say, love these books with all my heart—and I love you, too." It was quite a presumptuous letter for Browning to write to a woman he had never met, particularly when the famous lady was known to be something of a recluse. For the past seven years she had barely ventured out of her second-story bedroom at 50 Wimpole Street in London.

Elizabeth was astonished but thoroughly excited by the romantic audacity of the letter. At thirty-nine she was a small, delicate woman who had spent many years recovering from an illness, probably due to a spinal injury that she suffered when she was fifteen. While Elizabeth's life had been devoid of any serious male suitors, she was no stranger to romance. Her passionate poetry had been published in a number of literary magazines, and her *Poems* had earned her enviable status among the ranks of England's poets. A great admirer of Browning's work, she was overwhelmed that such a handsome, thirty-three-year-old bachelor was courting her.

Hardly a day had gone by before Elizabeth replied to Browning's letter. She thanked him for his kind words, told him of her love for his poetry, and responded to his comment about an occasion, several years past, when they had almost met. She wrote, "What I lost by one chance I may recover by some future one. Winters shut me up as they do a dormouse's eyes; in the spring, we shall see. . . ." The hint of a spring meeting so encouraged Browning that his next letter was more flattering, more intimate. For the next four months the two poets became frequent correspondents. He kept urging, if ever so gently, for a face-to-face meeting; she was thrilled by the blossoming romance but was tormented by the thought of the inevitable encounter. When she could hold him off no longer, Elizabeth invited Browning to her home on May 20, but cautioned, "There is nothing to see in me, nor to hear in me—I never learnt to talk as you do in London. . . . If poetry is worth anything to any eye, it is the flower of me. . . . The rest of me is nothing but a root, fit for the ground and the dark. . . . Come, then. There will be truth and simplicity for you in any case, and a friend. . . ."

Their first meeting lasted for an hour and a half. He saw a petite, delicate woman with large, luminous eyes and cascading ringlets of lustrous black hair. She saw a slim, good-looking man with a dark beard, wavy hair, and crystal-clear gray eyes. While she was soft-spoken and shy, he was spirited, self-assured, and witty. There was no witness to the meeting, but their ensuing letters showed that neither party had been disappointed.

One of Browning's subsequent letters, however, was so alive with unabashed, joyful love that it propelled Elizabeth into an agitated, fever-ish state. After a sleepless night, she answered with trembling hand, "You do not know what pain you gave me in speaking so wildly. . . . You have said some intemperate things . . . fancies, which you will not say over again, nor unsay, but forget at once. . . . Now if there should be one word of answer attempted to this, or of reference, I must not—I will not—see you again. . . ." But Browning refused to be discouraged, and it was not long before he was regularly visiting Elizabeth once a week, then twice a week. On the days Browning did not see her, he wrote to her. He even kept a diary of his visits, carefully recording each date and the number of hours and minutes they had spent together.

While Elizabeth was hopelessly in love, she remained frightened. She was too old for Browning, too inexperienced in social circles. He would someday fall prey to a beautiful, captivating woman, and she would be left with a broken heart and a handful of memories. She told him of her doubts, and he patiently dissolved them one by one. He wrote, "I was made and meant to look for you and wait for you and become yours forever." And she responded, "You cannot guess what you are to me—you cannot—it is not possible. . . . It is something between dream and mira-cle, all of it—as if some dream of my earliest, brightest dreamingtime had been lying through these dark years to steep in the sunshine, returning to me in a double light. . . ."

Slowly Elizabeth's health improved. Encouraged by her lover, she rose from her bed and moved about her room. Soon she walked downstairs, to the amazement of her brothers and sisters who had become quite adept at carrying the frail woman around the Barrett house. Finally she sum-moned the courage to step out into the streets for short walks and car-riage rides through the city.

When Browning proposed, Elizabeth accepted. Even though she had erased thoughts of her ill health and personal inadequacies from her mind, she could not overcome the fear of informing her father of the upcoming marriage. While Edward Barrett was a responsible, devoted father, he demanded total obedience from all of his children and was adamantly opposed to any of them marrying. Never did he think he would have a problem with Elizabeth. Convinced that he would never approve of their union, Elizabeth insisted that she and Browning marry in secret. Not even her brothers and sisters were informed; only her personal maid, Lily Wilson, knew, so that she could help them carry out the elopement plans and accompany them to Italy.

On Saturday, September 12, 1846, Elizabeth and Lily Wilson left the house on Wimpole Street for St. Marylebone Parish Church. Along the way Elizabeth, who had been unable to sleep the previous night, almost fainted and had to be revived in a chemist's shop. After the short wedding ceremony, she and Lily stopped to visit a friend (the cover-up excuse for the day's outing) and then returned to the Barrett home. Browning returned home, took out Elizabeth's last letter, and wrote on it the date and the hour of the wedding. Next to that he wrote the number 91 to indicate that it had been their ninety-first meeting.

Since Elizabeth could not endure the physical and mental upheaval of a wedding and a journey in one day, the couple planned to meet on September 19, when they would leave for Italy. In the interim week they agreed not to see each other, since Elizabeth was afraid that her emotional state might betray her, causing an accidental disclosure of their secret. On the appointed day they slipped away, leaving a note behind for Edward Barrett. When he learned of the marriage, he flew into a rage, ordering that his daughter's name never again be spoken in his presence.

Elizabeth Barrett and Robert Browning enjoyed fifteen years of marital bliss and had one child, Robert. For most of their married life they lived in Florence, Italy. On their first anniversary Elizabeth wrote to her sister Henrietta, "The only difference is from happy to happier and from being loved to being loved more." In 1861, Elizabeth died in her husband's arms, "smiling happily, and with a face like a girl's."

Elizabeth's greatest work, *Sonnets from the Portuguese*, was probably begun in 1845 when she was in the throes of her romance. It chronicled her deepest and most private feelings. She did not tell her husband about the poems until she had completed them. One morning she shyly put the poems into the pocket of Browning's jacket and whispered, "Do you know I once wrote some verses for you?" Years later Browning was asked if he had any reservations about publishing such an intimate account of their love. He supposedly replied, "I dared not keep to myself the finest sonnets written in any language since Shakespeare's."

Of the many beautiful, sentimental pieces in *Sonnets from the Portuguese*, one has become the most often quoted, the one most synonymous with the names of the eternal lovers:

> How do I love thee? Let me count the ways.
> I love thee to the depth and breadth and height
> My soul can reach, when feeling out of sight
> For the ends of Being and ideal Grace.
> I love thee to the level of everyday's
> Most quiet need, by sun and candle-light.
> I love thee freely, as men strive for Right;
> I love thee purely, as they turn from Praise.
> I love thee with the passion put to use

In my old griefs, and with my childhood's faith.
I love thee with a love I seemed to lose
With my lost saints—I love thee with the breath,
Smiles, tears, of all my life!—and, if God choose,
I shall but love thee better after death.

Gala—Dali's Magic Mirror

SHE was phantasmagoric. Salvador Dali, the painter, created her—image after image—and was inspired by his own inspirations. Her heart and intelligence were a "diamond prism," transforming him. She was "the salt of my life . . . my double—ME." Did she walk bare-breasted in a fishing village near Malaga? Could she foretell the future? As a child, did an optical theater give him a prevision of her: a little Russian girl in a troika, riding wildly through an enchanted forest and accompanied by wolves with phosphorescent eyes? Did she save him from impotence? We know only what he says. The magic box of Dali's brain transformed his fifty-three-year love affair with his wife, Elena, nicknamed Gala, into a surrealist myth. The reality? It doesn't matter.

Who was this miraculous creature who once wore a lobster on her head? She had, according to her first husband, surrealist poet Paul Eluard, a "look that pierces walls." Her lynxlike eyes changed color. With her dark, wasp-waisted beauty and strange moodiness, she was the surrealist muse, and her effect on artists was extraordinary.

Dali first heard of her at a meeting in 1929 with Eluard at the Bal Tabarin in Paris. He did not actually meet her until later that year in his hometown, Cadaques, Spain, when she and Eluard came to visit. When Gala got out of the car, Dali had one of the fits of hysterical laughter that afflicted him in those days. He fell in love instantly, a sensation "strangely resembling certain gastric sensations at the first signs of seasickness."

At that time, he was in a bad way—"drowning," without control. Naked, he painted and masturbated for hours on end in his room. When he came out he wore outrageous "bachelor-girl" outfits and jewelry, and his hair was plastered down and lacquered like that of an Argentine tango dancer.

The day after Gala arrived, Dali dressed to meet her and Paul on the beach. It took much thought. Intimidated by Gala's Parisienne ways—

"unfolding valises that turned into wardrobes and spewed out gowns and fine lingerie"—he needed to impress her. Finally, he cut his shirt to show off his hairy chest and nipples, covered himself with a stinking mixture of goat manure and fish paste, shaved his armpits and knees until they bled, then let the blood coagulate for further decoration. To top off his creation, he stuck a flower behind his ear.

Then he opened the window, saw her "sublime" back as she sat on the sand, and felt a surge of desire. Changing his mind about his costume, he washed himself off and dressed more normally, still with a flower and pearls. At the beach, all he could do was laugh with his usual hysteria and sit at her feet.

Their first real conversation was about one of his paintings, *Le Jeu Lugubre*, which featured underpants festooned with excrement. She questioned him: Was he a coprophagic (feces eater)? Contrary to his usual habit, he told her the truth—that he was actually afraid of the manure and other hideous things he painted. He painted them to control them, he said. She took his hand.

When Eluard went off to Paris, Dali and Gala were alone together. He was fascinated by her numerous clothes changes and watched her eat grapes while sitting on a stone wall. Obsessed, he dreamed of impaling her on his penis, but in the daylight he could only kiss her and fantasize about pushing her off a cliff. As if she could read his mind, she incited his fantasy—she told him she *wanted* him to kill her. No longer could he imagine such an act. "From that moment on, I was cured of my haunting obsessions, my laughter, my hysteria. . . ," he later said. In making love to Gala, Dali experienced a kaleidoscope of inspiration: "Gala is like a magic mirror toward which the most marvelous moments of the successive presents of my life converge. Just before I explode inside her . . . I can feel mounting in me a power of imagery that dazzles me vertiginously. . . . As if ruled by the gridwork of a decoding system, these images soon become orderly and convey to me a unique truth. . . . At the moment when I melt into Gala . . . my orgasm at one and the same time occurs in three dimensions: Gala's body, my own, and a kingdom that is the present of all my presents." It brought forth "this sheaf of projections of images . . . to produce the diamond of Dalinian reality . . . my elixir, my semen, and the substance of the strength that enables me to conquer and domi-nate the world." (At sixty, talking with Alain Bosquet, a different time, a different age, he sang a different tune, saying, "For the divine Dali, if one drop of jism leaves him, he immediately needs a huge check to compen-sate for the expenditure.")

Though Dali always remained an outrageous character, he felt that Gala had saved him, for the rest of his life, from real madness. When he began to slide off the edge of sanity, where he was always poised, she snatched him and brought him to safety.

Dali believed in refraining from lovemaking during the conception of an idea, but in performing the act frequently during "periods of realization." He once claimed that he lived in a ménage à trois with his thirteen-year-old wife, Painting, and his wife-mistress, Gala.

From that stay in Cadaques, they were together. Eluard gave them his blessing and stepped out of the picture. When Dali and Gala returned to Paris, Dali's highly successful exhibit at Goeman's gallery was in full swing and a huge success. Film director Buñuel was talking about a scenario for a new movie, *L'Age d'Or*, in collaboration with Dali. Yet, in spite of all that was happening, the two lovers did not stay in Paris, but instead stole off to the Hôtel du Château at Carry-le-Rouet on the Riviera and holed up indoors, "two monks of sex," for two months. They finally surfaced for lack of money. Gala read cards and predicted that a letter with promises of money would come. It did—from the Vicomte de Noailles, wanting to buy a painting.

It was the beginning of a long life together, which they lived sometimes in Paris, London, or New York, sometimes in a house they built at Port Lligat, not far from Cadaques. (Dali attached one of his milk teeth to a string and hung it in the exact center of the ceiling.)

Gala was absorbed with his painting, so integral a part of the process that one day he said, "It is mostly with your blood, Gala, that I paint my pictures." From then on, most were signed "Gala Salvador Dali." Gala appears in nearly all his paintings; for example, early in the 1930s, at Port Lligat, he balanced two lambchops on Gala's shoulder, then painted the scene. Why? His answers are varied and imaginative—and probably all true, in some sense. He said that the "edible" was part of his paranoiac-critical representation of the world. He said that "by observing the movements of tiny shadows produced by the accident of the meat on the flesh of the woman I love while the sun was setting, I was finally able to attain images sufficiently lucid and appetizing. . . ." He said that he loved both Gala and the lamb chops, so why not paint them together in "perfect harmony"? He said that the chops were "expiatory victims of abortive sacrifices," meaning that he really wanted to eat her, but he later remarked, "That was the age of the imagination's raw meat. Today, now that Gala has risen in the heraldic hierarchy of my nobility, she has become my basket of bread." To show her as the basket of bread, he painted her with one breast exposed (the bread) above folded arms (the basket).

Dali painted Gala as *Leda Atomica*, floating naked with a swan, in accordance with "the 'nothing touches' theory of intra-atomic physics." At the foot of the Cross in his *Crucifixion* is a kneeling woman—Gala. In the *Last Sacrament*, Christ's face is hers. She is the focus of the painting *My Wife, Nude, Contemplating Her Own Flesh Becoming Stairs, Three Verte-brae of a Column, Sky, and Architecture*.

His love of her was all-encompassing. For her, he created a magnifi-cent gold and ruby heart, now in the Cheatham Collection.

Gala kept their life together. Early in the 1930s, she acted as a door-to-door salesman in Paris for the devices he had created: mirror finger-nails, baroque bathtubs, transparent mannequins with goldfish swim-ming in them. She never complained about the ridicule, the slammed doors, and the waits in the anterooms.

Everyday matters were her province: choosing his clothes, answering correspondence, driving the car, and cooking, though he claimed her food tasted like his handkerchief. She handled all the money, which was a good thing. Money literally slipped through Dali's fingers: Once, he put a $50,000 check between the pages of *Time*, then absentmindedly threw the magazine into a trash can.

Gala was his devoted collaborator, patient but strong, making sugges-tions yet never criticizing. Dali told an interviewer, "Before knowing her, I didn't even know how to blow my nose, and I didn't go to the cinema because I was afraid of the box office." She taught him pleasure and reality and helped him get rid of "tics, tics, tics."

If Gala sounds like the epitome of prosaic common sense, one must remember that she wore Minnie Mouse hats and shoes on top of her head. She once dressed in a transparent red-paper dress and put boiled lobsters and an ant-eaten doll on her head for a "surrealist dream" party in New York. And neither did she stop him from sporting his long, waxed mustaches "like an aerial stretching out to capture genius and inspira-tion," nor did she stop him from coming out of a large white egg at a press conference, from wearing double-paned glasses filled with live ants at an autograph party, from donning a helmeted diving suit at a London lecture (he had to be pried out of it with a billiard cue and hammer).

George Orwell once said that Dali had as good a set of perversions as anyone could hope for—and he did. He liked to stage sex acts and then watch them without participating. This, however, had nothing to do with the "magic circle" of his love for Gala. He said, "My work is but the setting of my erotic theater of which Gala is the soul."

Analytical critics have doubts about his sexuality, in spite of his ecsta-tic description of his coupling with Gala. As a child, Dali found his penis "small, pitiful, and soft," and he knew he would never "crack a woman like a watermelon." Reviewer Robert Hughes has spotted Dali's "love of anything flaccid," and arguments have been made about the significance in *Persistence of Memory*, perhaps his most famous painting, of the limp pocket watches, which he says were inspired by runny Camembert cheese. But, if only in his mind, Dali was potent with Gala—magnificently so.

Whatever the realities of their love life, they were first married in a civil ceremony in 1935, then again in a Catholic ritual in 1958. In 1979, they planned to marry again in a Coptic ceremony, "something useless and sacred," but were unable to because of health problems. He was then seventy-five, suffering from Parkinson's disease and depression, and she, at eighty-eight, was old and fragile. Gala died three years later at a castle in Spain he had given her. Years before, he had said he did not think he could face the thought of her death. But he lives on.

A. E. Housman's Secret Love:
A Shropshire Lad

WHO was the person to whom the mousy classics professor, A. E. Housman, wrote many of the enormously popular poems of *A Shropshire Lad*? Try as they might, contemporary critics could not identify a muse in the shadows that inspired the verses about doomed young men, suffering, and sorrow. However, there was such a muse—a man who remained forever beyond Housman's reach, "too dear for my possessing."

His name was Moses John Jackson, and Housman's unrequited love for him, which lasted almost sixty years, was the fountainhead of his inspiration. On the flyleaf of a copy of *Last Poems*, which he sent to Jackson in 1922, when Jackson was dying of a terminal illness, Housman wrote, "From a fellow who thinks more of you than anything in the world . . . you are largely responsible for my writing poetry and you ought to take the consequences."

Housman, born in 1859, knew about loss early: his mother died on his twelfth birthday, and his father squandered the family fortune. It is possible that the circumcision his father forced him to submit to at the age of fourteen traumatized him for life.

It was during his third year at Oxford that he met Jackson, a year older, a handsome athlete and science major with a sensual mouth. Jackson had no interest in literature and teased Housman for his lack of interest in sports. In 1880, Housman, Jackson, and another classmate shared rooms in an old house in St. Giles. After Housman failed at Greats (classics), he left school, but later boned up enough to obtain a Pass.

His path and Jackson's continued to cross. They worked at the same London Patent Office together for ten years, and again lived together, this time with Jackson's brother Adalbert for three years. During the last year, 1885, something went wrong between Housman and Jackson, and Housman, distraught, disappeared for a week. It is possible that he had finally declared his love and been rejected, for the friendship between the two cooled. Moses married, became a teacher in India, and finally moved to Vancouver.

A Shropshire Lad, published in 1896, was written in a short period of "continuous excitement," "a ferment so terrific that the nervous reaction was well-nigh insupportable." It made Housman famous. Meanwhile, he read Greek and Latin at the British Museum, became a Professor of Latin at University College, London, and in 1911 was given a Chair at Cambridge, where he taught until his death. His most noteworthy book in classics was his translation of works by the mediocre Latin poet Manilius. Housman sent Jackson a special morocco-bound copy of his translation. His "Epithalamium" (1902) was dedicated to Jackson.

Jackson's photograph hung over Housman's fireplace. When Housman's brother Laurence asked who the man in the photograph was, Housman replied, "That was my friend Jackson, the man who had more influence on my life than anybody else." On Jackson's last letter, Housman wrote, "Mo's last letter," then went over the writing in ink.

This private, reticent, pale-eyed man kept his love life a secret. It is possible that he had an affair with Jackson's brother Adalbert, who died tragically in 1892 of typhoid and who inspired Housman to write, "because I liked you better than suits a man to say." He also had an eight-year, on-and-off affair with a one-eyed Venetian gondolier, Andrea, who was twenty-three when Housman met him in 1900. Housman sent Andrea money when he needed it. And in Paris, Housman frequented male brothels where he made love with sailors, ballet dancers, and male prostitutes, then returned to his life of rectitude in England. Yet it was Jackson whom he loved. Housman was a man whose public life was without event, but whose private life was teeming, exotic, and passionate. Life, he said, was a "long, fool's errand to the grave." It is probable that the object of his love, the source of his inspiration, never understood him and never could.

Postcript: Housman wrote, about writing poetry, "I could no more define poetry than a terrier can define a rat, but we both recognize the object by the symptoms which it provokes in us. . . . Experience has taught me, when I am shaving of a morning, to keep watch over my thoughts, because, if a line of poetry strays into my memory, my skin bristles so that the razor ceases to act. . . . I have seldom written poetry unless I was rather out of health, and the experience, though pleasurable, was generally agitating and exhausting. . . . Having drunk a pint of beer at luncheon—beer is a sedative to the brain, and my afternoons are the least intellectual portion of my life—I would go out for a walk of two or three hours. As I went along, thinking of nothing in particular, only looking at things around me and following the progress of the seasons, there would flow into my mind, with a sudden and unaccountable emotion, sometimes a line or two of verse, sometimes a whole stanza at once, accompanied, not preceded, by a vague notion of the poem which they were destined to form part of. . . . The source of the suggestions thus proferred to the brain was . . . the pit of the stomach." Yet inspiration was not always so generous to Housman—he wrote a stanza for one poem thirteen times, and it took him a year to "get it right."

The Taj Mahal: The Monument to Love

QUEEN NUR JAHAN of the Indian Empire, found it politically expedient to arrange a marriage between her stepson, Prince Khurram, heir to the throne, and her niece, the princess Arjemand. The two had only met once, if at all, at a bazaar. No one could have predicted the magnitude of their love for one another.

They were married in 1612, she nineteen, he about a year older, to "magnificent processions by day and expensive fireworks by night. . . . The entire city of Agra was *en fête*," according to a contemporary report.

It was a pearl among marriages. When he became king of the Indian Empire as Shah Jehan and she queen as Mumtaz Mahal, she helped to make his rule harmonious and tranquil. More than his lover, she was his friend and advisor, inspiring him to be benevolent and charitable. He discussed matters of state with her, and it was she who stamped drafts of state documents with the royal seal.

Their wealth was legendary. Shah Jehan sat for audiences on the Peacock Throne, whose canopy was supported by twelve jewel-studded emerald posts. The capital city of Agra shone with marble palaces and was sweet with the smell of flowering gardens. The Shah owned thousands of horses and hundreds of elephants.

Mumtaz Mahal traveled everywhere with her husband. They were never apart. She even rode at his side on the battlefield. In the nineteenth year of their marriage, they traveled south to put down a rebellion by the Khan Jahan Lodi and the kingdoms of Ahmednagar and Bijapur. After several successful campaigns, they camped in the town of Burhampur in Deccan. Mumtaz Mahal was pregnant, due to deliver her fourteenth child. She heard the child crying in her womb and supposedly said to her husband, "Sir, I believe that no mother has ever been known to survive the birth of a child so heard and I fear that my end is near. O King, I have lived with you in joy and sorrow. God has made you a great emperor and given you many worlds to rule. And now there are only two things I have to say to you: Do not take another wife, and build me a tomb to make my name memorable."

As she had predicted, she died in childbirth not long after. He was disconsolate. After grieving for years, he finally began to plan the tomb she had asked for.

It took seventeen years to build. Twenty thousand workmen were employed, and they used 466.55 kilograms of gold, tons of fine marble, and baskets of precious stones, including jade, lapis lazuli, turquoise, sapphire, topaz, jasper, emerald, and ruby.

Shah Jehan supervised the construction. When his architect warned that the tomb was costing ten million rupees, he shouted, "Make it cost ten million more! The Crown of Mahal must be the one perfect thing."

Today many people agree on its perfection. The tomb, crowned by a double dome and flanked by four delicate minarets, seems to float in the water channel in front of it. Facing it are a red sandstone mosque and its "answer," another sandstone building. The buildings are set in gardens, with fountains and avenues of cypress. The central lotus pond is surrounded with dozens of fountains.

The magnificent tomb is built of pure white marble, with Persian silver doors. The room in which the casket of the Mumtaz Mahal resides is eighty feet tall. There, a whisper seems to float away in slow echoes.

The walls are closed with screens made of bits of milk glass that filter the light and are inlaid with a floral bas relief. Around the tomb is a delicate, intricately carved marble screen of open fretwork.

It has been said that Shah Jahan planned for himself a tomb just like his queen's, to be on the other side of the river and made of black marble, joined with hers by a silver bridge. But if he did plan it, he never had a chance to build it, for his son led a rebellion against him, and he was driven from the throne. Jailed for seven years, he could see the Taj Mahal from his balcony in the Jasmine Tower of the Agra Fort. He died there on June 22, 1666, at seventy-five, leaning against the arms of his eldest daughter Jahanar, and gazing at the Taj Mahal, where his love lay.

The Many Men in the Life of a Recluse

EMILY DICKINSON spent much of her life on an island of unattainable dreams. The two things she craved most in life—the love of a man and recognition as a poet—seemed consistently to slip from her grasp. From a charming, ambitious girl she evolved into a recluse who penned more than 1,800 poems, some of them the world's most dazzling, imaginative verse. The contrast between the romance of her poems and the reality of her life has stirred up a number of mysteries that will probably never be solved.

Born in the isolated town of Amherst, Massachusetts, in 1830, Emily grew up in a close-knit family. Edward, her father, was an attorney and U.S. congressman. Her mother, also named Emily, was a pious, retiring woman dedicated to the correct upbringing of her children. Emily had two siblings: William Austin, an older brother, and Lavinia, a younger sister who, like Emily, never married and never left home.

As a young girl Emily was known for her wit, abounding energy, and nonconformity. Educated at Amherst Academy and Mount Holyoke Female Seminary, she was a social asset at the Dickinson home where many prominent people were entertained. Emily had no shortage of friends, many of them male, and displayed a healthy, optimistic attitude toward the future. Though disappointed with her lack of conventional beauty, she described herself as follows: "Am small, like the wren; my hair is bold, like the chestnut burr; and my eyes, like the sherry in the glass that the guest leaves."

Gradually she drew inward and remained hidden in her home for about the last twenty years of her life. Also, in her later years she wore only white dresses, giving the local citizenry a source of endless gossip. Most concluded that poor Emily had had a disastrous love affair which caused her to shun the human race.

This theory, delectable all by itself, was further enhanced by the discovery of the "master letters" many years after Emily's death. In these three undated letters, probably written in the late 1850s and/or early 1860s and sent to an unidentified "Master," Emily shows herself to be a rapturous, anguished woman in love. For more than a hundred years Dickinson biographers have examined Emily's metaphors to find the mystery man, but the clues are too vague, the language too elliptical. There were three men who played prominent roles in Emily's romantic life. Any of the three could have been her Master, but more importantly, all three inspired her poetry.

The first man was Samuel Bowles, editor of the *Springfield Daily Republican*. Tall, shaggy-browed, and with magnificently deep-set eyes (Emily called them "isolated comets"), Bowles turned the heads of many women. His powerful personality, infused with charm and humor, made him an instant success at social gatherings. In addition, he seemed to hold a particular fascination for women like Emily. As one female observer pointed out: "To everybody his manner was gracious, but especially to plain and unattractive people—he had a knack of drawing them out, so that they became agreeable and entertaining."

Gifted with inexhaustible energy, Bowles was a dedicated newspaperman who took his father's small, weekly *Springfield Republican* and transformed it into one of the most influential daily papers in the country. He knew most of the political figures of the day and traveled extensively to cover local, state, and national stories. Usually on Bowles's agenda were the yearly commencement exercises at Amherst College, only twenty-five miles from his home in Springfield. It was inevitable that Bowles would someday find himself a guest at the Dickinson home.

While Bowles probably knew Emily's father before 1858, it was not until that year that he began to regularly visit the family, often accompanied by his wife Mary. All of the Dickinsons encouraged the visits, particularly Austin and his wife Sue, and, of course, Emily. The twenty-eight-year-old budding poet was mesmerized by the dashing, handsome, intelligent thirty-two-year-old Bowles. Not only did he find a permanent niche in her fantasies, but he also became an outlet for her poetic aspirations. For shy as Emily could sometimes be, she did want her poems to be recognized, and Bowles was the editor of a very important newspaper.

Emily's voluminous correspondence with Bowles began shortly after she met him. Poems were often enclosed in her letters. Emily was too scared to ask Bowles directly what he thought of her work or whether it was worthy of publication, but he did not miss the message. Neither could he possibly have misinterpreted Emily's passionate letters. However, no clear record of Bowles's attitude toward Emily exists in his letters. Worse, even though Bowles complimented Emily on her writing, he never truly appreciated the quality of her work, though he did print five of her poems in his newspaper.

Another possible choice for Emily's Master was the Reverend Charles Wadsworth, pastor of Arch Street Presbyterian Church in Philadelphia. In some respects Wadsworth remains the most mysterious of Emily's real and imaginary suitors. Only one piece of correspondence between the two—from the reverend to the poet—survives. That letter is undated, short, and reveals very little. However, in extant letters to other friends and relatives, Emily recorded some of her feelings for Wadsworth, calling him "the beloved clergyman," "my shepherd," and "my dearest earthly friend."

The two probably met in Philadelphia in 1855 when Emily made one of her rare trips outside Amherst. Supposedly, Emily attended church and was first exposed to the charms of the forty-one-year-old reverend. According to those who contend that there was an amorous Dickinson/Wadsworth liaison, Emily "met her fate" the moment she set eyes on the minister, and her love remained steadfast until Wadsworth died in 1882.

Wadsworth was slim, stood about five feet, ten inches tall, wore eyeglasses, and had dark eyes and hair. Actually, he was quite homely, but his appearance disguised a powerful inner self that he dramatically revealed in the pulpit. One newspaper reporter stated: "His sheer moral intensity penetrated the most sealed and obdurate hearts, and his congregations were shaken as if by a whirlwind."

While some Dickinson biographers are certain that Wadsworth was the impetus for much of Emily's passionate poetry, others claim that her love for the married reverend was of a spiritual, platonic nature. Wadsworth visited her only twice—in 1860 and again in 1880—and it is unlikely that on either occasion she was the primary reason for his being in Amherst. In the one surviving letter that the minister wrote to Emily, he misspelled her last name and did not even sign the note.

Regardless of their few face-to-face encounters, Wadsworth was definitely an important figure in Emily's life. When she died, a picture of the reverend and a book of his sermons were found among her most cherished possessions.

The third candidate for the poet's affections was Judge Otis Phillips Lord, Associate Justice of the Supreme Court of Massachusetts. Emily Dickinson fans utter a sigh of relief when reading about her and Lord, for in this relationship Emily loved and finally was loved in return. It is impossible to date the beginning of the romance since Lord, like Bowles, was a long-time family friend and over a period of years made numerous trips to Amherst from his home in Salem. Even though their "affair" was officially launched after the death of Lord's wife Elizabeth in 1877 (Emily was forty-seven; Lord was sixty-five), the couple may have been in love as early as the 1860s.

Lord was a well-known public figure with a long, distinguished career. A lawyer from Amherst College, he was quite successful in private practice before he entered politics, serving in both the Massachusetts House of Representatives and the state Senate. In 1859, he was appointed to the Superior Court of Massachusetts, and in 1875, he was chosen to sit on the Supreme Court. While Lord was very straitlaced, his dignity and conservatism were somewhat tempered by a kind, generous spirit. A robust sense of humor lay beneath the ironclad exterior, as evidenced by the cartoons he drew to alleviate boredom while presiding as Speaker of the House in 1854. Add to that a love of Shakespeare, and Lord seems an undisputable candidate for Emily's adoration.

Her letters to Lord—even though someone mysteriously cut out portions of them—are happy, passionate, and very intimate. For a woman of limited sexual experience, Emily was surprisingly bold, coy, and erotic, even though it is almost certain that the relationship was never consummated. She wrote:

Don't you know you are happiest while I withhold and not confer—don't you know that "No" is the wildest word we consign to Language?

You do, for you know all things . . . to lie so near your longing—to touch it as I passed, for I am but a restive sleeper and often should journey from your Arms through the happy night, but you will lift me back, won't you, for only there I ask to be—I say, if I felt the longing nearer—than in our dear past, perhaps I could not resist to bless it, but must because it would be right.

The "Stile" is God's—my Sweet One—for your great sake—not mine—I will not let you cross—but it is all yours, and when it is right I will lift the Bars, and lay you in the Moss—You showed me the word.

I hope it has no different guise when my fingers make it. It is Anguish I long conceal from you to let you leave me, hungry, but you ask the divine Crust and that would doom the Bread. . . .

Dickinson and Lord may have considered marriage, but too many obstacles prevented the union. First of all, family obligations were insurmountable. Some members of Emily's family were embarrassed and scandalized by the reclusive woman's late blossoming. In addition, Emily was primarily responsible for the care of her invalid mother. On the judge's side, relatives who had long expected to inherit Lord's estate were vehemently opposed to a woman who might jeopardize their financial future. But probably the largest roadblock to the marriage was the couple themselves. Each had established a life pattern that was impossible to alter.

Otis Lord died on March 13, 1884, following a stroke. Emily died two years later on May 15. She was buried in a white flannel robe. Before the casket was closed, her sister Lavinia placed two heliotropes in the poet's hand "to take to Judge Lord."

The Golden Woman

A DREAM WOMAN with troubling sensuality and delicate features, Simonetta Catteano drove many illustrious Florentines into ecstasy. At sixteen, she was adored by poets, scientists, seamen, and artists. All the virtues were hers: gentleness, goodness, beauty. Poets composed for her, knights jousted for her, and artists, among them Sandro Botticelli, painted her. Botticelli was obsessed by her and continued painting her image long after she was in her grave.

Giuliano Medici fell in love with Simonetta even though she was married to nobleman Marco Vespucci. When Giuliano asked if he could champion Simonetta as his lady in the jousts at the yearly Courts of Love, Vespucci encouraged him. He even suggested that Medici's thin, introverted genius-cousin Botticelli be commissioned to paint Simonetta's likeness on a banner for the joust.

For the banner painting, Simonetta wore a long, gold tissue tunic, her blond hair spread over her shoulders—a golden girl. After seven preparatory sketches of her and Giuliano, Botticelli interpreted her as the goddess of war with a blazing sun behind her. When Giuliano won the joust, she became the Love Queen of Florence.

In 1476, at age twenty, she died. Dressed in her wedding gown, lying in an open bier, she was carried through the streets while hundreds of mourners tossed flowers and sang songs for her. Lorenzo the Magnificent wrote one of the songs and the last stanza became her epitaph:

How love is youth's Springtime day
Which flies on every side away;
Who would be glad, let him be
Of tomorrow there's no certainty.

Set to music, it was the theme song for memorials held in her honor.

Three years after her death, Botticelli started painting Madonnas with Simonetta's face. By 1480, according to a contemporary chronicler, he was "running a large shop for the production of gentle and devout Madonnas. Teams of employees were turning them out en masse copied from his original drawings of Simonetta."

But he also captured her as a sensual woman of classical Greece. The central figure of his *Primavera* (Springtime) is Simonetta. So, too, is the Venus of *Birth of Venus*, naked but with a hand modestly placed, rising from a seashell on the shore.

Though Botticelli had loved Simonetta's beauty, as a follower of the religious fanatic Savonarola he had a change of heart and came to consider Simonetta a Satan-possessed temptress. At the Burning of the Vanities ("frivolous" books and works of art) in the Piazza della Signoria one Sunday afternoon, he threw all his Simonetta paintings and drawings into the raging fire. Still, her memory consumed him. Years later she appeared as Beatrice in his illustration for Dante's *Inferno*. He painted more pictures of her after her death than when she was alive, and could not stop. Whether he wanted her or not, she was his inspiration.

Dumas and La Dame aux Camélias

IN the early morning hours of February 3, 1847, a twenty-three-year-old courtesan, Marie Duplessis, died of tuberculosis in her apartment at No. 11 Boulevard de la Madeleine in Paris. The exquisitely beautiful and stylish woman, once the most sought-after courtesan in the city, spent her last days alone except for the comfort of her maid and nurse. She was placed in a coffin filled with flowers and yards of billowing white lace. In her hands was a bouquet of camellias, her favorite flower, and a cross. Amid the small group of mourners in the funeral procession to the Montmartre cemetery were her husband Viscount Édouard de Perregaux and several of her former lovers, including a Russian count and a notable

French banker. Conspicuously absent from the group was twenty-three-year-old Alexandre Dumas, son of the famous French author Alexandre Dumas. His short but intense love affair with Marie Duplessis would soon be permanently recorded in his most famous book, *La Dame aux Camélias*, and a subsequent play, *Camille*, one of the most popular stage productions of the nineteenth century.

Born in the village of Saint-Germain-de-Clairfeuille in 1824, Marie Duplessis (born Alphonsine Plessis) was the daughter of Marin Plessis, an immoral, brutal alcoholic, and Marie Deshayes, a modest, timid woman who deserted her husband and died when Alphonsine was nine years old. Unable and unwilling to care for his daughter, Marin Plessis sent her to various relatives or apprenticed her to a laundress, a dressmaker, a milliner—anyone who would take in the young girl.

By the time Alphonsine reached her early teens, she was strikingly attractive and charming, and by the time she was fifteen, she was living in Paris and taking care of herself. Although at first she worked at menial jobs, she soon realized that there were more than enough successful men who were willing to care for her. A restaurant owner provided her with an apartment in the rue de l'Arcade. Then a new lover found her more fashionable lodgings. Eventually she moved to the Boulevard de la Madeleine, her apartment paid for by yet another suitor. She had found a new and very reliable profession, one that guaranteed her the life-style she so desired. As she once said to a friend: "Why did I sell myself? Because honest work would never have brought me the luxury I craved for, irresistibly. Whatever I may seem to be, I promise you I'm not covetous or debauched. I wanted to know the refinements and pleasures of artistic taste, the joy of living in elegant and cultivated society."

Aware that beauty alone might not capture the aristocratic benefactors that she required, Alphonsine changed her name to Marie Duplessis and set out to transform herself into a refined lady. She learned to read and write, and her library included the works of Victor Hugo, Molière, and Alfred de Musset. She recited poetry, learned to play the piano, and attended the most noted theaters and opera houses. All of Paris was soon aware that Marie Duplessis was not a common courtesan.

During the day she rode through the streets of Paris in a splendid blue carriage pulled by two thoroughbred horses, often stopping at the most fashionable shops to make a few extravagant purchases. In the evenings she went to the theater or opera and commanded a box near the stage. Beautifully attired in the latest fashions (she commissioned a new dress every day) made from the choicest satin, velvet, silk, and brocade, she accented her clothing with exquisite diamonds and emeralds, strings of the finest pearls, and magnificent gold bracelets. As she gaily chatted with the steady stream of visitors who came to make her acquaintance, she held an ever-present bouquet of camellias and nibbled on expensive candy provided by her male companion.

It was on such an evening in the fall of 1844 at the Théâtre des Variétés that young Alexandre Dumas met Marie Duplessis. While gazing longingly at her throughout the performance, he noticed that Marie waved to a dressmaker who knew the man who had accompanied Dumas to the Variétés. Using the chain of acquaintances, he asked for a formal introduction. To his delight Marie invited Dumas and the two intermediaries to her apartment for an after-theater supper. At the supper, Dumas was so enchanted by Duplessis that he hardly spoke a word as Marie and the other two guests drank champagne and laughed uproariously at each other's stories. Dumas could not take his eyes from her. She was perfect—oval face, flawless complexion, dark eyes, tiny waist, and long curls of brilliant black hair.

By the end of the evening, however, the courtesan drank too much, laughed too hard, and suffered a coughing attack. As she quickly fled to her dressing room, Dumas followed her. After she recovered, he professed his love for her and his desire to look after her. While Marie had heard many such declarations, she was overcome by his genuine concern for her health. She agreed to see him but set a condition: "If you promise to grant all my wishes, without saying a word or making a comment or questioning me, I may perhaps come to love you."

The twenty-year-old Dumas blithely agreed but had no idea of the consequences that awaited him. At the time he was a struggling writer living in the shadow of his illustrious father, the author of *The Three Musketeers* and *The Count of Monte Cristo*. An extremely handsome young man with auburn hair, penetrating blue eyes, and broad, square shoulders, he was one of the city's most eligible dandies, but he depended largely on the earnings of his father for support. The cost of courting a woman like Marie Duplessis was exceedingly high. He took her out to dinner and the opera, bought her flowers and expensive gifts, and gave her money to gamble at the horse races or the roulette tables.

In less than a year Dumas was frustrated and heavily in debt. For a while he had believed that Marie had given up other men and belonged exclusively to him, but she had lied to him and was still involved with a number of suitors. When he demanded that she see no one but him, she answered simply that she would, if he alone could afford to support her.

Consumed with jealousy and depressed over his financial woes, Dumas decided that he must end the torturous relationship. On August 30, 1845, he wrote her a letter:

My dear Marie—I am neither rich enough to love you as I would wish nor poor enough to be loved by you as you would. Let us both, therefore, forget—you, a name which cannot mean very much to you, I, a happiness which is no longer possible for me. There is no point in my telling you how sad I am, since you already know how much I love you. Farewell, then. You have too much heart not to understand the reasons for this letter and too much intelligence not to forgive me. A thousand memories. A. D.

Marie never answered his letter. She continued to live a lavish, active life in spite of her deteriorating health. Not only did she continue to entertain her old lovers, but she found a few new ones, including Hungarian pianist Franz Liszt. On February 21, 1846, she married one of her admirers, Édouard Perregaux, in London, but they separated a week later, and Perregaux did not see his wife again until shortly before she died.

In the last year of her life, Marie Duplessis was beset with ill health and financial problems. Her benefactors, once so quick to attend to her whims, ceased to call. She was forced to sell some of her jewelry in order to pay her debts. Physically unable to attend social affairs, she often sat at her bedroom window in a white nightgown and cashmere shawl, with her arm around her favorite dog, watching the crowds on their way to the theater. In desperation she pleaded with Liszt to take her into his home. He quoted her as saying: "I shall not live. I'm a strange woman; I won't be able to cling to this life that I cannot live and cannot endure. Take me away. Take me anywhere you like. I won't be in your way. I sleep all day; in the evening you can let me go to the theater, and at night you can do what you like with me." Liszt, who was deeply in love with the courtesan, was moved, but he had a reputation to protect and was unwilling to make public his liaison with Marie. He did, however, promise to take her on a trip to Constantinople—a promise he failed to keep. In the depths of despair she even wrote to her husband begging for his forgiveness.

When the mortal men in her life failed her, she turned to God. She had always been religious, attending mass on Sundays, but now she became a fervent worshiper. For her boudoir she bought a handsomely upholstered prie-dieu and placed beside it a gilded statue of the Virgin Mary. But her prayers did nothing to improve her physical state. A week before she died she made a final appearance at the opera. One observer who watched her being carried to her seat wrote: "What was the shadow which attracted general attention by its comsumptive pallor and a large bouquet of white camellias? Marie Duplessis was going to the theater for the last time; for the last time she and her white camellias were presenting themselves to the public view."

Alexandre Dumas was in Marseilles when he learned of Marie's death. Grief-stricken, he returned to Paris and shortly afterward attended the auction of her estate. Huge crowds pushed into the apartment on the Boulevard de la Madeleine to bid for her possessions. He watched as the familiar objects—the rosewood piano, Dresden china, Venetian mirrors, antique clocks, her gowns and cashmere shawls—passed into the hands of strangers. Dumas bought only one remembrance, a simple gold chain necklace.

The following year, 1848, Dumas published *La Dame aux Camélias*, a fictionalized account of his love affair with Marie Duplessis. She became Marguerite Gautier, and Dumas portrayed himself as Armand Duval. The sentimental, tragic story with its heartrending death scene was an instant success, especially since the memory of Duplessis was still fresh in the public's mind. In 1852, the book was adapted into a play, *Camille*, that starred many famous actresses in the title role, including Sarah Bernhardt.

Even though Marie Duplessis had inspired his greatest work, Dumas was not permanently affected by her rejection of him or her death. He had numerous other love affairs and married twice. While in *Camille* he showed great compassion for the courtesan, Dumas later spoke out against prostitution and became a staunch moralist when writing of social issues such as divorce. But he could never erase his immediate identification with the lady of the camellias. When he died in 1894, Dumas was buried in the same cemetery as Marie Duplessis. Mourners took flowers from his grave and placed them on the grave of the woman he had once loved.

"Down by the Old Mill Stream"

ONE of America's favorite songs and a standard for barbershop quartets is "Down by the Old Mill Stream." Appropriately enough, this simple song was inspired by a teenage love affair.

In 1906, by an old gristmill near Findlay, Ohio, two lovers, Buda Goodman and Tell Taylor, spent many summer afternoons strolling and gazing into each other's eyes. On one of those occasions, Taylor, a frustrated songwriter, was overcome with love for Buda and wrote the song that would make him rich.

The couple's marriage was far less successful; after four years they got a divorce. Taylor had no idea that his young wife was the daughter of a race sheet writer and had grown up around the fast crowds at the Chicago racetracks and gambling dens. Taylor, a backward farm boy, could not accept her life-style. Of his angel-faced bride Taylor said, "I married Buda when we both were drunk, and I found out she was quite incapable of loyalty to anybody."

Taylor put all of his energies into songwriting. After several years of peddling his music in Findlay, Taylor went to Chicago and became a part-time actor, appearing with Sophie Tucker and Al Jolson. From there he moved to New York and set up a music publishing house with Jimmy Walker (later to become mayor of that city) and composer Ernest Ball. Financial difficulties forced the business to close, and Taylor subsequently returned to Chicago where he began another publishing house. There, his luck changed.

One day a famous male quartet, The Orpheus Comedy Four, came to Taylor's office and asked him for a new song. Taylor dusted off the yellowed pages of "Down by the Old Mill Stream" and convinced the group that the ballad was a winner. The sentimental tune was an instant hit, and soon Taylor was collecting $1,000 a month in royalties.

But Taylor, naive in money matters, wasn't able to hold on to his fortune. He made no solid investments and was a soft touch for financially troubled friends. In 1920, after most of his money had been spent, Taylor moved to a farm in his native Findlay. There he hoped to make a comeback by developing a movie based on "Down by the Old Mill Stream." He was still trying to negotiate a movie deal on November 23, 1937, when he died.

The lovely Buda became part of an extortionist ring in New York. Using her voluptuous body as bait, she conned many an unsuspecting businessman. Local police called her the "Queen of the Badger Game." Caught in a jewelry robbery, she was tried, convicted, and served two years in Auburn Prison. After that she disappeared.

7. People: Real and Ideal

It's quite a cast of characters—murderers to sexpots. These real-life models for artistic creations often bear little resemblance to the works of art they inspired. The real Bluebeard killed more people than his counterpart, and for different reasons. Dracula's prototype was bloodier than the seductive fictional villain ever thought of being. The flesh-and-blood Auntie Mame, *enfant terrible* of Newport, surpassed in outrageousness the character she inspired. The actual Man Who Came to Dinner may have been even more obnoxious than the character in the play.

But, on the other hand, creators have been known to gild the lily. While the model for Goldfinger was just as rich as the movie villain, he was nowhere near as diabolical. Time has enhanced some of the originals, as in the case of the inspirations for national symbols.

Some creators were favored with only passing glimpses of the inspirations for their works. One of Upton Sinclair's most moving scenes was based on a fleeting look at celebrating strangers, and big-eared, dim-witted Alfred E. Neuman's original was a stranger to the man who made him famous.

Is truth stranger than fiction, or is it the other way around?

The Man with the Midas Touch

THE SCENARIO for British author Ian Fleming's 1959 best-seller *Goldfinger* and its subsequent movie adaptation: Auric Goldfinger already possessed a large portion of the world's gold—most of it taken illegally from England. Greed, however, ruled this powerful and diabolical man, and with his gang of all-women cat burglars—led by the exotic Pussy Galore—the sinister genius plotted his grandest scheme: to steal the U. S. gold supply from Fort Knox. Only one man could stop him—James Bond, the finest double-o agent in the British Secret Service.

Of little concern to adoring audiences was the fact that Fleming modeled the Goldfinger character after his good friend, Charles Engelhard, industrialist and precious-metal tycoon. In reality, Engelhard and Goldfinger had little in common—except a lavish life-style and a love of gold. Engelhard's story, though not a spy thriller, is nonetheless an exciting one.

Born in New York City on February 15, 1917, Charles William Engelhard, Jr., was the son of Charles William and Emy Canthal Engelhard. After graduating from Harvard and serving as a bomber pilot in World War II, Charles joined the senior Engelhard in business—a precious-metal business that made the Engelhards one of the richest families in America. Of his father, Charles later recalled: "My father was very thorough, very Germanic. He controlled every detail of the business. He visited every plant he owned every day, punching in and out by the time clock. In some companies he signed every check for more than fifty cents. I can't ever remember having a personal conversation with him."

In 1950, after his father's death, Charles took over the reins of the Engelhard Minerals and Chemicals Corporation, which was controlled by Engelhard Hanovia, Inc., the family holding company. Before long Engelhard Hanovia had investments in fifty companies located on six continents. As one family friend observed: "Charlie put his trust in gold, platinum, and diamonds."

The portly, double-chinned Engelhard, who suffered from gout (but consumed vast quantities of Coca-Cola and Hershey kisses) and arthritis, thoroughly enjoyed his opulent, yet tasteful, life-style. His primary residence was a Rhinelike castle (complete with turrets) called Cragwood, which was set on a 172-acre hill in Far Hills, New Jersey. It was here that Engelhard, his wife Jane (always on the Ten Best-Dressed Women list), and five daughters felt most at ease. He also had four secondary residences: in Johannesburg, South Africa; in Boca Grande, Florida; on the Gaspé Peninsula in Quebec; and at the Waldorf Towers in New York City. All of the homes were decorated in pastel colors and adorned with the works of Dégas, Cézanne, Modigliani, Monet, Manet, Renoir, and Winslow Homer. An avid horse-racing fan, Engelhard had a stable of three hundred horses (an investment of $20 million).

Engelhard was constantly on the move—for business and pleasure. Always accompanying him was an entourage of chefs, valets, butlers, and secretaries, plus friends and favorite animals. Travel arrangements were never a problem since Engelhard owned a fleet of boats and airplanes (including a transoceanic jetliner). As fellow aristocrat Alfred Vanderbilt once said: "Charlie is a mogul. My wife and I have gone to Africa and Asia with the Engelhards, and you go first class. Every place we went we met *the* important people. . . . Charlie is a bright and curious man."

Also a generous man, Engelhard made large donations to various groups and charities, among them Boys Town, Rutgers University, the New Jersey Symphony Orchestra, the World Wildlife Fund, and the Democratic party. Many a campaigning Democrat was treated to an extravagant barbecue at Far Hills. Regulars on the guest list were John and Jacqueline Kennedy, Robert and Ethel Kennedy, Lyndon and Lady Bird Johnson, Hubert and Muriel Humphrey. At one such party the conversation turned to starvation in India and an upcoming $300 million loan that would help remedy the disaster. Charles's mother Emy—paying only peripheral attention to the discussion—innocently asked, "Is Charlie giving the money?"

Ian Fleming and Charles Engelhard were friends in the 1940s. It was at that time that Engelhard was shipping solid gold dishes, pulpit tops, and jewelry out of South Africa—to circumvent international trade restrictions on bullion sales. These gold dealings fascinated Fleming and eventually led him to create *Goldfinger*. Engelhard was relatively good-natured about his Goldfinger image. He once attended a formal party in a bright orange sweatshirt (a Goldfinger trademark) and often joked that he employed a stewardess, Pussy Galore, on one of his planes.

Unfortunately, the Fleming-Engelhard friendship did suffer one setback. On Fleming's suggestion, the two invested in African timber land on the banks of the Zambesi River in Mozambique. For a while the undertaking seemed lucrative as trees were cut down and readied for shipment to a nearby port. Then came the dry season when the Zambesi reverses direction and flows inland—a fact that came as a complete surprise to Fleming and Engelhard. Unable to ship the lumber, business came to a standstill, and the two friends quickly planted vegetables on the fertile land in an attempt to salvage part of their investment. The plan might have worked had it not been for the hungry hippopotami who greedily surged out of the water and devoured all the crops.

Charles Engelhard died at the age of fifty-four of a heart attack on March 2, 1971. In two decades he ballooned a $20 million inheritance into a $300 million corporate empire. A fitting epitaph is a description he once gave himself: "Other men may have made larger capital gains, but few men have earned more economic power."

The Real Bluebeard

GILLES DE RAIS, who was probably the model for the wife-killer Bluebeard in Charles Perrault's fairy tale, was actually a flesh-and-blood
nobleman, one of the richest in fifteenth-century Europe. His monstrous
crimes, beside which the fictional Bluebeard's paltry murders of seven
wives pale, were so loathsome that many of his biographers found them
too unspeakable to discuss, except in euphemisms.

As a small child, Gilles did not seem to be a monster. He was born in
1404 in the Black Tower of Champtocé, one of the family castles. At age
eleven, he was orphaned. His father was gored by a wild boar while
hunting; the manner of his mother's death is not known. Gilles was
brought up by his reprobate grandfather, Jean de Craon, who spoiled him
rotten—literally. When Gilles was still a teenager of sixteen or seventeen,
he kidnapped the unwilling Catherine de Thouars, whose parents' estates
bordered the Craon lands, and forced her to marry him. It was not love
but avarice. He did not kill her.

In his twenties, Gilles excelled as a warrior in battles against the
English. He was there in 1429 at the Day of the Herrings when the
French attacked an English supply train carrying fish for the troops to eat
during Lent, then fought the enemy among broken barrels and slippery,
stinking herring. The French lost. He was at Chinon when Joan of Arc
announced she was coming from Vaucouleurs to save the city of Orléans
and crown the Dauphin in Rheims cathedral. While she was making her
spectacular entrance into Orléans, wearing white armor and riding a
white horse, proud banners being borne before her among crowds of
torch-bearing townspeople, Gilles, as the one in charge of her armies, was
engaged in a far more mundane activity—finding supplies. However, he
later showed himself a true hero. When Joan was trapped by the English
after she impulsively rode out from Orléans to battle, Gilles came out of
the city on a prancing horse to save her. At twenty-five, he was made
marshal of France and given the right to add the royal arms, a fleur-de-lis
on blue ground, to his own.

In 1430, he was at Louviers, not far from Rouen, where Joan had been
imprisoned. Romantic tales place him there to rescue her, but records

reveal that he was in Louviers to buy a horse. Joan was burned at the stake on May 20, 1431. So ended the heroic stage of Gilles's life.

The man was immensely rich. After his grandfather died in 1432, Gilles could lay claim to twenty-four estates. On many of them, imposing, dark castles loomed, ruling the land from above. He lived in six of the castles, traveling from one to the other. They were filled with golden cloth, stained glass, and jewel-studded gold and silver objects. The 200-person retinue which accompanied him included jugglers, singers, actresses, and servants. His house was open to all—anyone could find a free meal there. Gilles de Rais, rich beyond imagination, garlanded with the honors of France, seemed to have all anyone could desire. It was not enough.

Sometime between the spring of 1432 and the spring of 1433, he killed a child, the first of at least forty, perhaps as many as two hundred, most of them young boys. The murders were not simple killings but the work of a monster, and they followed a pattern. They began with a feast and the drinking of hippocras, a stimulant, after which the chosen child was taken to an upper room and told what was to happen to him so that Gilles could delight in his terror. Gilles then rubbed his erect penis over the child's belly to orgasm. After that, he might hang the boy by the neck with a hook, only to take him down and comfort him. Often he sodomized the child. Eventually, after further debauchery and torture, he or his accomplices (his cousins Gilles de Sillé and Robert de Briqueville, or his servants) killed the child by one of various means, sometimes beheading. After the child was dead, he often performed sexual acts on the body. In his confession of the crimes, Gilles admitted, "When the said children were dead, I kissed them, and those who had the most handsome limbs and heads, I held up to admire them." His pleasure lay in seeing the children die. The clothes and bodies were burned in a huge fireplace, and the ashes and bones were thrown in moats or cesspits.

In that first year, Gilles killed at least four children. His procurers were his cousins and an old woman, Perrine Martin, also known as *la Meffraye* (the Terror). Like some evil witch, she roamed the countryside, enticing children to the castle. The first documented case is of Jean Jeudon, about twelve, apprenticed to the furrier Guillaume Hilairet. Gilles's cousins asked the furrier to send Jean to Machecoul, another castle, with a message. Hilairet duly dispatched the boy. Jean never returned. When Hilairet asked about him, the cousins said he might have been carried off by thieves.

In 1433 or 1434, Gilles began a new enterprise. He built his own chapel at Machecoul, called, without intentional irony, the Chapel of the

Holy Innocents. It had a staff of thirty—choirboys, archdeacons, chaplains, curates, and a schoolteacher, all dressed in "trailing robes of the best quality furs." Along with portable organs carried by six men, the entire staff accompanied him on his travels. The chapel itself was decorated with cloths of gold and silk, candlesticks, censers, and crosses of precious metals. Among the religious relics in it was an enameled and jeweled head of Saint Honoré.

The choirboys were chosen for their looks and angelic voices. One of his favorites, Rossignol (Nightingale), sold by his parents to Gilles for three hundred écus, was blond, a "Greek type." Gilles gave the boy property and money, sexual violation, and eventual involvement in his crimes. Another choirboy, Perrinet, was Gilles's "little darling."

Obviously, he was extremely insane. He was able to get away with his insanity because of his inherited power. His enormous ego was never satiated. On May 8, 1435, he presented a show, *Le Mystère du Siège d'Orléans*, to commemorate the tenth anniversary of the taking of Orléans. In it, the character of Gilles was servant to Joan of Arc. There were 20,000 lines of verse, 140 speaking parts, 500 extras. Entire battle scenes were staged. To pay for his share (most of the cost), he sold estates and many of his possessions, including his favorite horse. On the day of the performance, he marched in the triumphal parade, scattering money to the crowds from a helmet, escorted by an armored honor guard. Several thousand people were fed at his expense.

Meanwhile, he continued to kill children. Many were probably poor refugees, victims of the Hundred Years' War, ragged waifs who went begging from town to town. One beggar who stood in line at Machecoul for free food was invited inside the castle and never seen again. Other children disappeared while playing pelota, picking apples, or walking to the fair. There was one boy who, when taken to Gilles, was carrying his inheritance of one silver mark in a little box. Gilles sent the box back to the boy's parents—without the mark.

In about 1436, Gilles became interested in black magic and alchemy, both forbidden by the king. Signing in blood, he made a pact with the devil.

Since his glorious fighting days, Gilles had with him a page, Etienne Corillant ("Poitou"), at ten a young angel and by 1437, a decade later, when Gilles decided to let him in on his grisly secret, a handsome youth of twenty. Gilles sexually abused him, then locked him up for four days. The boy had little choice but to become his accomplice. In that same year, Gilles sent his body servant, Henriet Griart, to Nantes to get the brother of Catherine Thierry, a painter's wife, ostensibly to serve as choirboy. Instead, the boy was murdered, and Henriet was trapped into complicity. He and Poitou joined Gilles's group of procurers.

A year later, Champtocé was taken away from Gilles by force, so he ordered Robert de Briqueville and Robin Romulart to take away the bones of children "from a tower near the castle" within forty-eight hours. De Briqueville allowed two ladies to watch the proceedings through a peephole. Though they counted the skulls of the children, they could not later remember the number—it was somewhere between thirty-six and forty-six. The bones were put in chests and taken to Machecoul, where they were burned and thrown into the castle water pipes.

Rumors were raging throughout the country around Machecoul. What was happening to the children? Why were they disappearing? "They eat children there," country people said. One wonders why parents allowed their children near the fateful castles. It was partly out of desperate poverty. It was better to take the chance: If the children were not killed, they would at least have enough to eat. Some parents thought that if they sent their children to beg for food in pairs, the children would be safe. They were not. After Gilles took one child of a pair sexually, he killed both "so that the other should not pine for the first." If a frightened mother complained when her child was taken, she faced the absolute feudal power of Gilles de Rais, Sieur de Laval, ruler of the domain.

In February or March 1438, young Guillaume Delit disappeared. His mother Jeanne overheard Jean Briand, who worked for Gilles, say he had told the cook it was a mistake to let a certain boy help the cook prepare a roast at the castle, implying that the boy himself might be roasted. In May, Mme Delit approached Briand's wife and said it was "rumored that the Sire de Rais had small children taken so that he could kill them"; she had heard of a boy being cooked. But Mme Briand, far from being sympathetic, cried out in the presence of two of Gilles's men that Jeanne Delit would pay for her words, so the distraught mother apologized and left.

Poitou told Peronne, mother of ten-year-old Robin Loessart, that her son would have a wonderful life with Gilles and would be allowed to complete his education. When Poitou offered her 100 sous for a new dress, she surrendered Robin, whom Gilles described as "well chosen and pretty as an angel." Poitou bought Robin a horse. Two months later, the previous owner saw the horse being ridden by another boy in Nantes. The story circulated that the wind blew Robin into a river while he was crossing a bridge.

In 1439, at least twelve children died because of Gilles de Rais. In 1440, at least ten more children met their deaths by his order, including ten-year-old Lavary, whose body, thrown into a cesspool, floated so that Poitou had to be lowered into the muck to push it under.

On July 29, 1440, Jean de Malestroit, chancellor of Brittany and bishop of Nantes, accused Gilles of murder and invocation of the devil, claiming that Gilles had engaged in child sacrifice. The latter accusation was probably not true, though Poitou, according to the servant Henriet, had put a child's head and heart in a cloth-covered glass on the chimney piece of the room in which Gilles practiced magic.

Gilles de Rais was put on trial. He confessed to his crimes, blaming them on his grandfather's indulgence of him. He was hanged and burned at Nantes on October 26, 1440. Henriet and Poitou were also burned, and Perrine Martin hanged herself in her cell.

Charles Perrault, secretary of finance under Louis XIV's minister Jean Baptiste Colbert, lived more than two centuries after Gilles de Rais. Ironically, though it was his greatest desire to be immortalized as an intellectual, he is best known as the writer of a book of fairy tales, *Contes de ma Mère l'Oie* (*Stories of Mother Goose*), which he wrote when he was nearly seventy under the pseudonym P. d'Armancour. Among the tales are "Cinderella," "Puss in Boots," "Hop o' My Thumb," "Little Red Riding Hood," and "Sleeping Beauty."

By then Gilles had passed into legend as bogeyman of the countryside. In one story, he forces a woman, "pale as a lovely lily and . . . trembling," to marry him at an altar lit by a thousand candles. She asks him to give himself to her body and soul, and when he promises to do so, she turns into a blue devil and changes his red beard to blue, saying that he shall be called Bluebeard and cursed forever.

In Perrault's story of Bluebeard, inspired by the legendary de Rais, Bluebeard leaves his wife with the keys to all the rooms in his castle, warning her not to use one which is for a closet. Of course, she cannot resist temptation, and in the closet, to her incredible horror, she sees the headless bodies of his seven previous wives ranged around the walls. Blood that she cannot wipe off appears on the key, so that when Bluebeard returns, he knows what she has done and decides to kill her. She gains time by begging to pray, asking her sister Anne, in the tower, if she sees help coming. "I see sun scattering and grass greening," says Anne at first, but then she spies puffs of dust and two horsemen—their two brothers—who save the wife from death just as Bluebeard is lifting her hair preparatory to beheading her.

No such saviors appeared for Gilles de Rais's child victims.

Marian Fish: The Real "Auntie Mame"

AUNTIE MAME was a smashing success—as a book in 1955, as a Broadway play in 1956, and as a film in 1958. The madcap adventures of the eccentric middle-aged terror of Beekman Place in New York City were the creation of writer Patrick Dennis (a pseudonym for Edward Everett Tanner), who based his central character on his aunt Marian Fish. While the fictional Mame was outrageous, she was but a dim facsimile of the showstopping real-life lady.

Born into a middle-class family in New York City in 1853, Marian Anthon suffered an early setback when at twelve her father died and her family had to move to Astoria to ease financial woes. However, money problems vanished when Marian married her childhood sweetheart, financier Stuyvesant Fish, who became a kingpin in the American railroad networks.

Tossed into the world of very fashionable, very proper high society, "Mamie" (as her friends called her) rebelled at the strict, stifling laws that governed the lives of the elite "Four Hundred." Refusing to cower under the pressure of the what-was-expected-of-you upper class, Mamie never hid the fact that she did not enjoy art or the theater or literature or music. As a matter of fact, she loved to shock her stodgy, rich friends with the facts that she had never even attended the first grade, was a miserable speller, and could hardly write a legible letter.

What Mamie lacked in education she more than made up for with her distinctive brand of style. In 1900 at Newport, Rhode Island—one of the most frequented watering holes of the wealthy—Mamie and her husband built a summer home, "Crossways," a colonial building adorned with four large Corinthian columns. Always scorning her status (only worth "a few millions," according to Mamie), she called the resort house a "cottage" and pointed out that she employed fewer servants (only fifteen) than her friends in Newport.

Parties at Crossways were always the talk of the town. There was the annual Harvest Moon Ball, which required farm costumes. There was the Mother Goose Ball, in which invited guests came as Little Jack Horner, Old Mother Hubbard, Jack Sprat, or any other favorite Mother Goose character. Some parties had no special theme but were a spectacle of dazzling decorations (such as the one that blanketed the ballrooms with American Beauty roses) or had a special guest of honor (such as the monkey in a white tuxedo who threw lightbulbs from the chandelier).

Called the *enfant terrible* of Newport's Golden Age, she reveled in breaking any long-established social rule. While most hostesses entertained guests with a three-hour dinner, Mamie limited her feasts to forty minutes. Some guests complained that they almost had to hang on to their plates, but Mamie boasted that her all-time record was an eight-course meal served in a half hour. However, no one disapproved when she introduced champagne to the meals. According to Newport's number one hostess, "You have to liven these people up. Wine just makes them sleepy."

Of all her trademarks, Mamie Fish's acerbic wit and sharp tongue were the most impressive. *Not* to be insulted by Mamie was a true insult. She addressed no one by proper name, preferring an across-the-board "Pet" or "Sweet Pet" or "Lamb" or "Sweet Lamb." In her traditional greeting she usually said, "Howdy-do, howdy-do. Make yourselves at home. And believe me, there is no one who wishes you were there more than I do."

The life of the irrepressible Mame is chronicled by Cleveland Amory in *The Last Resorts*, a book about the rich and their vacation spots. Included are many of Mamie's most memorable retorts, one-liners, and insults. For example: Mamie on occasion arranged ladies' luncheons even though she hated them. At one such affair she quipped, "Here you all are. Older faces and younger clothes." And another popular anecdote: When Henry Lehr, one of Mamie's best friends, suffered a nervous breakdown, she wrote and invited him to Crossways. "You know quite well, sweet lamb, that you won't need any mind to go with the people here," she concluded.

After years of barbs and banter, Mamie Fish succumbed to a stroke on June 8, 1915. A month before, she had written her own epitaph based on Matthew Arnold's poem "Requiescat":

> Strew on her roses, roses
>   And never a spray of rue,
> For in quiet she reposes
>   And I would that I could too.
> The world her mirth required,
>   So she bathed it in smiles of glee,
> But her heart was tired, tired,
>   So now they let her be.

For her life was turning, turning,
In mazes of heat and sound,
But for peace her soul was yearning,
And now peace laps her around.

The Sweetest Little Rosebud

"THE YELLOW ROSE OF TEXAS" was not a refined, pampered Southern belle or even the earthy dame in the famous 1955 Mitch Miller rendition of the song, but a beautiful mulatto slave girl. Her name was Emily Morgan, and she played a decisive role in the Battle of San Jacinto in 1836, a major clash in the Texas war for independence from Mexico. After that battle between the Mexican forces of General Santa Anna and the Texan forces of Sam Houston, Emily Morgan would have faded into obscurity except that someone whose identity is not known wrote "The Yellow Rose of Texas" in her honor.

Emily became Santa Anna's property after he forcibly took her from the home of Colonel James Morgan, at Morgan's Point (then called New Washington), Texas, where she was an indentured servant. Thereafter she became a "serving girl," providing the womanizing general with a great deal more than housekeeping comforts. Santa Anna, whether at home in Mexico or camped along a river in Texas, always maintained a high style of living. His personal quarters, a large carpeted tent, was filled with monogrammed china, silver teapots, and crystal stemware. In addition, it boasted an elaborate bed with silk sheets and was always stocked with an ample supply of champagne. The general's well-ordered life, however, was radically altered on April 21, 1836.

Approximately six weeks after Santa Anna had killed 200 Texans at the Alamo in San Antonio, the general and his 1,500-man Mexican army were camped on the banks of the San Jacinto River near what is present-day Houston. At three-thirty in the afternoon, an 800-man Texas army—fired up with revenge and yelling "Remember the Alamo"—attacked with lightning speed. The battle was over in less than thirty minutes. The Mexican army was resoundingly defeated—600 dead, 200 wounded, the rest captured.

Where was the great General Santa Anna? He was in bed with Emily.

As soon as he heard the gunfire, he raced outside, dressed only in his drawers and red slippers. At first he ran around wringing his hands and shouting a few useless commands. However, it took him only a few minutes to realize that the battle was lost, so he jumped on the nearest horse and raced off to safety, leaving his army behind. He was captured the next day.

Emily Morgan returned home to her former master and told him about her life with General Santa Anna. Morgan passed on the story, and Emily was soon a heroine. Many of Emily's admirers believed she had somehow known of Houston's planned attack and had schemed to have the general in bed at the appropriate time. Whatever the truth, she was immortalized as the "The Yellow Rose of Texas."

The original 1836 lyrics to the song:

There's a yellow rose in Texas
That I am a going to see
No other darky [sic] knows her
No one only me
She cryed [sic] so when I left her
It like to broke my heart
And if I ever find her
We nevermore will part.

Chorus:

She's the sweetest rose of color
This darky ever knew
Her eyes are bright as diamonds
They sparkle like the dew
You may talk about dearest May
And sing of Rosa Lee
But the yellow rose of Texas
Beats the belles of Tennessee.

Where the Rio Grande is flowing
And the starry skies are bright
She walks along the river
In the quite [sic] summer night
She thinks if I remember
When we parted long ago
I promised to come back again
And not to leave her so.

Oh now I am agoing to find her
For my heart is full of woe
And we will sing the song togeather [sic]
We sung so long ago

We will play the banjo gaily
And will sing the song of yore
And the yellow rose of Texas
Shall be mine forevermore.

"What, Me Worry?"

CALLED an imbecile, a moron, a jerk, at best a simpleton by adults, Alfred E. Neuman is a cultural hero to countless high school and college students. Since his face started to appear regularly on the cover of *Mad* magazine in October 1956, Neuman has portrayed an amazing array of characters, from Attila the Hun to Benjamin Franklin. In spite of his ever-changing costume and hairstyle, the recognizable face remains the same: partly closed eyes (the right eye and eyebrow are always a little higher than the left), a pushed-in nose, plump rosy cheeks, huge jug ears, and a toothy grin (one tooth is missing).

The very first issue of *Mad*—which appeared in 1952 and was titled "Tales Calculated to Drive you MAD: Humor in a Jugular Vein"—cost ten cents and was strictly a comic book. Inside was a variety of stories, including a horror tale, a Western, and a science-fiction sketch. Three years later, however, to sidestep restrictions imposed by a comic book code, *Mad* adopted a magazine format. Shortly afterwards, Neuman popped up on the cover.

Mad's creator, Harvey Kurtzman, a comic-book editor and cartoonist who had dreamed up *Mad* while he was recuperating from an attack of jaundice, was seated in an editorial office of a big New York publisher when he first saw the face of Alfred E. Neuman. He was there to discuss the first *Mad* paperback anthology, a collection of satires that was to be called *The Mad Reader*. As he glanced up at a bulletin board, he spied an advertisement. In it was the grinning face of the boy who would become Alfred E. Neuman.

The ad for a Kansas City dentist, based on a 1910 nickelodeon slide, showed a young boy with big ears, tousled hair, and a rather dimwitted, vacuous stare. Pointing to a hole in his front row of teeth (where the dentist had obviously been at work), the kid said, "What, me worry? Didn't hurt a bit." Kurtzman borrowed the ad, and a *Mad* staff artist, Norman Mingo, fine-tuned the face into a creation worthy to adorn *The Mad Reader*. Soon Neuman appeared in the magazine as the "What—Me

Worry? Kid." From there it was but a short step to resident cover boy for *Mad* magazine. (The origin of the name Alfred E. Neuman is a mystery.)

For more than thirty years publisher William Gaines and number one editor Albert Feldstein, the imaginative genius who is largely responsible for the magazine's success, have poked fun at everything that is a part of the American scene. Nothing escapes the cluttered pages of *Mad*—not movies, television, politicians, advertising, celebrities, music, drugs, alcoholism, war, fads, education, sports, crime, divorce, bigotry, the family— and more. As Feldstein said in an interview with *The New York Times Magazine*: "What we did was to take the absurdities of the adult world that youngsters were facing and show kids that the adult world is not omnipotent, that their parents were telling the kids to be honest, not to lie, and yet they were cheating on their income tax. We told them there's a lot of garbage out in the world, and you've got to be aware of it. Everything you read in the papers is not necessarily true. What you see on television is mostly lies. You're going to have to learn to think for yourself."

Over the years the satirical comic magazine has received some high-level complaints. Probably the most publicized was one that resulted from a 1950s parody of the British royal family in which Queen Elizabeth and Prince Philip discussed the proper upbringing of young Prince Charles. The outrageous dialogue was enhanced by the drawings of Prince Charles which showed him as an unruly, nervous child—who resembled none other than the prince of nerds, Alfred E. Neuman. One British newspaper, appalled at the impertinent behavior of the magazine, labeled the feature "a stupid insult" and commented, "What we have to say goes into two words—it's sickening." In addition, a letter, written on Buckingham Palace stationery, was sent to the *Mad* office in New York City. It read, "I jolly well do not look like Alfred E. Neuman." The note was signed "Charles, P." Only the stationery, not the signature, has ever been verified as authentic.

Mad magazine is zany, ridiculous, irreverent, subversive, and sometimes grotesque, and its popularity continues to grow. In the United States alone, *Mad*'s circulation averages 1.25 million copies per month; it is also available in twelve foreign editions. This enviable success is astonishing in light of the fact that the magazine carries no advertisements (publisher Gaines says that paid advertising influences the contents of a magazine).

What has *Mad* done for America? The world? Its avid readers need no long-winded answers. Or perhaps Andy Warhol said it all: "*Mad* made me fall in love with people with big ears. That's a good influence, isn't it?"

The Many Inspirations for Dracula

VLAD THE IMPALER, medieval warrior-prince of Wallachia, relished eating his dinner in the midst of a forest of impaled, groaning victims, arranged at different heights according to rank. Some were jammed on the stakes head up, others head down. It was said that Vlad drank his victims' blood and, riding on his black horse against the Turks, is supposed to have shouted, "I am invincible, for I have drunk the blood of one thousand Christians."

The warrior-prince was also called Drakula, which meant "son of Drakul," for his father was a member of the Order of the Dragon; King Sigismund of Hungary, who then ruled Wallachia, gave him the honor for his valor in fighting Turks. When the young Vlad was about thirteen, in 1444, he was captured by the Turks with his father and brother and imprisoned for four years. His brother Mercia was buried alive. In 1447, his father was assassinated. These experiences quite naturally turned him mean. When, in 1448, he became Prince of Wallachia, his career as a blood-thirsty villain began.

He was a striking man with large features, penetrating green eyes, long straight hair, and a sweeping mustache. Feared by all, he modernized Wallachia and terrorized his own people as well as the Turks. It is said that at least one hundred thousand non-military deaths can be laid at his feet. Impaling was not his only method. He flayed victims' feet, rubbed salt in their soles, then brought in goats to lick their feet. To punish Mohammedans who discourteously wore their fezzes indoors, he ordered the hats nailed to their heads. A moralist, he had unfaithful wives skinned alive and impaled other unchaste women through their vaginas on red-hot pokers. While in prison from 1462 to 1474, he tortured mice and birds for amusement.

Wolves and bats circled his Castle Dracula, built by forced labor on a mountain top. Once, after being surrounded by enemies, and his wife having committed suicide by leaping off a precipice, he escaped through a secret tunnel to temporary safety. But his life was soon over. He was killed at age forty-five, probably by one of his many enemies. His head was cut off and sent to the Sultan, who appropriately impaled it on a stake.

Bram Stoker, the nineteenth-century British author, came upon the best-known inspiration for his classic novel *Dracula* while doing research in the British Museum. But Vlad was not his only model for the fictional Count—another was an actor. Born in 1847, a sickly child bedridden until he was eight, Stoker grew up to love the theater. When he was nineteen, he was introduced to actor Henry Irving, whose performance in *The Rivals* took Stoker's breath away. The two became fast friends. Stoker used Irving's face as the model for Dracula. His description fits both: "His face was a strong—a very strong—aquiline, with high bridge of thin nose and particularly arched nostrils, with lofty domed forehead and hair growing scantily around the temples but profusely elsewhere. His eyebrows were very massive, almost meeting over the nose, and with bushy hair that seemed to curl in its own profusion. The mouth, so far as I could see it under the mustache, was fixed rather cruel-looking, with peculiarly sharp teeth; those protruded over the lips, whose remarkable ruddiness showed astonishing vitality in a man of his years. For the rest, his ears were pale, and at the tops extremely pointed; the chin was broad and strong, and the cheeks firm though thin. The general effect was one of extreme pallor."

But Irving was certainly not a vampire, and he did not have hair on his palms as Dracula did. And as for his personality—except for his appealing qualities, the differences between him and Dracula were night and day.

Arminius Vambery, a professor from the University of Budapest, provided Stoker with atmosphere for *Dracula* by telling him stories of vampires and Transylvania, "the land beyond the forest," a neighbor of Wallachia. Not long after, Stoker traveled to Transylvania. With its black, brooding mountains and sinister-looking castles, it was the perfect setting for a horror story.

Stoker's was not the first book about vampires. There were at least four others which he probably knew. *The Vampyre* (1819) featured a vampire named Lord Ruthven, modeled by author John Polidori after his friend Lord Byron, master lover. Like Ruthven, Dracula is strangely appealing to women. *Varney the Vampire, or the Feast of Blood* (1847) starred another nobleman turned vampire. His original name was Marmaduke Bannesworth, a suicide. His incarnation had eyes "like polished tin." The author, Thomas Preskett Prest, finished him off by having him jump into Mount Vesuvius. *The Mysterious Stranger* (1860) was the German Azzo, tall and pale with grey eyes. Like Dracula, he also attracted women. Countess Karnstein, a vampire-villainess, was the creation of Irish writer Sheridan Le Fanu in "Carmilla," a story in *In a Glass Darkly* (1872). Obviously, a best-selling vampire cannot be of the common folk.

Stoker's Dracula, too, was of the nobility.

The final inspiration for *Dracula*, published in brown paper cover in 1897, came from a nightmare induced by a shellfish dinner that Stoker ate. In the nightmare, a vampire ruled the world of the un-dead.

Nothing is as good as the original in Stoker's book: Dracula standing before the mirror and seeing no reflection; Dracula crawling down castle walls "face down with his cloak spreading around him like great wings"; Dracula saying these immortal lines to his love Minna before a mutual love bite, "And you, their best beloved one, are now to me flesh of my flesh; blood of my blood; kin of my kin . . . When my brain says, 'Come!' to you, you shall cross land or sea to do my bidding." He is the quintessential villain, subtle and dangerous, a far cry from his Wallachian namesake, which shows how an original inspiration can be transmuted by an artist into a much different work of art.

A Boy Named Sue

IN JULY 1969, Columbia Records released the single "A Boy Named Sue," taken from Johnny Cash's album *Johnny Cash at San Quentin*. Within six weeks the song had earned a million dollars and later was named "single of the year" by the Country Music Association. The record eventually sold three million copies.

The comedy hit, with its fast-paced lyrics and twangy guitar, tells of a man named Sue who roams from town to town looking for his father—to kill the man who gave him "that awful name" and then deserted him when he was only three. After a lifetime of embarrassment and fights, Sue finds his father playing cards in a saloon. They get into a fistfight, drag each other through muddy streets, and finally draw their guns. Sue is faster, but before pulling the trigger he gives his old man a chance to explain the name Sue. The world is rough, and defending the name had to make him tough, says the father; the name was to put "gravel in your guts" and "spit in your eye." The song ends amid laughter and applause as Cash tells how Sue puts down his weapon and forgives his "Pa."

The real "boy named Sue" was Sue Kerr Hicks, a distinguished judge from Madisonville, Tennessee. Born in 1895, the youngest of nine children, Kerr was named (by his father) in honor of his mother who died when the judge was born. At age thirty Kerr was the assistant prosecutor in the celebrated Scopes "monkey trial" of 1925 which tested the validity of a Tennessee law forbidding the teaching of any creation theories that contradicted the Bible. With chief prosecutor William Jennings Bryan, Kerr was pitted against Clarence Darrow who defended John Scopes, a high school science teacher who taught Darwin's theory of evolution to his students. While Kerr was on the winning side (Scopes was convicted and fined $100), the law was repealed more than thirty years later.

A devoted family man and community leader, Kerr served a term in the state House of Representatives and was a criminal judge in Tennessee for twenty-two years. He was also a past commander of an American Legion Post, belonged to the Kiwanis Club, and was an active member in the Madisonville United Methodist Church. The only thing Kerr had in common with Cash's Sue was his first name.

Had it not been for a loudspeaker, Kerr might have escaped the name notoriety that pursued him until he died in 1980. One afternoon, while attending a Bar Association meeting in Gatlinburg, Tennessee, Kerr was paged over a loudspeaker. Within hearing range was a songwriter for Johnny Cash, who happened to be at a meeting in the same convention hall. In an instant the idea for the song was hatched.

Judge Kerr never complained about his name. In fact, he was proud of it. Yet he once told a reporter, "It is an irony of fate that I have tried over eight hundred murder cases and thousands of others, but the most publicity has been from the name Sue. . . ."

The Man Who Came to Dinner

WHETHER friend or foe, most of Alexander Woollcott's acquaintances used the same words to describe him: self-centered, exasperating, insulting, arrogant, demanding, crotchety, irascible, eccentric, infuriating, and on and on. Above all, the 250-pound author, drama critic, and radio commentator had a sharp, ferocious tongue that was always poised, always ready to strike. The grand master of insults, quips, wisecracks, and one-liners, Woollcott enjoyed his controversial, flamboyant (though tarnished and battered) reputation. Even a vicious, totally biased portrait of him in a 1939 issue of *The New Yorker*—"His jowls would shame a bulldog with the mumps. . . . His head is as wide as a brood mare's rump"—failed to raise his blood pressure much (or cause him to cancel his subscription to the magazine).

It is not surprising that such a larger-than-life personality inspired the main character of a highly successful play, *The Man Who Came to Dinner*, by Moss Hart and George S. Kaufman. The plot of the play is relatively simple: A prominent broadcaster, Sheridan Whiteside, while on a Midwestern lecture tour, slips on a piece of ice after a dinner party in his honor and breaks a leg. Confined to the home of a reluctant couple in Mesalia, Ohio, the overbearing, impossible-to-live-with Whiteside butts into everyone's business and for two weeks disrupts the entire household. Finally the recuperation period is over, the meddlesome Whiteside says his farewells, and exits out the front door—only to slip once again on the ice. . . .

The idea for *The Man Who Came to Dinner* evolved from Alexander Woollcott's overnight visit to Moss Hart's home in January 1938. The outrageous episode, which became one of Hart's favorite, most repeatedly-told stories, is undoubtedly Woollcott at his best/worst.

The versatile Woollcott, who was testing out his acting skills in a play in Philadelphia, accepted a weekend invitation to visit George Kaufman and Moss Hart; the collaborating playwrights both had farms in Bucks County, Pennsylvania. From Saturday night through Sunday afternoon Woollcott stayed with Kaufman and his wife at Barley Sheaf Farm, then drove over to see Hart at his nearby Fair View Farm.

As soon as he got out of the car Woollcott began to make disparaging comments to Hart about Hart's house. Upon entering the house he discovered, much to his displeasure, that he was not the only guest. Also present was Broadway producer Max Gordon. Refusing to share the spotlight with anyone—particularly Gordon, whom Woollcott disliked—the audacious "Aleck" informed everyone that he was not staying for dinner but was returning to the Kaufman farm.

Later that Sunday evening, after learning that Gordon had left Hart's farm, Woollcott made a surprise return visit. Though a bit taken back, Hart did his best to be a gracious, accommodating host. But it was not an easy role to play with a guest like Woollcott. First of all, Aleck asked to stay in Hart's bedroom and demanded that all the heat in the house be turned off. Too shocked to refuse, Hart moved out of his bedroom. Woollcott then declared that he was hungry and insisted that the servants make him a frosted milk shake and a large chocolate cake. After these requests were filled, the venomous critic went into a long, loud monologue on the dishonesty and incompetence of Hart's servants. When the long evening was mercifully at an end, Woollcott asked to sign Hart's guest book. He wrote: "I wish to say that on my first visit to Moss Hart's house I had one of the most unpleasant evenings I can ever recall having spent."

The next day, after Woollcott was back in Philadelphia, Hart met with Kaufman and gave him a blow-by-blow account of the disastrous dinner party. As a humorous aside, Hart remarked that things could have been worse. What if Woollcott had broken a leg and had been forced to stay at the farm for an indefinite time? As the two writers enjoyed a good laugh, the same thought struck them. As Hart later recalled, "Both of our rosy little faces lit up at the same time. The germ of the play had been born, and out of the warp and woof of Mr. Woollcott himself."

Upton Sinclair's The Jungle: A Story in Search of Some Characters

FOR SEVEN WEEKS beginning in October 1904, Upton Sinclair—muckraker, propagandist, and socialist—wandered through the filth and stench of the Chicago stockyards. On assignment for a socialist weekly, *Appeal to Reason*, the twenty-seven-year-old writer, disguised in shabby clothes and carrying a dinner pail, was investigating the working conditions within the meat-packing industry. It was an ordeal that resulted in a best-selling book filled with characters that became symbols of oppression in America.

In the evenings he visited the workers in their homes and listened intently as they spilled forth tales of exploitation that made his mind reel and his stomach churn. Eager to have the truth known, many laborers risked losing their jobs by helping Sinclair gain access to employees-only areas of the plant. "I went about, white-faced and thin, partly from undernourishment, partly from horror," the journalist later wrote.

What Sinclair saw was indeed shocking: the "killing beds" where men stood ankle-deep in the blood of cattle, hogs, and sheep; the pickling rooms where one drop of spilled acid could eat away all the joints of a man's fingers; the fertilizer rooms (the most hated part of the plant) where the fine dust of the waste products covered a man from head to foot, seeped into his skin, and caused fits of vomiting; the cooking rooms where a man occasionally fell into a vat, was boiled to death, and became just another ingredient of Durham's Pure Beef Lard.

And the quality of the products? Tubercular steers, hogs dead from cholera, and "steerly cows" (those covered with boils) were everywhere. Spoiled, white, moldy sausage, returned from Europe, was dipped in borax and glycerine, thrown into the hoppers, and reprocessed for American consumption. The plant was a nightmare of steaming blood, polluted water and, as Sinclair observed, "walls, rafters, and pillars caked with the filth of a lifetime." Added to the nauseating visual experience were the haunting, terrifying shrieks of animals being led to their slaughter.

Sinclair was ready to write his exposé—except for one major problem. His autobiography tells of his dilemma and vividly recreates its resolution:

At the end of a month or more, I had my data and knew the story I meant to tell, but I had no characters. Wandering about "back of the yards" one Sunday afternoon I saw a wedding party going into the rear room of a saloon. There were several carriages full of people. I stopped to watch, and as they seemed hospitable, I slipped into the room and stood against the wall. . . . There were my characters—the bride, the groom, the old mother and father, the boisterous cousin, the children, the three musicians, everybody. I watched them one after another, fitted them into my story, and began to write the scene in my mind, going over it and over, as was my custom, fixing it fast. I went away to supper and came back again, and stayed until late at night, sitting in a chair against the wall, not talking to anyone, just watching, imagining, and engraving the details on my mind. It was two months before I got settled at home and first put pen to paper; but the story stayed, and I wrote down whole paragraphs, whole pages, exactly as I had memorized them.

Thus, a Lithuanian wedding (or *veselija*) filled the opening pages of *The Jungle*—one of the best scenes Upton Sinclair ever wrote.

The immigrant couple, Jurgis Rudkus and his young bride Ona Lukoszaite, and their familes became the central characters in Sinclair's exposé. For three months he fervently developed a story around them— one that told of workers kept in bondage by a "wage slavery" system that destroyed human dignity.

The first installment of Sinclair's indictment of the meat-packing industry appeared in *Appeal to Reason* on February 25, 1905. Reader support for the serialization was strong, and Sinclair became determined to turn his story into a book. However, even with the aid of Jack London, Sinclair was rejected by five publishers because the book was too full of "blood and guts." Finally, Doubleday, Page and Company accepted *The Jungle*—provided Sinclair's facts could be verified. The company sent a representative to Chicago, and he not only substantiated the facts but added a few gruesome tales of his own.

The Jungle was published in February 1906 and immediately became front-page news. An outraged public, obsessed with thoughts of putrid and poisonous meat, clamored for immediate reform. More than 100 letters a day arrived at the White House, and President Theodore Roosevelt was forced to take action. Within six months the Pure Food and Drug Act and the Beef Inspection Act were passed.

Only 12 of *The Jungle*'s 309 pages were devoted to the grisly details of meat production; Sinclair never intended it to be the focal point of the novel. As he later admitted: "I failed in my purpose. . . . I wished to frighten the country by a picture of what its industrial masters were doing to its victims; entirely by chance I had stumbled on another discovery—what they were doing to the meat supply. . . . In other words, I aimed at the public's heart and, by accident, I hit it in the stomach."

"But I Am the Real Casey"

"CASEY AT THE BAT" was written by Ernest Lawrence Thayer—Harvard graduate, son of a wealthy New England textile manufacturer, and friend of William Randolph Hearst—in a scant two hours when he was twenty-five years old.

Hearst had just gotten control of *The San Francisco Examiner* from his father when he asked Thayer, a classmate at Harvard, to write for the paper. For two years Thayer wrote a variety of amusing pieces, many of them ballads under the name "Phin" (short for his college nickname, "Phinney"). However, when Thayer went to work for his father in Worcester, Massachusetts, he ended his short and not very illustrious literary career. "Casey at the Bat" was the last of his contributions to the *Examiner* and appeared in print on June 3, 1888.

The poem would have had a life span of only one day had it not been for William De Wolf Hopper, singer and comedian, and his friend, novelist Archibald Clavering Gunter. On August 14, 1888, Hopper—who was appearing in the operetta *Prince Methusalem* at Wallack's Theater in New

York City—needed some special material to add to that evening's performance, because it was "Baseball Night" and the theater was playing host
to the Chicago White Stockings and the New York Giants. Gunter saved
the day when he pulled a yellowed, tattered newspaper clipping from his
pocket and showed it to Hopper. The clipping was a copy of "Casey at the
Bat" which Gunter had read while on a business trip to San Francisco.
Impressed with the ballad, he had cut it out and carried it around with
him for more than two months.

Between acts at that night's performance Hopper recited the poem.
Following the last line, "But there is no joy in Mudville—mighty Casey
has struck out," the crowd broke into thunderous applause. For the next
forty-seven years the entertainer made "Casey" a regular part of his act.
According to his own estimate, he recited the poem at least ten thousand
times.

As soon as Hopper began to popularize the poem, newspapers and
magazines started to reprint it. Sometimes the work was attributed to
"Phin"; usually it carried no by-line. Before long a number of writers
claimed credit for "Casey," and finally Thayer stepped forward to set the
record straight. He said: "During my brief acquaintance with the *Examiner*, I put out large quantities of nonsense, both prose and verse, sounding the whole newspaper gamut from advertisements to editorials. In
general quality 'Casey' (at least to my judgment) is neither better nor
worse than much of the other stuff. Its persistent vogue is simply unaccountable, and it would be hard to say, all things considered, if it has
given me more pleasure than annoyance. The constant wrangling about
the authorship, from which I have tried to keep aloof, has certainly filled
me with disgust."

The scramble for authorship was not the only matter that aggravated
Thayer. Various baseball players now climbed aboard the bandwagon,
each claiming to be the bona fide Casey, the baseball player who had
inspired the poem. Once again Thayer felt compelled to speak out. In a
letter to the *Syracuse Post-Standard* he wrote: "The verses owe their
existence to my enthusiasm for college baseball, not as a player, but as a
fan. . . . The poem has no basis in fact. The only Casey actually involved—I am sure about him—was not a ball player. He was a big, dour
Irish lad of my high school days. While in high school I composed and
printed myself a very tiny sheet, less than two inches by three inches. In
one issue I ventured to gag, as we say, this Casey boy. He didn't like it and
he told me so, and as he discoursed, his big, clenched, red hands were
white at the knuckles. This Casey's name never again appeared in the

Monohippic Gazette. But I suspect the incident, many years after, suggested the title for the poem. It was a taunt thrown to the winds. God grant he never catches me."

But Thayer's statement did not dissuade major league ball player Daniel M. Casey of Binghamton, New York, from claiming that he was the real Casey. Of all the Caseys he was the most vocal and the most convincing. For more than fifty years Casey called upon sportswriters, baseball managers, and players—anyone who would listen—and told them that he was without a doubt the real Casey of "Casey at the Bat."

At the age of seventy-six, after he had retired from his second full-time job as a trolley-car conductor in Binghamton, Casey moved to Silver Spring, Maryland, where he continued to mount an active campaign to ensure that he would go down in history as one of baseball's giants, if only in literature. In a 1938 interview with *Collier's* magazine, Dan Casey gave his version of the historic strike-out:

I was a left-handed pitcher for the Phillies. I guess you'd call me the Hubbell of my time. We were playing the Giants in the old Philadelphia ball park on the afternoon of August 21, 1887. Tim Keefe was pitching against me and he had a lotta stuff, but I was no slowpoke myself.

It was the last of the ninth, and New York was leading, 4–3. Two men were out, there were runners on second and third, and it was my turn at bat. Brother, I was a scared man! They called me the Mighty Casey, but I was never much of a hitter. I could pitch mighty well, but I never batted better than .183. . . .

When that first ball came over, it was fast and a little low. I just stood looking at it as it hit the catcher's glove. I couldn't have hit it with a shovel. . . .

Then came the next pitch. I hadn't even seen it! I was too busy getting my head out of the way! I didn't wave my bat at it, either. Those were two swell-called strikes. By then I wished I was somewhere else. . . .

Two men on, two strikes on me, and the last inning! I knew I had to swing on that next one—so I shut my eyes and swung! You know the rest.

Casey's story, at best doubtful, delighted baseball fans who were always ready to welcome a new hero. Everyone wanted to believe Dan Casey's claim, including Ford Frick, president of the National League, and Will Harridge, president of the American League. Together the two baseball executives presented Casey with a silver lifetime pass to all ball parks.

Marianne, John, and Sam:
The Symbols of Nations

BARE-BREASTED Marianne may be a French saint or a French trollop. John, a red-faced Englishman, epitomizes practicality. Sam, a lanky American meat packer in a flashy getup, is addicted to pointing. An ill-assorted trio, they have two things in common: They are symbols of their country, and they were inspired by real people.

Marianne

She is a Frenchwoman of a special kind: hard, young, and fierce. On her head defiantly sits a Phrygian cap, like those given to Greek slaves with their freedom. Her dress is short. A revolutionary of the lower class, she tramples on the Crown.

Though her more remote ancestors are Greek and Roman goddesses, Marianne is all the women who, during France's four main revolutions of the eighteenth and nineteenth centuries, manned the barricades with the men and bore the revolutionary standard high. When the fighting was over, the same women, riding in decorated carriages or borne on the shoulders of revelers, often starred as the symbolic Mariannes of victory festivals. When they grew old, they were revered for their revolutionary past.

Marianne is anonymous. She is the woman who led a bread riot, gave her dowry linens to make bandages, donated her wedding ring to raise money. She is the unknown woman who organized a mass protest meeting at Café de Foy in Paris, the one who beat a drum to rouse others to march to Versailles.

Maurice Agulhon, who traces the significance of Marianne in his book *Marianne into Combat*, cites a report of the 1830 insurrection in which a woman exemplifies the spirit of the French symbol:

A young girl, a latter-day Joan of Arc, fought with extreme valor on the Place de la Bourse. There, despite the hail of bullets, she secured a piece of artillery. Her companions in this glorious moment, marveling at her behavior, carried her to a throne in the Hôtel-de-Ville and crowned her with laurels. Then, on the twenty-

166

ninth, in the evening, she was placed in a triumphal chariot adorned with palms, laurels, myrtle, overturned white flags, victorious tricolor standards, and the spoils of the conquered army, and paraded through Paris. Young men drew the chariot along, and with their aid it passed over the entrenchments. The picturesque ceremony took place by torchlight amid cheers, cries of joy, and singing.

On February 24, 1848, a day of victory over Louis Bonaparte, tall and inspired women at the barricades held flags amid rains of bullets. Some died. A young girl stood motionless holding a flag, a living statue of freedom. She may have been, as the account read, a "public prostitute," like many other Mariannes.

During the 1870–1875 revolution when the Third Republic was proclaimed, women sewed sandbags for defense, fought along with their men, and participated in live allegories afterwards. Children, from a window, saw "their former governess marching in the front line, vigorously brandishing the staff of a red flag."

Many artists portrayed her. Delacroix painted her bare-breasted, leading the people at the barricades and carrying a banner, with a smile that Balzac described as "red lips turning up in the almost ferocious smile." In Daumier's *Republic*, in the Louvre, she is naked from the waist up, nursing two infants.

According to an art critic, sketches of Marianne submitted to a national contest in 1848 were extreme: "Most of the competitors depicted veritable viragoes, furies, shrews, enraged female devils with disheveled hair and ragged clothing. Their look was fiery, their mouths hurled abuse. . . . They were bristling with standards, pikes, and bayonets, and to cap it all, brandished exterminatory flares as they scrambled, in the ruddy light of fireworks, over paving stones, beams, stove-in barrels, and overturned coaches as if the Republic had ever to be storming eternal barricades." But the alarm of moderate Frenchmen was assuaged by another Marianne—conservative, older, wiser, with ears of corn on her head. An 1848 editorial stated: "The Republic will wear no red cap; she will be no camp-follower but a serene, glorious, and fertile mother who will hold festivals and shed smiles upon her children."

Her name was common in Catholic France—a combination of the names of Christ's mother and grandmother. Though scholars have attempted to link her to a specific Marianne, none has succeeded in making a strong case.

However, some individual women did exemplify the spirit of Marianne. Théroigne de Méricourt, a singer-adventuress-feminist of peasant stock, was a fervent revolutionary of the First Republic. She wore a sword and a red-and-white riding habit, saved starving Paris women from being shot by soldiers, leapt on a cannon in the fighting of August 1792, and later went mad. Marie Charpentier, according to a 1789 decree of the Constituent Assembly, was given a pension for "distinguishing herself in the siege of the Bastille, where she fought with the men and showed remarkable courage." Louise Michel, a revolutionary and anarchist of the Third Republic, participated in the Paris Commune of 1871 as *la Pétroleuse*, acclaimed for setting fire to many Paris buildings. Fiercely committed to revolution all her life, she said, "The first time one defends one's cause with arms, one sees the struggle so clearly that one seems to be a bullet oneself." When the commune failed, she was sent to New Caledonia in exile for eight years. Thin and masculine (she resembled Frederick the Great), she was too well educated to be a real prototype of Marianne.

In the 1870s, pottery and papier-mâché statuettes of Marianne in her Phrygian cap, symbol of revolution, began to appear all over France, especially in the south. Sold in back rooms, sometimes over the counter, they were banned from public places but appeared anyway, were carried in processions, hung in Trees of Liberty, hidden in closets and brought out for ceremonies. In the 1880s, it seemed that every town hall displayed a bust of Marianne. A contemporary writer noted: "Our town hall possessed a Marianne that had escaped the notice of the master. There she was, on her plinth, looking as if she was cocking a snook at the Moral Order. It couldn't last." It didn't—Marianne was removed by force.

But Marianne still lives, in spite of Verlaine's cynical poem:

> Marianne is very old, getting on for a hundred.
> In the flower of her youth she was a bold young hussy,
> Drinking and loving, her nights spent in the arms of soldiers;
> But now she is a garrulous crone with thin hair and no teeth.

John Bull

> The bull for Force
> In fielde doth Raigne,
> But Bull by Skill
> Good Will doth Gayne.

—Toast to the real John Bull, seventeenth century

> The world is a bundle of hay,
> Mankind are the asses that pull,

> Each tugs in a different way—
> And the greatest of all is John Bull!
>
> —Lord Byron, in a letter to Thomas Moore,
>   June 22, 1821

John Bull, the beefy, red-faced symbol of the ordinary practical and pragmatic Englishman, is the namesake of a real-life character who was his opposite in many ways, though no less a symbol of Britain. As Britain changed, so did the concept of John Bull, which shows how far a symbol can stray from its original inspiration.

The real John Bull was born of yeoman stock about 1563. He was a musician, composer, and secret agent for the English government. His character—humorous, imaginative, volatile—was typical of his age. Physically, he was a far cry from his modern namesake, for he was dark and lithe, with black eyes and a little mustache.

At ten, he was appointed one of the eight children of Queen Elizabeth's chapel royal. Ten years later, he became master of choristers and organist at Hereford Cathedral. The choirboys liked him—he taught them old tunes, sailors' chanties and knots, and fencing.

Bull could be testy and difficult, but also charming. Though he enjoyed Hereford, he was not in tune with the incessant bell ringing from the cathedral and scratched on the glass of the window in his room an irritated verse:

> Soules nothinge haue to feare
> Of greater griefe in Hell
> Than hee who hath to heare
> This thrice accursed bell.

Once, he became so engrossed in copying music that he forgot the Countess of Pembroke was coming to hear him play the organ. When he finally showed up, the Countess remarked acerbically, "A musician shoulde keep more juste tyme." Bull played a prelude he had written and then, ink-stained and wild-haired, presented it to her. When she laughed at his messy appearance, he stamped away, enraged. Later, as an apology, he wrote a piece of music for her and tossed it through her open window late at night. She was touched by this romantic gesture and used her influence at court to help his career.

Finally, he was called to the court of Elizabeth I, who was charmed by him. Before a private audience with him, she was practicing some of his music on the virginals, an early keyboard instrument. When he overheard her playing from outside, he eagerly entered the room, tripped over something, and fell on his face. In explanation he said that when majesty and music were so well combined, no man could prostrate himself too much. She replied, equally as courtly, that so rare a bull had song as well as bird. Their relationship was not always sunny, but she always forgave him his peccadillos, though once she remarked, "Of all the bulls that live, this hath the greatest asses' ears."

It was Sir Francis Walsingham, Elizabeth's secretary of state, who probably enlisted Bull as a secret agent, initially to help investigate the possible involvement of Mary, Queen of Scots in the Babington plot to murder Elizabeth. Bull traveled incognito on the Continent, ostensibly for his health, though he also went from city to city as a virtuoso musician. For example, when in 1601, Catholic-Protestant tensions were high, the Queen, worried about the relations of English Puritans with foreign Protestants, may have sent Bull to Europe under cover. As an anonymous visitor, he called on a famous musician at a cathedral music school, who showed him a forty-part song and challenged him to add further to it. Bull added forty more parts, doubling it. After the musician played this amplified version, he swore that whoever added the parts must be the devil or John Bull.

Bull could compose music that could be played upside down, backwards, or forwards. His manuscripts were black with notes. Curiosity about this almost caused his exposure as a spy. Henry IV of France figured out that a cipher existed within the thicket of notes on a page of Bull's music—it was not just an "excess of music" but some kind of message. However, he kept the secret and said that appreciation of art between friends was no bad thing.

Called the "father of keyboard music," Bull wrote more than two hundred compositions. His most famous piece was an anthem he wrote to celebrate the victory over the Spanish Armada. It was played at St. Paul's Cathedral during Elizabeth's triumphal procession down the long aisle on the day of celebration. Long after, for another state occasion, Ben Jonson supplied the words, and it became "God Save the King." Bull died in Brussels in 1628.

Now John Bull, the symbol, is pictured as a stocky Englishman, short on imagination and long on common sense, the salt of the earth, prosaic rather than witty, fat rather than thin, more phlegmatic than tempestuous, a rock of stability. Probably first "born" during the Napoleonic wars at the turn of the nineteenth century, he is very different from the impassioned individual who gave him his name.

Uncle Sam

Uncle Sam, in striped pants and top hat, the symbol of the United States government and national character, had a real-life prototype who was a meat packer and politician.

The man, Samuel Wilson, was born in Massachusetts in 1766, ten years before the beginning of the American revolution. At age fourteen he joined the army and fought for independence. In 1789, he and his brother Ebenezer went to Troy, New York, where they set up a meat-packing business known for its fair-dealing.

During the War of 1812, Northern troops were quartered near Troy, and Wilson was given the contract to supply the troops with meat and to inspect beef and pork for military use. He stamped his own casks and those he inspected for the army with "E.A.–U.S.," the E.A. standing for Elbert Anderson, the contractor of the job, and the U.S. for United States. An affable man, Wilson was affectionately known as Uncle Sam to his relatives, neighbors, and friends. On October 2, 1812, when visitors to the plant, including the governor of New York, asked what the initials on the casks stood for, a workman joked that the U.S. stood for "Uncle Sam" Wilson. Soldiers, many of them local boys, picked up on the joke and called themselves Uncle Sam's men. Wilson became active in Democratic politics, was a popular toastmaster, and died in his nineties. His tombstone, put up in 1931, reads: "In loving memory of 'Uncle Sam,' the name originating with Samuel Wilson 1766–1854—during the War of 1812 and since adopted by the United States." The name caught on because Sam Wilson fit the American ideal—honest, independent, and loyal to his country.

Even before the Civil War, Uncle Sam was portrayed in cartoons with a variety of appearances and attributes: round- or thin-faced, old or young, bearded or clean-shaven. Currier and Ives, the lithographers, made him look like Benjamin Franklin. It was Thomas Nast, a German-born cartoonist of the Civil War and Reconstruction period, who originated the Uncle Sam we know today: tall, thin, hollow-cheeked, and bearded. It is a coincidence that Nast's Uncle Sam resembles Sam Wilson, for Nast's model was actually President Abraham Lincoln. The World War I poster, "I Want You for U.S. Army," perhaps the most famous portrayal of Uncle Sam, was painted by James Montgomery Flagg. It sold more than four million copies in World War I and half a million copies in World War II. Flagg's Uncle Sam is a self-portrait.

In 1961, Congress adopted a resolution stating that Sam Wilson was the "progenitor of America's national symbol." But Sam had played that role informally for years. He promoted tobacco, pens, stoves, songs, and politicians. He appeared riding on a glass mustard jar shaped like a battleship, on a carousel seat, and on weather vanes. He was a toy bank and a mailbox holder.

Now he wears a tailcoat, striped pants, long hair, and goatee. Stars and stripes decorate his top hat. And promotion, not meat packing, is his real profession.

8. *Trains of Thought*

It's as though an inexorable force took them by the hand and led them. Some of the greatest people have been dragged through life by a series of linked inspirations when they might very much have liked to go another way. Louis Pasteur, for instance, wanted to discover a grand principle for the universe, but instead ended up dealing with tiny microorganisms. If Martin Luther had any idea of leaving his lifework of engineering a Reformation, his inspirational moments would have nudged him back on the path—God got to him even when he was on the privy. Alexander Graham Bell, inventor of the telephone, and the eccentric biologist Elie Metchnikoff were always prodded back on the trail by flashes of intuitive genius.

William Booth's fateful walk through London's noisome East End started a process that ended in the conversion of many sinners—an infinite chain reaction that continues today. Many extant gadgets helped Gutenberg assemble the puzzle that was the printing press.

One person's great idea can spark that of another. A millionaire's curiosity about how horses run began a chain that ended in the invention of movies. Margaret Mitchell's title *Gone with the Wind* came from a poem inspired, in its turn, by a most unlikely love object. And who would guess the sober end of a poet's obsession with ink blots and the macabre? And who would have anticipated that a 1960s song, beloved by hippies, could end up inspiring the naming of an old, old lady?

The Visions of Martin Luther: A Lightning Flash, the Inspirational Privy, and Fighting the Devil

A TERRIFYING FLASH of lightning, then a deafening thunderclap—the wrath of God. He was hurled to the ground by a thrust of air pressure, a powerful, divine hand. He shouted in mortal fear, "Help, dear Anne, I will become a monk." He did not die—whether or not his savior was Anne, mother of the Virgin Mary. There, a mile from Erfurt where he was a law student, Martin Luther had experienced the first of three major linked inspirations that altered his life and, with it, the course of history. It was July 2, 1505. He was twenty-one years old.

Earthy, with a hot temper and a coarse sense of humor, he was hardly the type to become a monk. The hospice he had joined at the university was called the Beer Bag; Luther drank his share, and more. But he believed his vow to the Virgin's mother was unbreakable. Thirteen days later, already regretful but determined to honor it, he threw for himself a great farewell party, at which he played the lute and sang songs to entertain his friends. On the following day, those friends, weeping, led him to the Black Cloister, a chapter house of the Hermits of Saint Augustine. He said, "Today you see me for the last time and then no more," a prophecy which turned out to be anything but true. The doors clanged shut behind him.

Luther's father, who was angry at his decision (he wanted his son to be a lawyer), said when Martin was ordained a priest two years later, "Would that it [the thunderclap] may not have been a mere illusion." This question occurred to Luther, too. He was given to hallucinations. Perhaps he imagined the thunderclap.

The second experience, in 1513, happened, many say, while Luther was sitting on the privy, trapped by a bout of constipation, a lifelong problem for him. (He had a related hang-up on cleanliness: "The more we wash, the less clean we become.")

For years after joining the monastery, even after he left to study at the

University of Wittenberg in 1508, Luther wrestled with his own over-whelming sense of sin and his doubts about the medieval image of God—"an angry judge sitting on a rainbow." As a child he had quaked before the Cross, sick to his stomach with fear of the Lord, and though his first year in the monastery was calm, he was wracked thereafter, sometimes confessing to his superiors as long as six hours at a time. In 1511, he took a forty-day journey to Rome on foot, where he was shocked by the corruption of the church. On the stairway of Pilate, he ascended on his knees, one step at a time, saying an Our Father on each for his dead grandfather, only to think on the top step, "Who knows if this is true?"

After he went to Wittenberg, he sometimes locked himself up in a square tower of the monastery, his workroom, with all its surfaces piled with books. There he often spent three days at a time completing his breviary. "Every time a little temptation came of sin or death, I was down and out," he wrote. "Neither baptism nor monastic vow seemed of any avail, as I had lost Christ and my baptism long ago. There . . . in the convent I was bathed in my monkery and had a real 'sweating sickness.' . . . For I no longer knew Christ except as a stern judge from whom I wanted to flee, yet was unable to escape." He experienced the "temptations of the flesh" and "tried all kinds of remedies, confessed daily, but it was of no avail."

While he was wrestling with these demons, he was also studying the Scholastics, who irritated him with their constant analyzing and debating. In the margins of their books he wrote epithets, like "pig-theologizer," "rancid Aristotle," "maggots!" "parasite-philosophers!" and "fetid logicians!" He was studying the Bible, too, interpreting passages that puzzled him.

Two passages bothered him because they seemed contradictory: one concerning the "righteousness" of God and the other which said that "the just shall live by faith." He "raged with a wounded and confused spirit . . . thirsting with a most ardent desire to know" through days and nights of uninterrupted meditation—and constipation. Then, suddenly, he had a "wonderful experience," while sitting on the privy, in which he was able to reconcile the two: the just God and the merciful one. The answer was faith, not good works. "Now at this I experienced such relief and easement, as if I were reborn and entered through open gates into paradise itself. The whole Bible all at once seemed different. . . ." He was euphoric: "And, then, what a game began! The words came up to me on every side, jostling one another and smiling in agreement. . . ."

The experience led to his formulation of Protestant principles: God is merciful; man is saved by grace, not good works; people can talk to God directly. In the end, for many, these ideas would topple Rome from its throne, for if one could talk directly to God, there was no need for an intricate ecclesiastical superstructure. Luther later added that secular authorities should be given the power to correct the excesses of the church if the church did not, that the Bible was the sole record of God's commandments, that the popes could not lay claim to a direct tie with Christ's apostles. It was, of course, considered heresy.

In 1517, Luther tacked the famous 95 Theses on indulgences to the church door at Wittenberg. In them he claimed that if it was by God's grace one was saved, then the corrupt practice of selling indulgences (sin cancellations redeemable at the Pearly Gates) was doubly corrupt. The indulgence-selling business had begun with religious rivalry during the Crusades. A Mohammedan soldier went to heaven straight off if he died in battle, no matter how sinful his life. The Christian, if he had any outstanding sins on the books, might not. To even things up, popes of the eleventh century granted absolution for all sins to soldiers who died in battle. Later, someone who paid to sponsor a soldier was also given absolution—an indulgence. When the Crusades were over, Pope Boniface VIII, unhappy with the loss of revenue, announced a jubilee indulgence which had nothing to do with soldiers. The recipients of indulgences, which became more and more available (for a price), were given papal certificates plastered with signatures and seals. One could also earn indulgences by viewing relics of saints. At Castle Church in Wittenberg on All Saints' Day, November 1, twelve rows of relics (a total of 17,443 pieces) were laid out—9 thorns from Christ's crown, 35 splinters from the Cross, a piece of bread from the Last Supper, a vial of Virgin's milk, a twig from the Burning Bush, Saint Jerome's tooth, 204 parts and a whole body from the Holy Innocents of Bethlehem . . . and more. By praying in front of them, the sinner could earn 127,709 years and 116 days of indulgence in the hereafter.

Luther made sense when he asked, "Why do we have to pay for holy love?" But as Erasmus said, "Luther sinned in two respects, namely that he attacked the crown of the Pope and the bellies of the monks." If the monks didn't like the Theses, the peasants and civil authorities did. Originally written in Latin and translated into German, the Theses were spread throughout the land. Luther became a hero to the laity. And the church, alarmed, began to harass him.

In Augsburg, he faced the papal legate and had to escape in the middle of the night by horseback, without pants or boots, to a stable in a town fifty kilometers away. He debated theologian Johann Eck at Leipzig. Yet, in spite of all his stage presence, he was not free of doubt. He asked himself, "Do you mean to say that all the previous teachers knew nothing? Do you regard all our fathers as fools? Are you alone the nest egg of the Holy Ghost in these last times? Could God have permitted all these years that His people should be in error?" But when a papal bull threatening to excommunicate him reached Wittenberg, he burned it and the canon law.

In 1521, at Worms, church repression of Luther culminated in an interrogation attended by Holy Roman Emperor Charles V and various dignitaries. The arrogant Luther came in a two-wheeled cart with an entourage of four, including a plumed herald wearing a tabard with a red eagle on it. "The Devil saw clearly the mood I was in when I went to Worms. Had I known as many devils would set upon me there as there were tiles in the roofs, I should have leapt among them with joy. I was undismayed and trembled at nothing—so foolish can God make a man!" Luther later said. Much of the world was on his side. Broadsides showed the Pope as an ass playing the bagpipes and Luther as an angel with a harp. But the Emperor, noting Luther's stocky, coarse appearance, re-marked, "That one will never make a heretic of me!"

In a torch-lit room with stone benches, Luther faced the Emperor with confidence and refused to recant. Placards endorsed by both the Pope and the Emperor condemned him, "Oh you fool, Luther! You have the effrontery to harp on old errors without finding anything new to say for yourself." His supporters tacked up their own, retaliatory message: "We, four hundred knights, have sworn not to abandon the just man Luther, and to declare war on the princes and the Romanists, particularly the Archbishop of Mainz. I may write poorly but intend great destruction. With eight thousand men we shall fight . . ."

Though he earned another hearing, where he again refused to recant, an edict was issued calling for him to be seized. Outside the meeting hall, he raised his arms. "I am through! I am through!"

In a sense he was a dead man, for ecclesiastical authorities, by order-ing his capture, had declared open season on him. On his way back from Worms, on a detour ostensibly to see relatives in a mountain village in Thuringia, he was kidnapped (willingly) with the connivance of Fred-erick III of Saxony, who opposed the power of the papal states. It was reported that Luther was hauled from his cart and thrown into a salt mine, where he died. Actually, he was hidden away in Frederick's castle at Wartburg, under the pseudonym Squire George. Two nobles' sons brought him his food, and he ate prodigiously and drank a good deal of beer. His heavy-framed skeleton began to fill out. He let his dark hair grow over his tonsure and sprouted a beard.

Chafing at his captivity in a room 20 feet by 15 feet, Luther engaged in a three-month fight with the Devil, who appeared to him in the "flesh" with a black dog beside him. Sometimes, especially when he was "sluggish in prayer," Luther broke wind to drive the Devil away. Part of the reason he ate so much, he said, was to fill up so that the Devil could not invade his insides.

After ten months at Wartburg, he returned home to Wittenberg, where he spoke out against the excesses of the infant Reformation. In 1524, he left the monastery. A year later, he married Katharine von Bora, a nun whom he had helped escape from a convent in a burgher's cart full of empty herring barrels. She was twenty-four, with delicate features, though plump. They grew to love one another. In 1526, he declared that he was so happy he "would not change my poverty for the wealth of Croesus." The Devil was still with him, but he warded the monster off by touching an intimate part of Katie's body. He won his biggest battles against the Devil "right in bed next to Katie," he said. However, his nemesis was not entirely defeated. A few days before his death in 1546, he saw the Devil sitting on a rainpipe right outside his window.

Doctors and Inkblots—The Kleksographien Chain

TO JUSTINIUS KERNER, a German physician and poet born in 1786, truth resided as much in the *Schattenseite der Natur* (the shady side of nature) as in science. He found much significance in chance. In 1804, weary of his menial job in a Ludwigsburg cloth factory, Kerner filled a knapsack with books and walked the long distance to the town of Tübingen, where the local university was. Having arrived late at night and exhausted, he fell asleep on a bench across from the pauper's hospital and dreamed a "strange dream." A blustery wind awoke him. Shortly after, a gust of wind blew a piece of paper within his reach. It was a prescription signed by the chief physician of Tübingen. Kerner later wrote, "Now I said to myself, 'this paper is sent to you as a sign of your future profession; you are to be a doctor!' And it was with this thought and with this intention that I walked through the gate into the unknown town of the Muses."

While Kerner studied medicine, he also wrote poems and songs, practicing his tunes on a Jew's harp, and made friends with other poets such as Ludwig Uhland and Gustav Schwab. After completing his medical training, he stayed on in Tübingen to work on his doctorate, a study of hearing in animals. He "lived in his room in friendly company with dogs, cats, chickens, geese, owls, squirrels, toads, lizards, mice, and Heaven knows how many other animals, and only had the bother of keeping the doors and windows shut so his guests should not escape," remarked his friend Karl August Varnhagen, a scholar of the time, also a friend to Beethoven. (Kerner determined that geese had the best hearing of the lot.) His interest in research continued. Later in his life, he involved himself in researching the causes of sausage poisoning (*Wurstkerner*).

He married in 1812. From 1819 to 1851, he was resident physician at Weinsberg (near Stuttgart), a town of medieval ruins, narrow streets, and vine-covered hills. On land with an old tower, he built a house, in whose foundation stone he put a glass tube containing a piece of parchment on which he had written, in part, "This house was built, through God's blessing, by Justinius Kerner, the doctor, who also sang songs, and his wife Friederike, in the year eighteen hundred and twenty-two, at a time when the stars of heaven, heating as never before, looked down upon mountain and valley. . . ."

In 1826, Friederike Hauffe, the "seeress of Prevost," who was blessed with psychic gifts but cursed with nervous fits, came to live in the Kerners' house for two years while he treated her with the new science of hypnotism which he had learned from the Austrian physician Franz Mesmer. He was not able to do much for her, but he did keep track of all she said, and his notes became the nucleus of his most famous book, *Die Seherin von Prevost* (1830).

The seeress was only one of many visitors, among them the exiled Gustav IV of Sweden and Count Alexander of Württemberg. He and his friends were intrigued with spiritualism and in love with Nature. In Kerner's poem "The Grass," the narrator, lying in a meadow, envisions air ships and air trucks that fly through the blue sky, raining oil to kill the fish in the Rhine and driving the birds into extinction: an early polemic against technology. In 1840, Kerner began the magazine *Magikon*, "observations in the realm of spiritual knowledge," which was published for thirteen years.

Late in life, half-blind from cataracts, Kerner became fascinated with images he saw in inkblot pictures he made by folding paper accidentally splattered with ink. He doctored them up to resemble weird ghosts, devils, and other horrific creatures which had escaped from the underworld to bring bad news to those aboveground. Diabolical, evoking nightmares, the pictures were inspirations for poems more playful than the pictures but still grotesque. This practice, of writing poems around inkblot images, was called *Kleksographien* (inkblot art), and it became the rage among his poet friends.

When Hermann Rorschach was in high school in Zurich in the late 1880s, he was nicknamed "Klek" (inkblot) for his fascination with *Kleksographien*. Though he had leanings toward being an art teacher like his father, he went into medicine instead. Even before he graduated from medical school, he began his research with inkblot pictures, at first as the basis for testing the intelligence of children, then as a device to analyze the emotional problems of the sane and insane. A friend who had also liked to experiment with *Kleksographien* in high school assisted him. In 1921, when Rorschach was thirty-six, he published the results of his ten-year study which grew into the Rorschach Test, a landmark in projective psychology. The test is comprised of ten relatively simple and symmetrical inkblots. He said, "The construction of the blots consists only in throwing some blots of ink on a sheet of paper, folding it in the center, and smoothing the folded paper with the finger. . . . The arrangement of the design on the card must fulfill certain conditions of spatial rhythm. When that is not the case, the design lacks pictorality, with the result that many subjects put the design off as 'merely blots,' without offering interpretations." The figures are centered on 8 inch × 10¾ inch cards; five are in shades of black, two in red and black, and three in color.

In giving their reactions to inkblots in psychological testing, patients open a window on the stored past in their unconscious, affording the therapist a look into their inner emotions without doing any harm. The test is multi-dimensional, measuring many aspects of the personality, including originality, intelligence, and emotional conflict. Variations of responses to inkblots run the gamut from "two bull dogs standing at a bonfire, carrying on secret societies" (a psychotic fantasy) to "two children, with caps on, on top of two piles of snow" (an unoriginal but healthy response).

It seems a long way from macabre poetry to the laboratory, from literature to science, from the irrational to the rational. But remember the inkblots' purpose—to open the mind to the "shady side," a concern of poet and psychotherapist alike.

"Darling, I Have Found My Destiny":

The Origins of the Salvation Army

THE SALVATION ARMY was inspired on a summer night in 1865, not by a glorious blaze and trumpet-blast of religious revelation, but by stink, muck, flashing knives, feral faces in a barroom brawl, the despairing invitations of prostitutes, children's bodies crooked with rickets, and the unhappy din of souls crowded 290 to the acre in a tumultuous setting reeking of decay and poverty.

On that night, in front of The Blind Beggar, a red-brick public house in the London slums, free-lance preacher William Booth banged his Bible and threatened the sinners in the crowd before him with eternal hell fire, then seduced them with promises of the love of God if they would but repent. It is not known how many souls the charismatic Booth saved during his stint as a visiting evangelist that summer day in 1865.

After the meeting ended, Booth walked the eight miles to his temporary lodgings in Hammersmith, where his wife Catherine, pregnant with their seventh child, waited for him. They expected to return to their home in Newcastle at the end of the week. Booth's walk, a fateful journey through the East End—one of the worst parts of London—changed everything. Grimed with soot, it was an earthly hell, its souls in torment. Booth trudged through crowds of screaming, fighting, cursing slum dwellers. Little children in pubs climbed specially built steps to reach the counter, where they ordered penny gins. Others played in the gaslit alleys with garbage—a fish skeleton on a string served as a kind of pull toy. Women sold flowers for pennies or their bodies for not much more. Cheering crowds watched cornered rats battle terriers for their lives in rat pits.

The air stank of must and mildew, old grease, excrement, urine spattered against filthy walls, and the open sewer of the Thames (whose waters would cause the deaths of some eight thousand Londoners from cholera and other waterborne diseases in the following year).

The East End—ugly, brutish, terrifying. Booth saw it and smelled it as if for the first time.

When he reached home, his first words to Catherine were, "Darling, I have found my destiny." If the purpose of his ministry was to save souls, he said, where could he find any more wretched and savage than those in East London? It was a bold, visionary proposal. It was also impractical. The Booths were in debt. William's connections to an established church had been broken. The philanthropists who so gladly supported missions to Africa were not likely to part with money to save the unlovely slum dwellers, whose illiteracy and desperate poverty could, with a little imagination, be laid at their own doorsteps.

But Catherine, an ardent feminist who did not automatically agree with her husband, agreed wholeheartedly. They stayed in London to found the Christian Mission, which was the genesis of the Salvation Army.

Though the final decision to begin the Christian Mission was made that summer night in 1865, the seeds had been planted long before when William, now thirty-six, was just a boy.

When he was fourteen and away at school, William was informed of the death of his bankrupt and bitter father, whose grandoise schemes of making a fortune as a building contractor had come to nothing. Mrs. Booth opened a pins-and-notions shop. With no money for school, William was apprenticed to a Nottingham pawnbroker, which brought him face to face with the desperate poor who hocked their pitiful possessions—tools, wedding rings, and other items valuable only to themselves—in order to survive.

About a year later he joined the Methodist Church. By age seventeen he was preaching, at first in dim alleys, then at cottage meetings held in parlors, his pulpit an overturned wooden box. His friends nicknamed him Willful Will. It suited him. Once he escorted a group of his shabby converts through the front doors of the Wesleyan chapel to the front pews, ordinarily reserved for the "respectable" middle and upper classes. The church establishment did not approve of William's actions. On the other hand, William did not approve of the church's attitude. His hero, and the church's founder, John Wesley, had worked with the poor, and Christ had honored them.

When his apprenticeship ended, William, then nineteen, went to London, where he found work with another pawnbroker and saved souls in his spare time. Tall, with a commanding eaglelike profile, he was a compelling preacher. Edward Harris Rabbits, owner of a chain of shoe stores, gave him a weekly stipend so that he could preach full-time. Converting the fallen was a grueling job, and Booth fortified himself for it by eating raw eggs for breakfast and massaging his chest with cold water.

In 1855, he married Catherine Mumford, a brilliant and articulate Quaker who came from a line of religious women. Her grandmother as a frivolous girl had lightheartedly and callously rejected a suitor who, turned from her door, rode his horse until it dropped dead; he later went insane. Her shamed response was to cut the ribbons from her dresses, quit playing cards, and embrace the Church. The family kept embracing it.

Catherine herself showed an early propensity for compassionate tenderness toward the unfortunate. As a child she once trotted hand-in-hand with a drunk being escorted by a policeman in order to give him a small offering of comfort. Incensed at seeing a boy beat his donkey with a hammer, she gave him a taste of his own medicine, then fainted. She was frail, tubercular, and afflicted as a teenager with curvature of the spine, but her spirit never flagged. When it was considered unbecoming for a woman to preach, she preached, in spite of her dread at facing an audience, and made "a fool of myself for Christ."

William became an official minister for the New Connexion, a Methodist splinter group, and was assigned to Newcastle. His enormous success at converting sinners made his colleagues jealous. His dramatic approach seemed not quite proper, somehow vulgar. At the 1861 New Connexion conference, when he asked permission to become a full-time evangelist, he was refused. Catherine encouraged him to break his ties with the group rather than acquiesce. Six months later, William was preaching on his own. He was a free-lance minister when he exhorted the sinners in front of The Blind Beggar.

From July to December 1865, Booth walked from Hammersmith to the East End and back nearly every day. Sometimes he preached in the open air. It has been said that he poked his umbrella in the ground and harangued it to attract crowds of the curious.

Later, he and his family moved closer to his congregation. Meetings were held in a wind-whipped tent in a Quaker cemetery, in Professor Orson's Dancing Academy and Assembly, in the Effingham Theater, in an old warehouse, in a hayloft behind a pigeon shop, even in stables. Drunken hecklers pelted him and his few followers with stones, fireworks, dead cats, mud, and bags of flour. By the end of the year, Booth had sixty converts—former prostitutes, thieves, and drunks, for the most part. Though the original intent of the Christian Mission was to bring the poor to the established church, it soon became clear that the established church did not want the poor, and the poor did not want the church.

A saloon, the Eastern Star, became Christian Mission headquarters, with a reading room, a bank, and seats for three hundred. At meetings, Booth gave his fiery sermons, and his converts told their stories of conversion, testifying about their past sins and present state of grace. The rousing lyrics of the hymns were often set to music-hall tunes; when the straightlaced complained, Booth quoted Martin Luther's remark that he didn't see any reason why the Devil should have all the best tunes.

At first Booth, with his socialist leanings, set up a governing board for the Christian Mission. But the war against sin demanded quicker strategies than could be planned in a ponderous committee, and his natural autocratic tendencies came to the fore. He was the Mission's general in spirit as well as name. He set up Orders and Regulations, with the objective of "getting saved and keeping saved and then getting somebody else saved." In an age of military metaphor, mission houses became "forts"; prayer "knee-drill"; shouting amen "firing a volley"; babies "reinforcements"; death "promotion to glory." And in a way, the war was a real one. Workers were harassed and often injured by hecklers. The black coal-scuttle bonnet worn by the women was a practical device that protected their heads against policemen's clubs and pranksters' rocks.

Catherine died in 1890. In 1912, shortly after an operation which left him blind, William joined her. Their son Bramwell became the next General of the Army and, under his guidance, it spread to the far corners of the world and became famous for its street bands, rousing street parades, and compassion. Wherever it has gone, it has never turned its back on the downtrodden and forgotten. Today, its soldiers counsel teenaged mothers, provide shelter for battered wives and abused children, aid the handicapped, rehabilitate drug addicts and ex-convicts, house and feed victims of disaster, and save souls. Booth's destiny has reached thousands of others and has been fulfilled many times over.

The Enchainment of Louis Pasteur

Fortune favors the prepared mind.
　　　—LOUIS PASTEUR

　　He had sudden inspirations which bore him on toward unexpected discoveries; he had instincts of divination which pushed him forward along unexplored paths; he had swift, headlong rushes of thought that overleaped and anticipated the establishment of truth, prepared the way for it, made its attainment more rapid, and more sure. But when a scientific problem had taken shape before him in one of those general flashes of illumination, he never considered it solved until he had questioned all nature; until he had classified or eliminated all the facts; until he had forced each and every one to give him an answer.　　　—JULES HENRI POINCARÉ

"ENCHAINED" was the adjective Louis Pasteur used to describe his inexorable scientific progress—inspirations and discoveries seemed to be linked in a chain of inevitability that held him captive. Implicit in the word is a true reluctance. He would have preferred, at least in the beginning, to spend his life pursuing his first scientific love: the investigation of crystal and its beautiful, abstract qualities. Instead, he was forced by his enchainment into matters far more mundane, like the illnesses caused by beer and swine. He stuck his head in beer and wine vats, tramped through hog pen muck, analyzed slime and stink and disease.

Early in his career he tried to elicit from the heart of the crystal an all-encompassing principle of the universe, a marvelous echo from galaxies back to the stone. In 1844, when a student at the Ecole Normale in Paris, his artist's eye was caught by a piece of Iceland spar, crystallized carbonate of lime. Through this pure and transparent stone, two images of an object were refracted. This fascinated the twenty-two-year-old scientist. He was also "attracted by the subtle and delicate methods used in studying these beautiful crystalline forms."

Most crystals are symmetrical—when broken on a plane, two identical halves result. But some, and these were the ones which interested Pasteur, are right-handed or left-handed, so one kind is the mirror image of the other. In the six years from 1847 to 1853, Pasteur earned his doctorate, moved from the Ecole Normale to the University of Strasbourg as a chemistry professor, and married Marie Laurent, the blue-eyed daughter of the rector of the Strasbourg Academy. In all that time he was also obsessed with the asymmetric crystalline shape of tartaric acids and the relationship between their form and optical qualities. Studying the tartrates microscopically, he noted that small facets were responsible for the asymmetry. He then examined the paratartrates (or racemates), which have the same chemical composition, specific gravity, and other properties—with one difference: the tartrates twist or rotate polarized light differently. Pasteur found that some paratartrate particles were right-handed and others left-handed. A solution made of right-handed paratartrates rotated the plane of polarization to the right, and left-handed to the left. The mixture of the two did not affect a polarized ray because they neutralized each other. When he made this discovery, he raced from his laboratory in the Ecole Normale, grabbed a laboratory assistant, and said, "I have just made a great discovery. . . . I am so happy that I am shaking all over and am unable to set my eyes again to the polarimeter."

He wrote about his discovery to J. J. Biot, a specialist in rotary polarization, through he had never met the man. Biot was skeptical, so Pasteur gave him a demonstration, using cork models he had made with colored edges and faces, a favorite method of his to demonstrate his findings. Convinced, Biot said, "My dear boy, I love science so much, and always have, that this sets my heart pounding."

The experiment led Pasteur to ask if molecules themselves were asymmetric, and in his investigation he broke ground in what became stereochemistry—the study of the arrangements of molecular chemical parts. Wanting to know if it was possible to change one form into another, perhaps because he always had a streak of alchemist in his soul, he decided to study paratartrates further. They were hard to find, so in 1852, Pasteur traveled through Germany, Austria, and Italy searching in wine cellars, breweries, and cattle breeders' barns with little success. Finally, he gave up and made some himself.

His studies had brought him to a question: Was asymmetry the key to understanding the chemical basis of life? From 1853 to 1858, he studied organic structure, theorizing that dissymmetry was fundamental at some level of organic matter even if it was symmetrical at another level. He tried to change the structure of chemicals with magnetism, and he planned bizarre experiments to introduce asymmetric forces to plant growth by subjecting plants to reversals of the sun's direction by using a clockwork heliostat (a mirror of the sun) to establish a mirror-image world. He felt that living forms were, "in their internal structure and their outward form, functions of cosmic dissymmetry. . . . The universe is a dissymmetrical whole, and I am persuaded that life, as manifested to us and observed by us, is directly or indirectly a function of the dissymmetry of the universe . . . . Terrestrial magnetism, and magnetic and electrical polarity, are probably resultants of dissymmetrical forces and movements." Excited, he felt himself to be "on the verge of mysteries, and the veil which covers them is getting thinner and thinner. . . ."

However, he was led into the realm of tiny life—from chemistry to biology—instead of into the vast universe. In an experiment fermenting paratartrate (a mixture of right- and left-handed molecules), he noticed that it was rotating polarized rays to the left at an increasing rate. At the end of the fermentation, only left-handed molecules remained—the organisms doing the fermentation had "eaten" all the right-handed ones. They could react chemically only with right-handed tartrate, indicating an asymmetry of their own. So he began to study fermentation, which took him to pasteurization, the process that kills pathogenic organisms in vinegar, milk, or fermented liquor through heat. Much of his fame in the world of the nonscientist stems from his creation of this process.

In 1857, he was appointed to the Ecole Normale faculty. His laboratory was an attic with a drying stove under the stairs, which he reached by crawling on his hands and knees. There he worked on alcohol fermentation for a few years.

His research brought about a head-on confrontation with believers in spontaneous generation, a theory curiously tinged with religious fervor. It was an old idea. Caterpillars, it was once said, sprang from leaves. Virgil thought bees arose from the body of a dead bull. Mice, said van Helmont, came from dirty sheets and wheat, but others claimed they crept out of a woman's dirty shift, full-born. Buonanni claimed that logs in seawater produced worms which turned first into butterflies, then birds. By Pasteur's time, scientists were finding miraculous unparented births in the world of the small. Pasteur would have loved to prove that spontaneous generation existed. His magnets and optical tricks were parts of his attempt to rouse life from dead matter. "I looked for spontaneous generation without finding it, but I do not believe it to be impossible," he once said.

The battles began in earnest in 1859. Pasteur's major opponents were several leading French scientists. Pasteur said that colonies of microorganisms did not arise miraculously but happened when microorganisms that had been floating in the air landed on something. He was at a disadvantage. As he said, "I do not pretend to establish that spontaneous generation cannot occur. One cannot prove the negative." Again, he started on an airy level—he was mainly interested in the debate because of the "relation to the impenetrable mystery of life and death." But he was soon brought down to hard experiment. He filled some sterile curved-neck flasks with a boiled infusion, sealed the necks while steam was coming out by melting the glass spout shut, then took them to various places where he unsealed them. He thought that if microorganisms existed in the air, there would be fewer in less populated, high, cold places, so the experiments took him on journeys from city to alps. As he walked on the road to his birthplace of Dole in the Jura Mountains, probably protecting hampers of precious vials on the back of his mule with one hand, vine laborers wondered what he was up to. An old schoolmate answered, "What would you have? It amuses him!"

In each place he visited, he snipped off the neck of a bottle or two, then resealed them. He found few or no organisms in the bottles he exposed to alpine air, more in those in the lowlands. It was as he expected. Pasteur won the debate, which culminated in his dramatic speech of April 7, 1864, in a crowded Paris hall:

And, therefore, gentlemen, I could point to that liquid and say to you, I have taken my drop of water from the immensity of creation, and I have taken it full of the elements appropriated to the development of inferior beings. And I wait, I watch, I question it, begging for it to recommence for me the beautiful spectacle of the first creation. But it is dumb . . . dumb because I have kept it from the only thing man cannot produce, from the germs which float in the air, from Life. For Life is a germ and a germ is Life. Never will the doctrine of spontaneous generation recover from the mortal blow of this simple experiment. . . . No, there is now no circumstance known in which it can be affirmed that microscopic beings came into the world without germs, without parents similar to themselves. Those who affirm it have been duped by illusions, by ill-conducted experiments, spoilt by errors they either did not perceive or did not know how to avoid.

Meanwhile, he pursued studies of fermentation. His researches saved vinegar makers millions of francs. He examined wines gone bad and concluded that each disease could be traced to a different organism. The cure? Heat.

In 1865, silkworm disease was ruining the French silk industry. From 1852 to 1865, production of cocoons dropped from fifty-two million pounds to eight million. Though growers tried sprinkling the worms with charcoal or rum, they continued to sicken and die. Because of Pasteur's success with wine, his old friend Jean Baptiste Dumas begged him to help. Pasteur wrote, "Consider, I pray you, that I have never touched a silkworm . . . [but] do with me as you like." He wasn't fooling about his lack of knowledge. The famous naturalist Fabre had to tell him what a chrysalis was. He arrived in Alais in the midst of the epidemic. Mulberry plantations were abandoned, and the land was dreary with poverty. The disease he was investigating—pebrine—manifested itself through a peppering of black spots. At first Pasteur wondered if it was caused by some internal chemical imbalance within the worm, but he found small oval organisms in silkworm blood. Having identified the cause and its spread through infected leaves and eggs, he suggested a cure: Look for parasites in the bodies of the worms after they laid their eggs and, if any were found, destroy the eggs.

The abstract dreamer was an industrial hero. But the hero was also experiencing tragedy: the death of two daughters (aged twelve and two) and his own cerebral hemorrhage, which left his left arm and leg paralyzed. He never completely regained the use of his left hand, but he kept working.

When the Franco-Prussian War broke out in 1868, Pasteur, who was extremely patriotic, searched for a way to serve his country and found it— in the improvement of French beer, so that it would rival that of German imports. "Oh, that I might begin a new life of study and work. Poor

France, dear country, what would I not do to relieve your distress!" he wrote.

His compassion for wounded soldiers dying from infectious diseases caused him to pioneer in antisepsis. His work influenced Joseph Lister, who campaigned for sterile hospitals. He also identified the cause of puerperal fever, which was killing ten percent of women admitted to maternity hospitals. Antiseptic procedures reduced death rates from puerperal fever, gangrene, and erysipelas to less than one percent each.

In studying swine plague, he discovered that the microbe that caused it increased in virulence as it was injected into pigeons, the blood from the first infected pigeon being injected into the next, and so on down the chain. The blood from an end-of-the-line pigeon could kill a pig faster than that from the initial pigeon. Inherent was an important principle: that the virulence of an organism can be manipulated in the laboratory.

His work with anthrax yielded rich scientific rewards. He not only developed a vaccine that protected animals from the disease but also, in proving an argument, discovered something about variation in death rates from animal to animal. M. Colin, a professor at the veterinary school at Alfort, claimed that chickens could die of anthrax. Pasteur challenged him. Bring a chicken dead of it, and I'll believe you, he said. No chicken was forthcoming and, after making excuses, Colin finally admitted he was wrong. Then Pasteur proved him right. He put a hen inoculated with the disease in cold water, with feet fastened to the bottom. Its body temperature fell, and it died. Noninoculated chilled hens lived. Conclusion: Anthrax germs thrived only at temperatures lower than that of a hen.* Pasteur packed up the experimental hens in a cage (including the dead one) and took them to the Académie de Médecine. He dropped the dead one on Colin's desk.

The work with disease, perhaps, made Pasteur finicky. Adrien Loir, who was his assistant from 1884 to 1888, remarked, "He minutely inspected the bread that was served to him and placed on the tablecloth everything he found in it: small fragments of wool, of roaches, of flour worms. . . . All the others ate the same bread without finding anything in it. This search took place at almost every meal and is perhaps the most extraordinary memory that I have kept of Pasteur."

In addition to pasteurization, named for him, Pasteur is perhaps best known for the coup of his old age: the conquering of rabies. Before Pasteur came up with a better one, the treatment for this dread disease,

---

*Later scientists have suggested that lower resistance because of cold is also a factor.

known at least since the time of Aristotle, was to apply a red-hot iron or acids to the wounds, or to sprinkle gunpowder on them and then light it. When Pasteur was a child, he witnessed the cauterization of victims of a rabid wolf at the blacksmith shop and was horrified at their screams of pain and the smell of burning flesh.

Experimenting with brain matter of rabid dogs and rabbits, he conjectured that the disease traveled through the nervous system. He dried the spinal cords of rabbits dead of rabies for varying lengths of time to develop vaccines of varying strengths. Would the vaccines work on someone already bitten? Pasteur wanted to try them on condemned criminals, but the law would not allow it.

In July 1885, nine-year-old Joseph Meister was attacked by a rabid dog. The frenzied animal threw the child to the ground and bit his face and hands in fourteen places. A laborer rescued the boy, covered with blood and froth, and a doctor washed and cauterized the wounds with carbolic acid, a relatively ineffective treatment. When it was determined that the dog was rabid, the doctor suggested the boy be taken to Pasteur for treatment. Joseph arrived in Paris on July 6. On July 8, Pasteur started treatment with vaccine from a spinal cord dried for fourteen days. Within ten days, the boy was inoculated twelve times, each time with a stronger vaccine. Madame Pasteur wrote to her children, "Your father has had another bad night. He can hardly bring himself to make the last inoculations of the child. And it is necessary to go on with it now! The boy continues to be very well." Every night, Pasteur dreamed of the boy suffering from rabies. Joseph lived. Through Pasteur's vaccine, mortality from rabies, which had been from 16 to 40 percent, dropped to less than 1 percent.

This was his last important discovery. In 1888, he gave up his tools. In 1895, he died, never having cracked the all-encompassing principle of the universe, but a master of the small world of microorganisms. His enchainment was relentless.

"Lucy in the Sky with Diamonds"
Meets Lucy in the Desert with Arthritis

AS SOON AS the Beatles' recording of "Lucy in the Sky with Diamonds" was released in 1967, the British Broadcasting Corporation (BBC) banned it. The song was about drugs, its detractors insisted. It was an acid trip of "tangerine trees," "marmalade skies," "newspaper taxies," "plasticene porters with looking-glass ties," and the title was cleverly constructed to stand for LSD.

While the Beatles repeatedly denied the drug connection, the rumors persisted, and the analyses of the song became more and more sophisticated. Years later in a *Playboy* interview John Lennon told of Lucy's origin, just as he had when the song hit the charts. It was very simple, he said: "My son Julian [age four] came in one day with a picture he had painted of a school friend named Lucy. He had sketched in some stars in the sky and called it *Lucy in the Sky with Diamonds*. The other images were from *Alice in Wonderland*. There was also the image of the female who would someday come save me—a 'girl with kaleidoscope eyes who would come out of the sky. It turned out to be Yoko, though I hadn't met Yoko yet. So maybe it should be 'Yoko in the Sky with Diamonds.' "

Seven years later Lennon's "Lucy" would inspire the naming of one of anthropology's greatest discoveries—a 3.5-million-year-old female hominid found at Hadar in the remote Afar Triangle, a desert region of northern Ethiopia. The hominid—unearthed by paleoanthropologist Donald Johanson on November 30, 1974—is the oldest, most complete, best-preserved skeleton of any erect-walking human ancestor. In his book *Lucy: The Beginnings of Humankind*, Johanson (along with coauthor Maitland Edey) gives a thrilling account of that eventful day when Johanson, accompanied by American graduate student Tom Gray, searched through the rubble of a small gully at Hadar. First Johanson spotted a piece of a hominid arm, then the back of a small skull, then a thigh bone. As he later wrote:

We stood up and began to see other bits of bone on the slope: a couple of vertebrae, part of a pelvis—all of them hominid. An unbelievable, impermissible thought flickered through my mind. Suppose all these fitted together? Could they be parts of a single, extremely primitive skeleton? No such skeleton had ever been found—anywhere.

"Look at that," said Gray. "Ribs."

A single individual?

"I can't believe it," I said. "I just can't believe it."

"By God, you'd better believe it!" shouted Gray. "Here it is. Right here!" His voice went up into a howl. I joined him. In that 110-degree heat we began jumping up and down. With nobody to share our feelings, we hugged each other, sweaty and smelly, howling and hugging in the heat-shimmering gravel, the small brown remains of what now seemed almost certain to be parts of a single hominid skeleton lying all around us.

The two men climbed into their Land Rover and raced back to camp. That afternoon all members of the expedition returned to the gully and carefully began to gather up the hundreds of bones and bone fragments that would eventually fit together and comprise forty percent of a human skeleton. After a long, exhausting—but exciting and rewarding—day, the scientists kicked off their boots and readied themselves for an evening of celebration. They stayed up all night, drinking beer and talking in rapturous tones of the discovery. The camp tape recorder was operating at full blast and one song, "Lucy in the Sky with Diamonds," was played over and over again. It seemed to echo the emotionally-charged mood of the scientists. It was not long before someone christened the female hominid "Lucy." When asked about the naming of Lucy, Johanson replied, "She was a female. And that Beatles song. We were sky-high, you must remember, from finding her."

While the physical characteristics of young Julian Lennon's schoolmate Lucy are not known, Johanson pieced together a very complete description of his Lucy (officially catalogued as AL 288-1 in the Hadar collection). She was three and a half feet tall (fully grown), weighed sixty pounds, and was between twenty-five and thirty-five years old when she died. Though she was more ape than human, Lucy was bipedal (she walked erect on two legs), and her hands were similar to human hands except for the fact that her fingers tended to curl more than human fingers. Lucy's brain was very small and encased in a head the size of a softball. Her vertebrae showed evidence of a bone disorder, probably arthritis. Her jaw was V-shaped and her arms were longer in relation to her body size than human arms. Probably dark-skinned, Lucy was definitely hairier than modern humans. As Johanson states, "Lucy was not human. No matter what kind of clothes were put on Lucy, she would not look like a human being. She was too far back, out of the human range entirely."

Mayflies, Starfish, and Intestinal Fortitude

FRAGILE INSECTS flying in a cloud in the light of a lantern near the Rhone Bridge caught Elie Metchnikoff's attention as he was taking a solitary walk, shortly after an attempt at suicide because he was depressed over the death of his wife Ludmilla. The insects, which he mistakenly identified as *Ephemeridae* (actually they were *Phryganidae*), changed his mind about dying. In another man, their pale flight might have inspired thoughts of the frail Ludmilla, so ill on their wedding day four years before that she had to be carried to the church in a chair, or thoughts of the tragically short life span of humanity. But instead the insects brought Metchnikoff, a twenty-eight-year-old Russian biologist, alive with a question: Could one apply the theory of natural selection from Charles Darwin's *Origin of Species* (published in 1859, ten years before the Metchnikoff wedding) to short-lived insects? Did they have time in their tiny life span to adapt at all?

He was intrigued, as were most scientists, with the implications of Darwin's theory (the research which could come from it!), with new discoveries about the cell, with warring philosophies in science (was science villain or savior?). Though the sight of the flying insects got him thinking again, he could not immediately go back to work at his chosen task of seeking genetic links in the cellular layers of sea animals, because his eyes were so inflamed he could not use a microscope. In fact, his sister-in-law found him cutting up paper in a dark room for lack of something better to do. So he went off the Kalmuk slopes for a fling at anthropology—the bodily measurement of natives who, he decided, were less developed than Caucasians, partly because they were always slightly tipsy from koumiss, the fermented mare's milk that was a part of their everyday diet.

After his eyes improved, he went back to teaching at the University of Odessa and to his research on cells. In 1875, he married a teenaged girl, Olga Belokopitova, the oldest of a boisterous family who lived in an apartment above him and annoyed him with their noise. During the following years, though by mutual consent they had no children of their own, the couple acquired a family of young orphaned relatives, who called Elie "the Prophet."

Five years after his marriage, Olga became ill with typhoid, and student protest against the repressive regime of Tsar Alexander II interfered with his work, and again Metchnikoff attempted to kill himself, this time by inoculating himself with *Treponema recurrentis* (relapsing fever). However, he survived, euphoric at coming out alive from the Valley of the Shadow. In 1882, the tsar was assassinated, and Elie, weary of the repressive regime which followed, took his family and left Russia in disgust to pursue biological research abroad. By then he was financially independent as a result of various inheritances, for in spite of his "red" leanings, he came from a family of rich landowners, as did his wife.

They lived in a suburb of Messina, Italy, in an apartment overlooking the ocean; they were very happy there. In a laboratory that had been converted from a drawing room, Elie studied the mobile digestive cells in starfish larvae, which he believed had evolved from similar cells in more primitive animals. He later wrote, ". . . it was in Messina that the great event of my scientific life took place. A zoologist until then, I suddenly became a pathologist."

In his own words, this is what happened:

One day when the whole family had gone to a circus to see some extraordinary performing apes, I remained alone with my microscope, observing the life in the mobile cells of a transparent starfish larva, when a new thought suddenly flashed across my brain. It struck me that similar cells might serve in the defense of the organism against intruders. Feeling that there was in this something of surpassing interest, I felt so excited that I began striding up and down the room and even went to the seashore to collect my thoughts.

I said to myself that if my supposition was true, a splinter introduced into the body of a starfish larva, devoid of bloodvessels or of a nervous system, would soon be surrounded by mobile cells as is to be observed in a man who runs a splinter into his finger. This was no sooner said than done.

There was a small garden to our dwelling, in which we had a few days previously organized a "Christmas" tree for the children on a little tangerine tree; I fetched from it a few rose thorns and introduced them at once under the skin of some beautiful starfish larvae as transparent as water.

I was too excited to sleep that night in the expectation of the result of my experiment, and very early the next morning I ascertained that it had fully succeeded.

That experiment formed the basis of the phagocyte theory, to the development of which I devoted the next twenty years of my life.

According to his theory, the mobile cells that ate the thorns in the starfish larvae were precursors of white blood corpuscles in mammals. Both kinds of cell were phagocytes (devouring cells) that acted as soldiers in an organism's war against invading bacteria. Also, he determined, the phagocytes played a part in the establishmemt of the body's immunity. Not all scientists agreed with him. Though most saw that phagocytes did indeed "eat" bacteria, many believed that they merely provided a kind of trolley car system whose purpose was to carry bacteria to another part of the body, where the invaders, let off, wreaked their havoc in new territory. Other investigators felt that something in the fluid part of the blood was a kind of essential sauce, without which the phagocytes could not do their work.

Metchnikoff fought like a tiger against opposition to his theory. Was he right? Yes, and so were the believers in the "sauce" in the blood, though modern thinking about immunology is more sophisticated—involving lock-and-key clumping of antigens (invaders) by antibodies (armies specifically equipped to disarm them) and the carrying of immunological messages by lymphocytes. The white blood cells *do* engulf bacteria, which are then destroyed by chemical agents in the cytoplasm. In broad outline, his ideas hold up.

But that is getting ahead of the story. After two years in Messina, Metchnikoff and family returned to Russia for a time. In 1888, Louis Pasteur invited Elie to work at the Pasteur institute in Paris. He accepted, and he and his wife spent the rest of their life in France, in a country house in Sèvres, from which Metchnikoff commuted to work at the institute.

Metchnikoff's theories about immunity led him to the conviction, close to modern-day autoimmune disease theory, that old age was a kind of immunological disease in which the phagocytes, unable to separate friend from enemy, turned against the body in which they resided. "Old age is an infectious chronic disease," Metchnikoff said, "characterized by a degeneration or an enfeebling of the noble elements and by the excessive activity of the phagocytes."

He also developed theories, largely erroneous, relating the length of an animal's intestine to its life span—the shorter the intestine, he said, the longer the life. Did not birds and bats have short intestines and great longevity? The intestine was a vestigial organ, he claimed, developed by Nature to allow creatures to "hold" feces while running from their enemies and then let them go at a more convenient time. From this he was led to implicate "bad" intestinal bacteria as villains in the life-shortening process. Why not "tame" the intestinal flora using lacti acid bacilli, antagonistic to "putrefying" microbes, which flourished in koumiss, yogurt, and other fermented milk products? After all, the Biblical patriarchs who ate sour milk lived to good old ages (Moses to 120, Aaron to 123) as did old people in Bulgaria who ate yogurt. Human beings, Metchnikoff claimed, should live to 120 or 150, provided they followed what he called orthobiosis (right living). He himself ate Bulgarian yogurt and cooked food (nothing raw), such as stewed fruit, legumes, grains, and a little meat. He was fanatic about hygiene. At his request the baker delivered rolls packed each in a separate bag, safe from contamination.

His theory of orthobiosis became popular, and people everywhere began to gulp down yogurt. Yogurt was sold in powder form, in tablets, and in soda-fountain drinks. Metchnikoff unwisely agreed to allow a commercial manufacturer, who employed his goddaughter and her husband, to label his yogurt containers "Sole Provider of Prof. Metchnikoff." He was later accused of making a profit from his theory. The press had a field day, asking rhetorical questions like "Who would want to live one hundred and fifty years if he had to drink sour milk three times a day?" and calling Metchnikoff "a modern Ponce de Leon searching for the fountain of immortal youth and finding it in the Milky Whey."

So the chunky little man with the bushy gray beard became a well-known figure. He must have enjoyed the acclaim, for he was always a proponent of bringing science to the people and attracted crowds to his lectures even before his fame as a health-food promoter.

In 1908, with Paul Ehrlich, he won the Nobel Prize in physiology and medicine for work in immunology. A believer in the power of rationality and science, he was shocked by World War I—he had thought the human race had progressed beyond such an unthinkable catastrophe. "With the help of science, man can correct the imperfections of his nature!" he had claimed. Shortly after the war began, he became ill, though not so ill that he stopped generating theories. One was that autointoxication (the result of metabolizing one's own fat) killed silk moths, who had no working mouth parts and could not eat. Another was that perhaps there were "invisible microbes" too small to be seen under a microscope. And still another was that "men of genius are but rarely the first-born" (not true). He examined the organs of an old diabetic dog while they were still fresh after its death to see if diabetes was an infectious disease.

Meanwhile, he kept track in a journal of his "psychical state" and symptoms: "I was thirsty and drank hot weak tea; I vomited; I felt wind in the stomach and intestines"; and "It is possible that having begun an intense life, I have attained at sixty-eight a precocious satiety of living, just as certain women cease to menstruate earlier than the great majority." He found that his theory of the death instinct—that at the end of their natural lives, people desire death—was proving true for him. One day, he felt, there would be "a new science—the science of death; it will be known how to make it less hard." Shortly before he died, of heart failure, on December 15, 1916, he said to a doctor friend, "You will do my postmortem. Look at the intestines carefully, for I think there is something there now." He was a scientist to the end.

Horse Sense and the First Movies

A BIG MAN with a beautiful smile, tycoon Leland Stanford had a controversial reputation encapsulated in Alfred Cohen's remark that he had the "ambition of an emperor and the spirit of a peanut vendor." Fabulously rich from his Gold Rush grocery trade, he was a prime mover in the building of the Central Pacific Railroad, served as governor of California from 1862 to 1864, sat in the U.S. Senate from 1885 to 1893, and founded Stanford University. But he is more interesting for his extravagance and eccentricity. His fifty-room mansion on Nob Hill in San Francisco, surrounded by a thirty-foot wall, had a seventy-foot-high glass-domed circular entrance hall and its own private railroad spur. When his son Leland junior was born in 1868, Stanford introduced him to friends by having him carried into dinner in a silver-covered dish and then with a flourish lifting the lid to reveal the baby lying on a bed of flowers.

It is not surprising that he was influential in the invention of such a magical process as motion pictures, though at the time he helped to develop them his mind was really on horses. An intuitive horseman, he owned a nine-thousand-acre horse farm in Palo Alto and raised race horses. In 1889, 775 horses plus yearlings were housed there. His methods of horse training proved so effective that other stables adopted them.

But Stanford also had a scientific mind. He was fascinated with machines. He owned an orchestrion, a mechanical orchestra in a ceiling-high cabinet, and a collection of tin mechanical birds which, operated by compressed air, sang when a button was pushed. In training horses he not only relied on intuition, but also asked anatomical questions: Through what actions did the horses run? Did a trotter ever have all four feet off the ground? To answer these questions he thought of photography. If a picture could be taken of a trotting horse with all four feet off the ground, he would know the answers to one of his questions. In 1872, he hired Eadweard Muybridge, a British photographer working for the U.S. government on the West Coast, to try to get a photo of one of his horses in action.

The experiment was not conducted until 1878. By that time Stanford had set up a photo studio. Its cameras were timed to take a sequence of stills of a running horse. Meant to answer Stanford's questions, they had an exposure time of 1/1,000th of a second. There were twelve of them, twenty-one inches apart. When horses hit a string, it would supposedly trigger the camera mechanism. A fine scheme, but it didn't work: strings broke or stretched, horses bolted, cameras were knocked out of position. So Stanford hired engineer and photographer John D. Isaacs to come up with a better system. For each camera, Isaacs arranged two shutters, one above and the other below the lens opening, with electronically operated latches and a rubber spring-triggering mechanism. Twelve pins spirally placed on a cylinder were connected in a magnetic circuit with the twelve cameras so that, as the cylinder revolved, each pin would in its turn make contact with one of the cameras. When a sulky wheel passed over one of the wires embedded every twelve inches in a rubber roadway and ex-posed at its edge, it activated the processes. In this manner a series of twelve exposures was made during one stride of the horse. To measure the height of hooves above the surface, a 50-foot-long by 15-foot-high wooden backboard covered with muslin was black-lined into 12-inch ver-tical spaces. About 1½ feet from the base was a 12-inch-high board with horizontal lines 4 inches apart to measure the height of the horse's foot from the ground.

The photographs that resulted answered several questions about the movement of trotters, not least among them that they did, indeed, some-times have all four feet off the ground at once. In the summer of 1878, Muybridge copyrighted the photographs. In 1879, he created a method of showing them in motion. He affixed silhouettes of horses' positions in sequence on a glass wheel, then passed them rapidly in front of a lighted camera projector slot. The first home movies were shown—in Leland Stanford's mansion.

In 1886, Muybridge gave Thomas Edison a demonstration of his zoo-praxiscope, developed from his original experiment. He became a celeb-rity lecturer in the United States and Europe, showing motion pictures to scientists and artists. In 1893, Edison invented the kinetoscope, and movies, originally inspired by a tycoon's curiosity about horses in motion, were born.

Inspirations of the Printing Press

A WINE PRESS, coin punchers, mirrors, and playing cards were the inspirations for Johann Gutenberg's inventions of the printing press and, in general, the printing process.

A brilliant synthesizer, he did not bring books to Europe's masses by himself. For a thousand years the Chinese had been practicing block printing, which was known in Europe as early as the 1100s, 300 years before Gutenberg. Books were being mass produced in the fifteenth century. One Venetian bookseller employed a staff of up to fifty scribes at one time to make books. So Gutenberg did not single-handedly propel civilization out of the Dark Ages, though certainly much of his life seems to remain buried in them.

That much is known. But much of the life of this pioneer of modern communications remains a mystery. What is available comes mainly from court records. A man involved in five lawsuits in his lifetime, Gutenberg was probably unscrupulous and hot-tempered. In one case, for example, he was fined fifteen guilders for calling a shoemaker "a poor creature leading a life of lies and deceit." His business associates sued him three times for matters regarding the printing press.

Considering the cloudy spots and total blanks in present knowledge of Gutenberg's life, it is amazing how easy it is to piece together the puzzle of inspirations which led to his great achievement. A letter he may have written to a friend provides some possible details: "I took part in the wine harvest. I watched the wine flowing, and going back from the effect to the cause, I studied the power of this press which nothing can resist." The wine press was an old invention, brought to the Rhineland by the ancient Romans. There was nothing new about it, except Gutenberg's use of it.

Gutenberg's father belonged to a patrician fellowship of coinmakers in Mainz, where Johann was born around 1400. The boy couldn't belong, though membership was hereditary, because his mother's father was from the merchant class, and he was, therefore, not a pure patrician, which was necessary for admission. But he knew how coins were minted, and later, exiled to Strasbourg, as were other patricians, he became a goldsmith and stone-polisher.

There in 1438, Gutenberg—for a price—agreed to include some of his paid goldsmithing pupils in a manufacturing scheme. Each paid him a premium as teacher and granted him half the proceeds from the enterprise, which was to sell mirrors to pilgrims traveling to Aix-la-Chapelle to view religious relics. The pilgrimage was a big event which took place every seventh year for two weeks. The pilgrims believed that the reflections of relics in mirrors would be magically captured behind the surface forever. So they could take back with them the holiness of the relics—Christ's swaddling clothes, Mary's birthing outfit, John the Baptist's bloody headcloth. At home, they nailed the mirrors to house and stable doors to keep evil away. Some mirrors were thrown into the melted metal used to cast church bells, where they left fossil-like impressions. Enormous numbers of people made the pilgrimage to Aix-la-Chapelle—142,000 in 1492, for example—so the potential profit was also enormous.

The mirrors were small with broad, fancy frames cast from molds of tin, copper, or brass or molded in a press. Some may have been incised with writing. The materials in mirrors—lead, tin, and antimony—and the methods of making the frames were employed by Gutenberg in typecasting.

Like many get-rich-quick schemes, the mirror manufacturing plan failed. The pilgrimage, originally scheduled for 1439, was put off for a year. So a new contract was drawn up among the participants for another project, which may well have been printing, perhaps Bibles for the pilgrims. Then one of his partners, Andreas Dritzhen, died. Gutenberg, afraid Dritzhen's heirs would find out his printing secrets, melted down the "forms" for the new project and asked that four pieces from the press, which were the key to his secrets, be taken apart and separated. Jorg Dritzhen, Andreas's brother, brought suit, claiming that Gutenberg was preventing him and his brother Claus from getting in on the enterprise or getting Andreas's money back. Gutenberg, of course, refuted the claim—Andreas, he said, had gotten his money's worth. From testimony at the trial, it is fairly certain that the project did involve printing and that the participants expected to make a great deal of money from it. The goldsmith, Hans Dunne, had received money from Gutenberg in 1436 "for what has to do with printing." Barbel von Zabern, a tradeswoman, said that Andreas Dritzhen had told her he had spent more than three hundred guilders (more than the annual salary of a high-living official) on the project and expected to get his money back in a year. Gutenberg won the lawsuit. Still, scholars are not absolutely certain that Gutenberg had developed the press because, as one of them said, when told that Strasbourg was the cradle of printing, "Yes, but it is a cradle without a baby." The baby? A press or books.

By 1448, Gutenberg was back in Mainz, his birthplace, working on printing something, perhaps the "42-line" Bible for which he is famous, certainly calendars and indulgences for sinners, those pieces of paper that were tickets to heaven. Starving for capital, he borrowed eight hundred guilders from one Johannes Fust in 1450. Two years later, he borrowed another eight hundred guilders, and Fust became his partner.

The Bible, which he did print sometime before 1455, was illuminated with animal and plant engravings, probably produced by intaglio on copper by someone known as the Master of Playing Cards. These engravings are scattered throughout the front of the Bible only, which leads us to believe that Gutenberg abandoned the idea of including illustrations, perhaps for financial reasons. However, it may be that one of Gutenberg's inventions was the use of printed illustrations in books and that he owed an inventor's debt to the Master of Playing Cards who helped him to develop the process.

In 1455, Fust demanded his money back, and, in yet another lawsuit, Gutenberg lost his business. It is possible that he went blind after 1460. Five years later, he was given a pension by the archbishop of Mainz. He died in 1468, poor and obscure.

What exactly did Gutenberg invent that produced this machine which in one day, with one worker, could reproduce the work of several scribes for a year? Surprisingly modern, his overall concepts involved mass production and the use of interchangeable parts. Previously, every letter on every page of every book was carved and set in place forever. It could not be reused on another page. Making letters which could be used over and over seems simple. But it was not. Gutenberg realized that letters had to made from metal rather than wood, that they had to be precise, that every letter had to fit with all the others tightly. His solution was a fairly complex process of typecasting—he was, then, the inventor of typography. For each letter he made a hard metal punch containing the letter's mirror image. The punch was used to impress the letter on a softer flat piece of metal. The softer piece of metal was inserted into a boxlike hinged instrument into which molten lead, tin, or antimony heated to 300°C was poured. This made a letter on a stick, a piece of type. The type was set in place, tied with string, and put under the screw and lever press, where it was inked with soot and gallnut ink. The paper was laid on top of it, then imprinted.

By 1500, forty-five thousand books had been printed in Europe. It was the beginning of a new age—books for everyone, not just the rich. Fifteen years after Gutenberg's death, Jacobus Philippus Bergomensis wrote, "Oh blessed printing. . . . Now at little cost anyone may become learned."

Bell's "Bridge Through Moving Air"

THE MARRIAGE of two obsessions led Alexander Graham Bell to create a device of great irony: an invention that was useless to those who inspired it. One obsession was his desire to teach the deaf to speak, and the other was to develop a harmonic telegraph.

As a boy, with his brother, Bell made a gutta-percha and rubber talking head with movable parts—tongue, jaws, and vocal cords—all activated with bellow lung power. It could say "Ma-ma." He also tried to teach his Skye terrier to say "How do you do," but failed. His father, a speech teacher, devised Visible Speech, a ten-symbol system that reproduced the sounds of any language or human utterance. Bell grew so adept in reading Visible Speech that he could say words in Sanskrit and Gaelic as well as capture the sound of a kiss in symbols.

At sixteen he moved to his grandfather's house in London, later to be joined by his father. Though he hated dressing up and carrying a cane, as London custom mandated, the city was invaluable to his future work. It was here that he first taught Visible Speech to the deaf, experimented further with acoustics, and became acquainted with the work of others in the field. Bell found a copy of a book by physicist Hermann von Helmholtz on simulating the human voice through electromagnetism and related experiments with vowel sounds. The book was written in German, so Bell could not read it. What's more, he misinterpreted some of the illustrations, assuming that they showed that Helmholtz *telegraphed* the sounds. Taking off from this erroneous springboard, Bell wondered: If Helmholtz had been able to telegraph vowel sounds, why not consonants or speech itself?

After tuberculosis killed two of his brothers, with Alexander himself in poor health, the family moved to Brantford, Canada, for the climate. For a year he did nothing but analyze the Mohawk language and teach Visible Speech to a tribe of Mohawks. They took him into the tribe and taught him war dances in return.

Bell's direction in life seesawed: Should he continue teaching the deaf to talk, or should he work on his invention for a musical telegraph with a tonal keyboard that could transmit messages of varying pitches in Morse code? He opted for a teaching job in Boston at the Horace Mann School for the Deaf. He taught there for two years and was appointed Professor of Vocal Physiology at Boston University. During that time he took up residence with the wealthy family of one of his students. In exchange for tutoring, they provided him with a workshop, so that during the day he earned his living while at night he pursued his inventions. Thomas Sanders, the student's father, later reported, "Often in the middle of the night Bell would wake me up. His black eyes would be blazing with excitement. Leaving me to go down to the cellar, he would rush wildly to the barn and begin to send me signals along his experimental wires. If I noticed any improvement in his machine, he would be delighted. He would leap and whirl around in one of his 'war dances' and then go contentedly to bed. But if the experiment was a failure, he would go back to his workbench and try some different plan."

In 1873, Bell met Mabel Hubbard, then fifteen, who had lost her hearing from scarlet fever when a small child. Bell instructed her teacher in his methods and four years later married Mabel. When Bell met Mabel he was leading a double life: inventor and teacher of the deaf. Then the two coincided when Bell attempted to solve one of the difficult problems in teaching the deaf: how to communicate voice quality and inflection to those who cannot hear. Bell had been trying to invent something—a precise vibration alphabet system to help his deaf students feel words. He wrote, "My original skepticism concerning the possibility of speech teaching had one good result: It led me to devise apparatus that might help the children . . . a machine to hear for them, a machine that should render visible to the eyes of the deaf the vibrations of the air that affect our ears as sound."

In early summer 1874, he started investigating new uses for two inventions already in existence: the manometric capsule and the phonoautograph. In the first, sound vibrations were transmitted to a membrane, causing a gas flame to flicker in a serrated pattern. This flickering, a visual representation of the sound, was reflected in a revolving mirror as a wavering band of light. Bell's idea was to photograph the shape of a speech sound in the band of light, then have the deaf person try to reproduce the shape by uttering the sound into the capsule. If the sound was right, the shapes would coincide. However, Bell found that photographing the light band was too difficult.

The other invention, the phonoautograph or sound-writer, consisted of a stretched membrane, a lever with a bristle at its end, a mouthpiece, and a blackened piece of glass. Vibrations from the membrane to the lever were traced by the bristle on the glass, which was made to move. The sound's shape was thus scratched out on the glass. Bell thought of making copies for the deaf of the sound tracings from the phonoautograph, which they would then try to reproduce on the manometric capsule. There was one great difficulty: Tracings from the phonoautograph did not match those of the same sound on the capsule. He would have to try to improve the phonoautograph.

Bell's friend Clarence Blake, Doctor of Otology at Harvard, suggested a way out of the problem: Why not use a real ear as a model? He gave Bell a dead man's ear with all its bones and eardrum to replace the phonoautograph membrane and lever. Bell took this grisly object, moistened with glycerine to give it flexibility, with him to Brantford, where he experimented with it by talking into it to make the drum vibrate, which, Rube Goldberg-fashion, would then activate a hay bristle to make marks on a glass. He was, as his father wrote, "full of new schemes."

The apparatus never did work right, but it gave Bell an idea: If the thin ear membrane could vibrate a bone, then an iron disk could vibrate a wire. Bell later wrote: "It did not enable the deaf to see speech as others hear it, but it gave ears to the telegraph, and today we hear in Boston what is spoken in New York and Chicago."

Hubbard, Mabel's father, who was backing Bell's experiments, did not think much of Bell's new idea, a machine to transmit speech over distances. It would be only a scientific toy, he said, and urged Bell to work on the harmonic telegraph instead. But luckily Bell was obsessed and worked on both, for each was essential to the final invention.

Meanwhile, he had acquired a co-worker, Thomas A. Watson, seven years younger and a mechanical genius, whom he had met at a Boston electrical shop. On June 2, 1875, the two were tinkering with the harmonic telegraph trying to tune it, Bell at the receiver and Watson at the transmitter sixty feet away. Listening, Bell heard something he was not supposed to hear—the overtones of a steel spring Watson was plucking. He rushed into the other room to investigate. A contact point which was supposed to produce make-and-break current had been screwed down too tight so that it produced a steady flow. It was this mistake that brought Bell to another revelation: Sound, complex sound, even speech, could be sent over a wire with a current of electricity varying in intensity. The harmonic telegraph was never perfected by Bell, but it had served its purpose.

The two men also experimented with disks to transmit sound—some tiny, others big as garbage can lids—using thin animal skin as membrane. Together they developed the membrane telephone with two eardrumlike iron disks connected by electrified wire. On March 10, 1876, Bell spilled acid on his pants and called in panic to Watson, three flights of stairs away, over the telephone, "Mr. Watson, come here, I want you." Excitedly, Watson replied, "I can hear you. I can hear the words." The telephone, patented three days before, was a working instrument.

That May, Bell exhibited his invention at the Centennial Exposition in Philadelphia. Again his experiences teaching the deaf played a part. A group of fifty judges touring the inventions arrived late at his narrow exhibit space between a stairway and a wall. Tired, they would have given the telephone only a cursory examination had not one judge, Dom Pedro de Alcantara, Emperor of Brazil, lighted up with recognition on seeing Bell. The two had met when Dom Pedro had visited Bell's class for the deaf at Boston University. In fact, the Emperor had later helped to organize the first school for the deaf in Brazil. So, impressed by a nod from royalty to the obscure inventor, the judges gave a fair hearing to Bell's demonstration: a recital over the telephone of Hamlet's soliloquy, "To be or not to be." He won a gold medal.

The telephone was not an instant success. Bell was called a crank, a ventriloquist, an impostor. The *London Times* printed a scientific explanation of why this "American humbug" could not possibly work. The telephone was called "Salem witchcraft" and a "playtoy."

To promote the telephone, Watson and Bell, aided by the impressive Hubbard with his patriarchal beard, staged publicity stunts. They sent a message 250 miles over a telegraph line from Boston to New York, Watson shrouded in blankets so his shouting would not upset the landlady of Bell's boarding house. They played "Yankee Doodle" over the phone and set up a telephone conversation between two Japanese. At New Haven, Connecticut, Bell persuaded sixteen Yale professors to join hands in a line, then talked through their bodies.

Adding to their difficulties, Western Union tried to infringe on Bell's patent. Eleven years and 600 lawsuits later, Bell was the clear winner.

In 1877, Bell married Mabel and gave her his telephone stock. He was interested in a vast number of other things and wanted to pursue those interests. Watson once reported, "One Sunday we found a dead gull at Swampscott. Bell spread it out on the sand, measured its wings, estimated its weight, admired its lines and muscle mechanism, and became so absorbed in his examination that, fastidious as he always was, he did not seem to notice that the specimen had been dead some time. As I was less enthusiastic, I was obliged to keep well to windward of the bird during the discussion. . . . I fancy if Bell had been in easy financial circumstances, he might have dropped his telegraph experiments and gone into flying machines at that time." Bell did go into aviation experiments later: tetrahedral kites, seaplane pontoons, and propellers that were precursors of helicopter rotors. He also used rockets for propulsion and promoted air mail. As president of the National Geographic Society, he saved the magazine from extinction by suggesting the use of photographs. Among his other inventions were the photophone (speech transmitted by light rays) and improvements on the phonograph. He bred four-nippled sheep, suggested radium to treat cancer, and experimented with seawater conversion. When President Garfield was shot, Bell offered to find the bullet with a metal-detecting device, the induction balance, which he had invented and tested on raw meat. Though Garfield's steel mattress made results impossible, and the bullet was too deep for extraction in any case, the device was later used in medicine.

However, in spite of the ironic fact that his invention, originally planned to help the deaf, was useless to them, he never lost his interest in their problems. He invented the audiometer, investigated the possibility of hereditary transmission of deafness, and continued to teach them speech.

Now devices exist so that deaf people can utilize phone communication. TTY/TTDs (Telecommunication for the Deaf) enable the deaf to make and receive calls. One version, like a teletype machine, prints out the message, and the other displays the message on a television screen. The communicator types out the message for both on a small portable typewriter hooked to the phone. The answer to a dialed number is a beeping sound instead of a voice. Deaf people know the phone is ringing when a light flashes or a fan begins to turn. But in actuality the real wonders of the telephone—the ability to hear someone talking and respond with speech over long distances—are forever denied to them.

Margaret Mitchell: "Cynara" and the Polish Waitress

MARGARET MITCHELL was totally unprepared for the publicity explosion that accompanied publication of her 1936 Civil War novel *Gone with the Wind*. An Atlanta journalist who found writing a painful chore ("I'd rather pick cotton than write"), Mitchell was utterly astounded by the American public's desire to know every detail of her personal and professional life. As she wrote to a friend: "I was asking for notoriety, I suppose, when I published a book, and it is only right that I should take the consequences. And short of any reflection of my personal integrity, I intend to take it with as good a grace as is possible, hoping to God that this miserable period will end quickly."

The period, however, did not end quickly, and Mitchell's aversion to the limelight only provoked additional grist for the rumor mill. Among the stories about her home and family life: She had a wooden leg, was dying of leukemia, suffered from a rare blood disease, and would have gone blind except for an emergency operation performed by a surgeon who had once operated on the King of Siam; her husband John Marsh was an invalid who had incurred enormous debts, and Margaret was forced to write in order to pay off the bills; she didn't live in Atlanta but was a claustrophobic who resided on a mink farm in Alaska.

The rumors about the book and the subsequent movie included: Mitchell was not the sole author of *Gone with the Wind* but wrote it in collaboration with her husband; she had written an unpublished, follow-up chapter about Scarlett and Rhett Butler which could be purchased for one dollar from her publisher; she personally was handpicking the cast for the David O. Selznick film of the book, and she would play Scarlett (whose original name, incidentally, was Pansy O'Hara) or Melanie.

Margaret Mitchell's mailbox overflowed with letters from well-meaning, inquisitive fans. The two most frequently asked questions were: "Did Scarlett ever get Rhett back?" and "Will there be a sequel to the book?" ("I don't know" and "No" were the respective answers from Mitchell.) Everyone, it seemed, wanted to know the stories behind the story. Was there a real Scarlett, Rhett, Melanie, Ashley? Where was the real Tara, the O'Haras' white, columned mansion? And how did she get such a perfect title?

Mitchell patiently wrote to her readers, answering as many as one hundred readers a week. Her characters, she said, were purely fictional even though the events and places were real. She had spent many pains-taking hours researching public records—including tax rolls, hospital records, and a catalog of tombstone names—to make sure that none of the names she chose for her characters duplicated the real names of anyone living in Atlanta or the surrounding areas at the time—1840 to 1873—that *Gone with the Wind* took place. Mitchell placed Tara about five miles outside of Jonesboro (thirty miles south of Atlanta) in Clayton County, an area familiar to Mitchell. While many readers insisted that they had found the real Tara, Mitchell could do no more than deny it. As she wrote to one "discoverer": "When I wrote of Tara I went to great pains to describe a house which had never existed in Clayton County. . . . In my imagination I located Tara on a road which I found in one of General Sherman's maps of 1864. This road no longer exists; it has fallen to pieces, and I had to travel it on foot."

The title *Gone with the Wind*: Where did it come from? Mitchell had a ready answer for this frequently asked question. The original title for the novel was *Tomorrow Is Another Day*, the last four words of the book. However, the word "tomorrow" appeared in the titles of thirteen books already in print, so the Atlanta story simply became *Another Day*. Still not satisfied with the title, Mitchell submitted more than twenty additional titles to her publisher, including *Bugles Sang True, Tote the Weary Load, Ba! Ba! Black Sheep*, and *Not in Our Stars*.

The perfect title finally came to her as she was reading an English anthology of poems and happened upon "Cynara" by Ernest Dowson. The full title of the poem in Latin is *Non Sum Qualis Eram Bonae sub Regno Cynarae* ("I am not what I used to be in the days of Cynara"). The phrase that caught Mitchell's eye appears in the first line of the third stanza:

> I have forgot much, Cynara! gone with the wind,
> Flung roses, roses riotously with the throng,
> Dancing, to put thy pale, lost lilies out of mind;
> But I was desolate and sick of an old passion,
> Yea, all the time, because the dance was long:
> I have been faithful to thee, Cynara! in my fashion.

After finding the title, Mitchell needed to fit it into the text of the story. She picked one of the book's (and the film's) most memorable scenes:

Atlanta had fallen to the Yankees. Rhett Butler had stolen a horse and wagon to carry Scarlett, Prissy, Melanie Wilkes, and her new baby away from the burning city and home to Tara. But before the journey was completed, Rhett decided to join the Army, leaving an angry but still spirited Scarlett to find her own way home. As Margaret Mitchell told it:

> She had never in her life been out in the sunshine without a hat or veils, never handled reins without gloves to protect the white skin of her dimpled hands. Yet here she was exposed to the sun in a broken-down wagon with a broken-down horse, dirty, sweaty, hungry, helpless to do anything but plod along at a snail's pace through a deserted land. What a few short weeks it had been since she was safe and secure! What a little while since she and everyone else had thought that Atlanta could never fall, that Georgia could never be invaded. But the small cloud which appeared in the northwest four months ago had blown up into a mighty storm and then into a screaming tornado, sweeping away her world, whirling her out of her sheltered life, and dropping her down in the midst of this still, haunted desolation.
>
> Was Tara still standing? Or was Tara also gone with the wind which had swept through Georgia?

Gone with the Wind was not the only book/movie title inspired by the words of Ernest Dowson. Another, almost equally familiar title taken from his poetry is *The Days of Wine and Roses*. But who was Ernest Dowson?

A shy, delicate man, Dowson was born in Lee, Kent, England, in 1867. Both of his parents suffered from tuberculosis, and much of his childhood was spent moving through England, France, and Italy in search of a suitable climate for his parents' health. While his early education was rather sporadic, he did enter Queen's College, Oxford, but in 1888, he dropped out after attending for only two years.

The force behind almost all of Dowson's love poems was a girl named Adelaide Foltinowicz. By most men's standards, Adelaide barely qualifies as "inspiration." The daughter of a Polish immigrant, Adelaide worked as a waitress in her father's restaurant, named Poland, in Soho. Not only was she plain-looking, she lacked education and sophistication. But Dowson was captivated by her youthful vigor (when he first met her she was twelve and he was twenty-four), charming innocence, and animated conversation. He decided to marry her when she grew older, and for the next six years he frequented the restaurant—usually four or more times a week.

Perplexed and upset over Dowson's obsession with such a mediocre female, one friend pleaded with him to find another, more suitable woman. To that Dowson erupted: "Can't you see that I loved her just because you and the others could find nothing in her; no beauty in her curving white neck and the way the dark tendrils curled on it; no sweetness in the pure eyes and mocking gay laughter; nothing. But I saw and knew she was mine, made for me and me alone to love and possess."

In 1897, at the age of eighteen, Adelaide married a waiter at her father's restaurant. She had two children, but after tiring of married life she left her family and became a prostitute. She subsequently died in the charity ward of a hospital in London—following a badly performed abortion.

Dowson was crushed by Adelaide's defection. By this time the distraught poet was himself plagued with tuberculosis, and his already disorderly life became an alcoholic nightmare. In late December 1899, a friend of Dowson's found the ailing, homeless, penniless poet in a London pub. He took Dowson in and cared for him until his death six weeks later at the age of thirty-two.

Non Sum Qualis Eram Bonae sub Regno Cynarae is undisputably the best of Dowson's poems. Filled with unrequited love for Adelaide, the poem takes its name from a line in the first ode of the fourth book of Horace. "Cynara," as the poem is popularly known, may seem a bit stilted and outdated today, but it certainly cast a spell over one old-fashioned lady from Atlanta who in turn has mesmerized millions of readers in forty countries around the world.

9. The Power of Suggestion

A casual conversation or a passerby's offhand remark often puts an idea in a creator's head. A tossed-off suggestion generated a horrible death machine. A conversation on a train would have been forgotten if one of the debaters had not used it as an important part of a novel that was to become one of the greatest motion pictures of all time. An obscure London comic acted out a drama that a psychologist translated into a controversial therapy treatment in humanistic psychology. A dim-witted blonde so infuriated Anita Loos that Loos wrote an unforgettable comedy. A boy and a dog searching for food in a garbage can sparked a great deed of kindness affecting millions. In a humorous book about a student paralyzed by writer's block, a young physicist found the beginnings of one of his profound insights.

Sometimes an animal provides suggestions. A fat dog became the symbol for a huge company. A totally exasperating woodpecker tapped his way into a creator's mind—and immortality.

From the wings of the stage that is fame, prompters whisper suggestions. They may not be remembered, but their ideas are.

Hiram Maxim's Killing Machine

HIRAM MAXIM, a self-educated Yankee inventor, went sightseeing in Europe after showing his prize-winning electric pressure regulator at the 1881 Electrical Exhibition in Paris. In his travels he met another American who inspired him with this advice: "Hang your chemistry and electricity! If you wish to make a pile of money, invent something that will enable those Europeans to cut each other's throats with greater facility."

The bumptious suggestion was right up Maxim's alley. In his forty-one years he had racked up an impressive list of inventions: an improved curling iron, a self-setting mousetrap for a rodent-ridden gristmill, a silencer for rifles, an automatic sprinkler fire extinguisher, a locomotive headlight, a gas lighting machine, a light bulb, and more. In addition, he had learned how to work with his hands in his jobs as a draftsman for a shipbuilder, as a scientific instrument maker, and as a wood turner. Another job—as a bouncer in a bar—brought out his pugnaciousness.

All in all, he was quite suited for his new enterprise, for he took up the American's challenge and decided to invent a machine gun—a weapon for mass killing. He moved to London and set up a workshop where he devised a spring-and-lever recharging mechanism, analyzed the force exerted by black powder on gun parts, and tinkered endlessly on the components of his gun. The result was a single-barrel, belt-fed, water-cooled working model. It was crude but good enough to give Maxim the confidence to start his own firm, the Maxim Gun Company. The improved version of the Maxim machine gun, weighing sixty pounds, was fed by a belt-and-sprocket-operated twelve-chamber magazine, triggered by the recoil of the barrel and housing. In other words, the force of the explosion of one cartridge was used to eject the empty shell and reload the gun with the next cartridge.

The Maxim performed magnificently against other machine guns. Its firing speed was 660 rounds per minute, more than fifty percent above that required by the British government for the Army, which initially bought a few Maxims for instructional purposes.

Maxim carried his demonstration gun in a suitcase and showed it to officials throughout Europe. Upon seeing it perform against three rival guns (the Gatling, Nordenfelt, and Gardner), the Kaiser said, "That is the gun. There is no other."

The Maxim proved to be a killing machine in European campaigns against native armies in India and Africa. In the Matabele War of 1893, for example, fifty Rhodesian police with mediocre training and four Maxims beat off five attacks from about five thousand tribesmen. And at the battle of Omdurman, Maxims operated by Anglo-Egyptian forces killed seventy-five percent of Dervish attackers.

In 1901, Maxim was knighted.

Maxims killed thousands of Japanese in the Russo-Japanese War and established a fantastic record of two hundred thousand rounds fired by sixteen guns without mechanical failure.

But during World War I the cynical American's suggestion—that there was money to be made in the invention of devices for Europeans to kill each other—really proved itself and, in fact, turned out to be too narrow a prophecy. Soldiers from all armies—American as well as European—

faced Maxims with enormous fear and wielded them with great efficiency. The gun mowed down soldiers in awesome numbers, stitching death across thousands of bodies.

In 1914, 12,500 Maxims were issued to German troops. The total holding was later said to be 50,000. On July 1, 1916, the first day of the British Somme offensive, British casualties, mostly from Maxim fire, amounted to 57,000. And nearly two months later, at High Wood, in just one day British soldiers manning the ten guns of the 100th Machine Gun Company fired off close to one million rounds, cooling their guns with water when it was available and with urine when it wasn't.

Maxims were also used in the air, some mounted on top of zeppelins. The Parabellum, a version of the Maxim designed in the munitions factory at Berlin, killed half the pilots and observers of the British Royal Flying Corps during Bloody April in 1917.

The total number of Maxim-caused deaths cannot, of course, be determined. What did Maxim think of the success of his invention? We don't know. It may be a blessing that he died at the end of November 1916, before the war was over and before he had full knowledge of his invention's true killing power.

Gentlemen Prefer Blondes: Henry Mencken and the Golden-haired Birdbrain

IN 1923, screenwriter Anita Loos was madly in love with journalist and critic Henry Louis Mencken. A vivacious, diminutive brunette, Loos was thirty-five and married when she set her sights on forty-three-year-old Mencken, a stocky five-foot, eight-inch bachelor whose literary reputation and masculine charm made him quite a popular personality, especially with women. Though Mencken lived in Baltimore, he made regular trips to New York City, where Loos resided, and on those occasions the couple usually dined with friends at one of Mencken's favorite restaurants, Luchow's, where the group took great pleasure in defying Prohibition laws by drinking beer served in teacups. (Loos had a Hollywood-type marriage—by definition, one that permitted dating.)

The Loos-Mencken romance, much to the screenwriter's disappointment, never got off the ground. Resigned to a solid, steady friendship,

Loos said that in Mencken she had found "an idol to adore for a lifetime" even though he regarded her as a "cute kid." She was not prepared, however, for the day when her intelligent, logical, sophisticated hero was bewitched by a "golden-haired birdbrain." Mencken's fascination with a dumb blonde provoked Loos into a fit of jealousy that resulted in her hit play *Gentlemen Prefer Blondes*.

It all started at a small dinner party in New York. George Jean Nathan, Mencken's friend and co-editor of the magazine *Smart Set*, brought as his date an attractive though dimwitted blonde. Anita Loos was aghast at seeing her beloved "Menck" captivated by the little blonde's idiotic remarks, idle chatter, and "naive, stupid viewpoint on everything." That same evening Loos and her husband John Emerson boarded a train headed for Hollywood, where she was to begin work on a new film. Much to her surprise, also on the train was the golden-haired birdbrain—on her way to the West Coast to make a screen test for a part in a Charlie Chaplin movie.

For the next five days Loos watched the men on the train fall all over themselves in an attempt to impress the giggly blonde. If the femme fatale so much as dropped a magazine, a dozen men charged to her aid. Meanwhile, Loos was single-handedly dragging around heavy luggage and fending for herself—all the while fuming at the men who seemed to have sent their brains on vacation. In her autobiography, *A Girl Like I*, Loos clearly recalls the exasperating experience:

> As our train raced across the plains of the Midwest, I watched her disorganize the behavior of every male passenger on board. I tried to puzzle out the reasons why. Obviously there was some radical difference between that girl and me, but what was it? We were both in the pristine years of youth. She was not outstanding as a beauty; we were, in fact, of about the same degree of comeliness; as to our mental acumen, there was nothing to discuss: I was the smarter. They why did that girl so far outdistance me in allure? Why had she attracted one of the keenest minds of our era? Mencken liked me very much indeed, but in the matter of sex he preferred a witless blonde. The situation was palpably unjust but, as I thought it over, a light began to break through from my subconscious; possibly the girl's strength was rooted (like that of Samson) in her hair. At length I reached for one of the large yellow pads on which I jot down ideas and started a character sketch which was the nucleus of a small volume to be titled *Gentlemen Prefer Blondes*. . . .

That sketch, which featured a diamond-hungry blonde, Lorelei Lee, was never intended to be a major literary work. It was simply a way of letting off steam in an attempt to get even with the man who had dared to trade her in for a dizzy blonde. For six months Loos forgot entirely about the scenario as she was caught up in the hectic world of movie-making.

But when she returned to New York she discovered the manuscript while unpacking and put it in the mail to Menck—to amuse him. On his next visit to New York, Mencken invited her to dinner and told her how much he had enjoyed the story and strongly advised that she try to sell it, which she did—to *Harper's Bazaar*.

The editor at *Harper's Bazaar*, Henry Sell, asked Loos to lengthen the story: "Take your blonde to Europe and let her have some more adventures." So Loos went to Europe and sent back monthly installments of the story. As soon as the feature was published, sales of the magazine began to increase; soon newsstand sales tripled, all because of Lorelei Lee. Editors at the magazine were delighted, especially since many of the new readers were men. It was not long before the publication—which catered to women—was attracting advertisers promoting men's clothing, sporting goods, cigars, and whiskey.

After her success with a magazine serial, Loos turned *Gentlemen Prefer Blondes* into a novel in 1926. It became such a best-seller that it paved the way for theater and movie versions. The most notable of these were the 1949 stage musical starring Carol Channing and the 1953 musical film with Marilyn Monroe. The lovable blonde became popular worldwide as the novel was translated into thirteen foreign languages, including Russian and Chinese. As millions of dollars flowed into Loos's bank accounts, she shook her head in amazement and said of Lorelei, "She has been harder to kill than Rasputin."

Just how dumb was Lorelei Lee? While much of the time she earned her birdbrain reputation, she did occasionally come up with sound philosophical advice, as when she said, "An American girl has to watch herself, or she might have such a good time in Paris that she wouldn't get anywhere. I mean, kissing your hand can make a girl feel very good, but a diamond bracelet lasts forever." Lorelei's friend Dorothy seemed to understand the blonde's special brand of intelligence: "Her brain reminds me of a radio," said Dorothy. "I listen to it for days and get discouraged, but just when I'm ready to smash it, something comes out that's a masterpiece."

Anita Loos and Henry Mencken remained close friends for many long years. She lived to be ninety-three and established an enviable literary output of plays, books, and more than 200 screenplays (including *San Francisco*, *Saratoga*, and *The Redheaded Woman*). Her sought-after talent made her a welcome guest in the homes of Hollywood's greats, including Irving Thalberg, D. W. Griffith, Douglas Fairbanks, Jean Harlow, Tallulah Bankhead, Joan Crawford, Clark Gable, Spencer Tracy, Helen Hayes, Lillian Gish, and Mack Sennett. Mencken died at the age of seventy-six after firmly establishing himself as one of America's foremost critics, leveling heavy attacks on American complacency, hypocrisy, and bigotry. Among his most enduring works are *Prejudices* and *The American Language*.

Anita Loos never tired of telling how she came to write *Gentlemen Prefer Blondes*. Over and over again she stated, "My only purpose was to make Henry Mencken laugh." And how she delighted in concluding the story with his much appreciated remarks: "Young lady, you have committed the great sin. You are the first American who ever made fun of sex. . . . It [the story] made me laugh like hell."

Heavy Theories from Light Reading

STUDENT: . . . and then I come to think of my thinking about it, again I think that I think of my thinking about it, and divide myself into an infinitely retreating succession of egos observing each other. . . . My head gets all in a whirl with dizziness as if I were peering down into a bottomless chasm, and the end of my thinking is a horrible headache.

STUDENT'S COUSIN: I cannot help you in sorting your many *I*'s. . . . My line is to stick to palpable things and walk along the broad highway of common sense; therefore my *I*'s never get tangled up.

STUDENT (explaining why it's taking him so long to write his paper): . . . certainly I have seen before thoughts put on paper; but since I have come distinctly to perceive the contradiction implied in such an action, I feel completely incapable of forming a single written sentence. . . . You see, my friend, a movement presupposes a direction. The mind cannot proceed without moving along a certain line, but before following this line, it must already have thought it. Therefore one has already thought every thought before one thinks it. . . .

STUDENT'S COUSIN: Bless me, while you are proving that thoughts cannot move, yours are proceeding briskly forth!

STUDENT: That is just the knot. This increases the hopeless mixup, which no mortal can ever sort out. The insight into the impossibility of thinking contains itself an impossibility, the recognition of which again implies an inexplicable contradiction. . . . Thus on many occasions man divides himself into two persons, one of whom tries to fool the other, while a third one, who is in fact the same as the other two, is filled with wonder at this confusion. In short, thinking becomes dramatic and quietly acts the most complicated plots with itself, and the spectator becomes actor.

—POUL MARTIN MØLLER:
Tale of a Danish Student

This clever tale satirizing the convoluted musings of a student who is putting off writing his paper was meant to be funny. The vaudevillian spectacle of the hero chasing his own intellectual tail in ever smaller and more frustrated circles while his commonsense cousin takes potshots at him has had Danes laughing from the beginning. It was written—and ironically never finished—by a young poet, Poul Martin Møller just back from two years of teaching in China, where he went to forget a broken heart.

A hundred years later, at the turn of the nineteenth century, Danish readers, among them the young student Niels Bohr, were still amused by it. Bohr saw himself in the tortured student and never forgot it. He gave the story credit for some of the inspiration which produced his great discoveries in physics, for rudimentary as Møller's tale was, it influenced Bohr's thinking. It helped him solve some tail-chasing problems of the structure of the atom and gave him ammunition for his heartfelt attempts to bring about an open community of nations. Complementarity, the umbrella principle which Bohr derived partly from his consideration of the ambiguity of Møller's simple ideas, is one of the most profound concepts of the twentieth century.

When we think about our own thinking, we operate on two different planes, Bohr thought (thinking about himself thinking)—we are both thinker and observer, object of our own gaze. So how, he wondered, can we possibly be objective with our use of language? And are some phenomena dual by their very nature?

While the young Bohr was pondering these deep thoughts, he was also studying science. Though he had a record for breaking laboratory glass ("It's Bohr," his instructor would say when something shattered), he was a fine student. His first paper, an investigation of the surface tension of water, won him the gold medal of the Danish academy of sciences. He had had trouble finishing it because he was so busy doing just one more experiment, then another. . . . His father sent him to a family mansion far from his laboratory where, unlike Møller's poor student, he was able to complete his work. At twenty-six, in 1911, he finished his doctoral thesis on the electron theory of metals. That year he went to England, at first to Cambridge, then to Manchester University, where he studied with

Ernest Rutherford. Rutherford, like Bohr, was unpretentious. He was known for his prodigious swearing at recalcitrant equipment, hated "pompous talk," and disliked being addressed by his title of lord. At the time he was investigating the behavior of particles of matter forced through thin metallic films. The boomeranging of positively charged alpha particles from the film led him to postulate that they were being repelled by heavy positive charges in the metal itself. Those charges, he further guessed, might be nuclei of atoms. From this he developed a model of the atom as a miniature solar system, with the positively charged nucleus as the "sun" and the negatively charged electrons as the "planets." Thrilled by his discovery, the big, hearty Rutherford marched into the office of his colleague, Hans Geiger (physicist, inventor of the Geiger counter), humming, "Onward, Christian Soldiers," then announced, "I know what the atom looks like."

However, appealing as it was, Rutherford's model didn't quite fit the *facts* about the atom. His atom, if it existed, would speedily decay and would emit a steady, continuously changing spectrum of colors as it did. Instead, atoms usually remained stable and gave off spectral lines in discrete color patterns.

The Alice-in-Wonderland world of the atom is different from the world of "big" things, like human beings, plants, and stones. It is full of ambiguities, paradoxes, rabbit holes. The rules by which it operates are different. Bohr started asking questions. Why did atoms remain stable? Why did they give off such a spectral pattern? The Rutherford model, he knew, was a product of classical physics, which had developed from Newton's work in the seventeenth century. But there was a new physics, quantum mechanics, developed by Max Planck and Albert Einstein, which stated that energy moves in packets (quanta)—discrete units—rather than in a continuous stream. What if the atom were ruled by *both* kinds of physics? Bohr proposed that the atom emitted radiation only when an electron made a quantum "jump" from one stationary state of higher energy (one orbit) to another stationary state of lower energy (another orbit). (According to quantum mechanics, it would not move through space as it did so.) This would explain the spectral line pattern and the fact that the atom did not quickly decay. Though, in classical physics, electrons could not "jump," classical physics was needed to explain the vibration of excited atoms which made the jump possible.

Bohr wrote his paper on these ideas and sent it to Rutherford. Rutherford thought it was too long and asked Bohr to work with him on shortening it. With "angelic patience" he tried to persuade Bohr to eliminate passages, but to no avail. The gentle Bohr was unbelievably stubborn.

He was also right—or at least "more right" than Rutherford. His work led to discoveries about the properties of atoms, elements, and radioactivity, which in turn brought about a major revision of the periodic table of elements. In it, he brought together two systems of ideas which, as further understanding of the atom developed, were still both needed, though they seemed mutually exclusive. Much was statistical: You could decide how many electrons would give off quanta of energy at a given temperature, for instance, but you could not determine when one *specific* electron would jump. That was the quantum world. But it was being measured by instruments of the classical physics world—fixed scales, regulated clocks. The result of an experiment was often a spot on a plate left by a moving electron. The interaction between apparatus and object had to be taken into account. How can you otherwise reconcile the inability to transfer the laws of momentum and energy (working on moving particles) to this unmoving apparatus? And in applying the laws of momentum and energy, you must renounce space-time coordination; that is, you can't know where the electron is and still know how fast it is moving. Conducting the experiment is a human being who, living according to the rules of classical physics (what human ever made a quantum jump?), is trying to enter a world that is not his. His measures of the quantum world can be only classical. And more, the human being must express in common, unambiguous language how he did his experiment and what he found out. No wonder Bohr said, "But if anybody says he can think about quantum problems without getting giddy, that only shows he has not understood the first thing about them."

Behind Bohr's contributions to atomic theory lay his fundamental principle, derived partly from his musings about the Danish student: Nature has complementary aspects which cannot all be studied in one experiment or from one point of view. That is, you can study the atom through both classical physics and through quantum mechanics, limiting each to its appropriate terrain; but you must take into account the observer as well as the observed. In 1927, he dignified the principle with the name *complementarity*.

In 1920, Bohr founded the Institute for Theoretical Physics (the Niels Bohr Institute), located on the edge of Copenhagen Park, where physicists from all over the world ("Bohr's Boys") came to work and study together. One of them, Leon Rosenfeld, wrote later,

Every one of those who came into closer contact with Bohr at the institute, as soon as he showed himself sufficiently proficient in the Danish language, was acquainted with the little book [*The Tale of the Danish Student*]: it was part of his initiation. Bohr would point to those scenes in which the licentiate [student] describes how he loses the count of his many egos, or disserts on the impossibility of formulating a thought, and from these fanciful antimonies he would lead his interlocutor—along paths Poul Martin Møller never dreamt of—to the heart of unambiguous communication of experience, whose earnestness he dramatically emphasized.

Even Bohr's jokes were usually based on heavy thought. He postulated that the innocent man had an advantage over the villain in a gun battle because the villain had to decide to draw his gun, while the good guy merely reacted without thinking. To prove it, he set up a demonstration using toy guns, with himself as the innocent. "We shot it out, and he killed us all," George Gamow, one of Bohr's Boys, later remarked.

Bohr said to a group of physicists after they all saw a Tom Mix picture together: "I did not like that picture. It was too improbable. That the scoundrel runs off with the beautiful girl is logical, it always happens. That the bridge collapses under their carriage is unlikely, but I am willing to accept it. That the heroine remains suspended in midair over a precipice is even more unlikely, but again I accept it. I am even willing to accept that at that very moment Tom Mix is coming on his horse. But that at that very moment there should be a fellow with a motion-picture camera to film the whole business is more than I am willing to believe."

In 1932, Bohr addressed a congress in Copenhagen with a lecture called "Light and Life," in which he applied complementarity to biology. Biological functions and physical-chemical reactions are, he said, complementary to each other. An organism cannot exist separate from its environment—air and nutrients, in particular. How can you tell if an atom of air in the lungs of a mammal is part of the animal or part of its environment? It is close to impossible to study a being without taking into account its life-support system. But, on the other hand, the creature is clearly discernible from its environment. Six years later, Bohr talked to a group of anthropologists about the complementary character of diverse human cultures and the possibility of intercultural cooperation.

In 1939, World War II began. For some time Bohr stayed in Denmark, though it was dangerous for him to be there. In 1943, he received a message from British Intelligence through the Danish general staff. As he had been forewarned, the message was hidden in a hole in a key. It invited him to come to England to work on atomic research. At first he refused, but in 1944, circumstances forced him to leave for Sweden. He then traveled secretly to England in the bomb bay of a Mosquito fighter, stayed there for a time, and finally came to Los Alamos, the atomic energy center in New Mexico, where he operated under the code name of Nicholas Baker, "Uncle Nick" for short.

Aware of the potential danger of atomic power, he hoped, idealistically, that it would, by its very horror, make war impossible. In 1950, he wrote a long, impassioned letter to the United Nations appealing to all the countries of the world to endorse international cooperation of science and to work toward an open, peaceful world. Groups of people with diverse views *could* be reconciled and work together, he said.

Bohr was a lovable, honest human being with many endearing characteristics, not the least of which was his ability to work with compromise, yet remain uncompromising. As Oskar Klein said of him, "It might be said that his original, innocently credulous way and his power of doubting entered his philosophy as complementary features." His alter ego, the Danish student, would probably agree.

A Debate over Christ

BEN-HUR, A TALE OF THE CHRIST was the best-selling book of the nineteenth century. A 550-page historical romance published in 1880, it has remained in print for more than 100 years, enjoying worldwide sales of well over 10 million copies. It has appealed to both young and old, the religious and irreligious, the elite as well as the common folk. When General Ulysses S. Grant, who hadn't read a book in ten years, received the novel from author Lew Wallace, he read it nonstop for thirty hours, sacrificing a night's sleep. Pope Leo XIII was so impressed with Wallace's handling of religious themes that he ordered a special Italian translation prepared, specifying some revisions "in the interest of piety." For Wallace the most welcome and heartwarming praise came from the thousands of letters he received from small-town Americans, many of whom had read very little or no fiction at all. In the illuminating and exhaustively researched biography *Lew Wallace: Militant Romantic*, authors Robert E. Morsberger and Katharine M. Morsberger quote one historian as saying: "[Ben-Hur was] an epochal book, because it was the first American novel to break through the rustic and village opposition to popular fiction. *Ben-Hur* rode that gilded chariot right through the front door to enter the homes of hard-shell Baptists, Methodists, and other non-novel-reading sects, and to an eager welcome. Thousands of back-country Americans first learned the charms of fiction from *Ben-Hur*."

The book's author, soldier-lawyer-statesman Lew Wallace, was overwhelmed by the religious zeal which *Ben-Hur* inspired in countless readers. An alcoholic from Kewanee, Illinois, wrote that his life was doomed until he read the novel which "brought Christ home to me as nothing else could. . . . I stood up . . . and was a man." Another man from Jamesville, Wisconsin, was moved to join the church and said he had "been blest with a new home, a new life, and a perfect piece of mind." In addition, Catholic and Protestant leaders, many of them proclaiming that the book was qualified to be a modern-day extension of the Bible, were eager to meet and confer with Wallace. The acclaim was somewhat ironic since Wallace was not a particularly religious man. In fact, he had never been affiliated with any church and he frankly stated, "I was not in the least influenced by religious sentiment. I had no convictions about God or Christ. I neither believed nor disbelieved in them." What then motivated Wallace to write one of the great Christian books of all time?

On September 19, 1876, General Wallace (a distinguished soldier in the Mexican War and in the U.S. Civil War) boarded a train in Crawfordsville, Indiana, where he lived and headed for Indianapolis to attend the Third National Soldiers' Reunion. Before long he was introduced to famed iconoclast Robert Green Ingersoll, who challenged Wallace to a debate on "God, heaven, life hereafter, Jesus Christ, and His divinity." Even though Wallace was far from a pious man, he quickly found himself defending religion as the magnetic, verbose Ingersoll logically and effectively presented his agnostic views. Wallace was no match for the irreverent Ingersoll, who was well-read on the issues and had become famous for his uncompromising, somewhat shocking beliefs. As Wallace described Ingersoll: "He was in prime mood; and, beginning, his ideas turned to speech, flowing like a heated river. His manner of putting things was marvelous; and as the Wedding Guest was held by the glittering eye of the Ancient Mariner, I sat spellbound, listening to a medley of argument, eloquence, wit, satire, audacity, irreverence, poetry, brilliant antitheses, and pungent excoriation of believers in God, Christ, and Heaven, the like of which I had never heard. He surpassed himself, and that is saying a great deal."

When the train arrived in Indianapolis, the two men went their separate ways, but Wallace remained affected by the intense debate. As he walked alone through the dark, gaslit streets of the city, he resolved to take a deeper look into the religious question. Years later he recalled that monumental decision: "I was ashamed of myself and make haste now to declare that the mortification of pride I then endured, or if it be preferred, the punishment of spirit, ended in a resolution to study the whole matter, if only for the gratification there might be in having convictions of one kind or another."

At the time, Wallace was working on a short story about the birth of Christ which he hoped to serialize in a magazine. Instead he decided to use the story as the opening scene for a full-length novel that would study the life and times of Christ, ending with the Savior's crucifixion. The bulk of the book would focus on the religious and political beliefs of the Romans and Jews during the Christian era. The two major fictional characters in the book, a Jewish hero and a Roman villain, were plucked from an incomplete novel Wallace had been working on since 1874. After the Ingersoll encounter, the short story and the unfinished novel were fused together to become "A Tale of the Christ."

For the next seven years Wallace lost himself in his majestic story. He poured over innumerable history, religious, and map books. Determined to be historically accurate, he was obsessed with the geography of Jerusalem and surrounding areas (where most of the action takes place) as well as the fine points concerning dress, customs, dialect—even animals and vegetation. (Apparently his devotion to detail proved worthwhile, for many years later when he was able to trace the life of his hero Ben-Hur from Bethany to Jerusalem, he concluded, "I find no reason for making a single change in the text of the book.") While most of the book was written in Crawfordsville, when possible in the shade of a stately old beech tree, Wallace completed the book in March 1880, in Santa Fe where he resided while governor of the territory of New Mexico. When the final draft (written in purple ink to symbolize Lent, the season of penitence before Easter) was ready, he personally took it to Harper & Brothers, a prestigious publishing company in New York. While most executives at the company were enthusiastic about *Ben-Hur*, they were skeptical about the idea of humanizing Christ, making him a character in a work of fiction. Wallace, however, was a persuasive man and convinced everyone that his portrait of Christ was biblically accurate and not even remotely blasphemous. When the two-hundred-thousand-word novel was published on November 12, 1880, it got off to a slow start, and the first few years showed disappointing sales. But word-of-mouth publicity intervened and soon boosted sales to heights that left Wallace—who expected to make $100 a year from both *Ben-Hur* and a previously published novel, *The Fair God*—astounded but exhilarated. At the age of fifty-eight Wallace reflected on his accomplishments in a letter to his wife Susan: "I have tried many things in the course of the drama—the law, soldiering, politics, authorship, and lastly, diplomacy—and if I may pass judgment upon the success achieved in each, it seems now that when I sit down finally in the old man's gown and slippers, helping the cat to keep the fireplace warm, I shall look back upon *Ben-Hur* as my best performance. . . ."

A Tongue-in-Beak Defense of Woody Woodpecker

ON AUGUST 29, 1941, cartoonist Walter Lantz and his wife had just settled into an idyllic cottage at Sherwood Lake, California, for the start of their honeymoon when a persistent, energetic woodpecker began to stir up an ungodly racket. He refused to be scared away and continued his assault on the cottage, making his way through the roof with no problem. While pursuing the noisemaker, Walter Lantz may have sacrificed a quiet honeymoon, but he gained a great deal more.

The Lantzes named the feathered intruder Woody Woodpecker and tried to convince dubious executives at Universal Studios that a new star had been born. "They told me I ought to have my head examined," Lantz later recalled. "They said he's noisy, raucous, obnoxious; he'll never go." But Lantz won the argument, put his pencils to work, and soon Woody appeared on the big screen. Today Woody Woodpecker cartoons are popular worldwide—showing in the movie theaters of seventy-two countries and on television in sixty countries. The cartoons are dubbed for the foreign market, but Woody's five-note wacky laugh, done for more than forty years by Grace Lantz, remains unchanged.

The Screaming Cure

IN JANUARY 1967, Dr. Arthur Janov, a psychologist and psychiatric social worker, developed a new treatment called Primal Therapy for psychological and psychosomatic disorders. Up until that time Janov, a native Californian, had been practicing conventional methods of treatment for seventeen years, but was not satisfied with the results. As he later stated: "I seemed to be doing a patch-up job. Whenever a leak appeared in a patient's defense system, I was there like the legendary little Dutch boy." But an incident involving a twenty-two-year-old college student during a group therapy session changed the course of his professional career. Three years later he described the incident in his best-selling book, *The Primal Scream: Primal Therapy—the Cure for Neurosis*:

He was not psychotic, nor was he what is termed hysteric; he was a poor student, withdrawn, sensitive, and quiet. During a lull in our group therapy session, he told us a story about a man named Ortiz who was currently doing an act on the London stage in which he paraded around in diapers drinking bottles of milk. Throughout his number, Ortiz is shouting "Mommy! Daddy! Mommy! Daddy!" at the top of his lungs. At the end of his act he vomits. Plastic bags are passed out, and the audience is requested to follow suit.

Danny's fascination with the act impelled me to try something elementary, but which previously had escaped my notice. I asked him to call out, "Mommy! Daddy!" Danny refused, saying that he couldn't see the sense in such a childish act, and frankly, neither could I. But I persisted, and finally he gave in. As he began, he became noticeably upset. Suddenly he was writhing on the floor in agony. His breathing was rapid, spasmodic; "Mommy! Daddy!" came out of his mouth almost involuntarily in loud screeches. He appeared to be in a coma or hypnotic state. The writhing gave way to small convulsions, and finally he released a piercing, deathlike scream that rattled the walls of my office. The entire episode lasted only a few minutes, and neither Danny nor I had any idea what had happened. All he could say afterward was: "I made it! I don't know what, but I can *feel*!"

This incident, Janov says, marked the beginning of Primal Therapy. Its theory is simple: An infant is born into the world with basic biological and emotional needs (that is, to be fed, to be loved). If parents fulfill these needs, a child will grow up healthy. However, if parents fail to carry out their responsibilities, the child becomes deprived and suffers Primal Pains which are unconsciously repressed. These pains can cause neurosis, and the neurosis can be cured only by reliving the traumas of infancy and reexperiencing the original pain. The reliving, or "Primal," can be accompanied by weeping, writhing, and vomiting. It often culminates with a Primal Scream, followed by "a relaxed feeling of well-being." And, as Janov says in the booklet that is distributed to potential patients, "Repressed early feelings do not disappear. They remain trapped inside and build up a lasting tension throughout the body. This tension drives a person into a continual struggle to symbolically fulfill his childhood needs and frequently brings on depression and anxiety. Every aspect of his life may suffer—from his work, to his relationships with friends and family, to his overall state of mental and physical health. . . . Primal Therapy, therefore, helps a person by encouraging the buried hurts to the surface so they can at last be faced, felt, understood, and learned from."

Janov, the author of seven books that support and expand upon his theories, has established a Primal Institute in Los Angeles. Treatment can require a year or more, and the patients are required to spend at least six months in the vicinity of the institute. During the first three weeks of intensive therapy, patients are asked to be "completely free of any job, school, or family obligations." After that, individual appointments, as well as group therapy sessions, are scheduled as needed. In addition, the institute offers follow-up retreats, a "buddy-system" program, seminars, and other special events.

From the start, Janov's theory, as well as his methods, have been under attack from members of the medical establishment. His critics are astonished by the list of ailments that advocates of Primal Therapy claim can be cured by Janov's treatment: alcoholism, drug addiction, sexual disorders, stuttering, asthma, stomach ulcers, ulcerative colitis, and more. In addition, Janov claims his therapy lowers blood pressure, pulse rate, and body temperature, thus prolonging human life. He even goes so far as to say that Primal Therapy could eventually reduce the population of mental hospitals and prisons; it could even bring about an end to war.

To counterattack his critics who claim that his theory, therapy, and cure rates are not scientifically valid, he points to his Primal Research Laboratory—with programs in neurophysiology, biochemistry, and psychology—and to his academic affiliation with Antioch College where his therapists are trained. But the skeptics remain unconvinced. As one noted research psychiatrist in Washington, D.C., wrote in a scathing appraisal of Primal Therapy: "If it is not a scientific system, then what is Primal Therapy? It is a religion, pure and simple, as are many of the other therapies being huckstered to the American intelligentsia. It has a leader whose authority cannot be questioned, for the leader offers Truth. . . . Arthur Janov, then, is pure American camp."

But Janov is undaunted as he continues to take his message to the public. Handsome and charismatic, his soft-spoken and commonsense approach remains persuasive and comforting to his patients. While his opponents continue to complain, Janov continues to write, to lecture, and to philosophize: "Primal people represent a new kind of human being, perhaps the first individuals in thousands of years of human life who can feel and who can grasp the meaning of feeling and its relevance to human existence."

RCA Victor and the Fat Fox Terrier

NIPPER, a fox terrier born in or near Bristol, England, in 1884, was sent to live with artist Francis Barraud when Barraud's brother died in the 1890s. The dog was the inspiration for one of the most famous trademarks in the world.

One day Barraud played a record on his "talking machine." As the music came out of the machine's morning glory trumpet, Nipper quizzically cocked his head to listen to the sounds. Barraud decided to paint the heart-catching sight. His painting, which he titled "His Master's Voice," differed from the final version most of us know: It depicted Nipper in his pose before the record player, while in the background his dead master lay in a coffin. To highlight the macabre painting, Barraud changed the black horn to a brass one; then, at the suggestion of an executive from London's Gramophone company, he replaced the cylinder-type machine with a disc phonograph. After persuading Barraud to dispense with the coffin, the Gramophone Company bought the painting and its copyright for 100 pounds sterling. In 1901, the Victor Talking Machine Company acquired U.S. rights to the use of Nipper. The painting was featured in a center-spread ad for Victor in the *Saturday Evening Post* for April 25, 1913.

The Gramophone Company prized the original painting. Company firemen had orders to take it down from the wall of the director's board room and carry it out in case of a fire. For most of the rest of his life, Barraud made a living copying "His Master's Voice" in watercolor and oils for the workers at Gramophone Company and Victor. Late in life he was pensioned. Nipper died at age eleven in 1895 and was buried under a mulberry tree behind Mayall's Photographic Works at Kingston-on-Thames.

When RCA acquired Victor Talking Machine Company in 1929, they also took on Nipper. Since then his likeness has been reproduced in the millions—on phonograph records, salt-and-pepper shakers, hooked rugs, china, belt buckles, mirrors, key chains, neckties, coin banks, T-shirts, and beach towels. He has been modeled in snow, plastic, papier-mâché, bronze, and sterling silver. In 1915, four stained-glass windows, each 14½ feet in diameter and showing Nipper and the phonograph, were installed in the Victor Talking Machine Company tower in Camden, New Jersey. The windows, lit at night, were a landmark on the Delaware River waterfront for fifty-four years. They are now divided up between the Smithsonian, Widener Hall In Pennsylvania, Pennsylvania State University, and RCA.

In the 1930s, twenty thousand images of Nipper, enough to fill fifty freight cars, were reproduced in papier-mâché in eleven-inch and thirteen-inch heights and given to RCA record and phonograph dealers for display in stores. Some dealers used Nipper as a sidewalk salesman by putting loudspeakers in his chest to beam the latest hits to the passersby.

The world's biggest Nipper weighs four tons and stands 25½ feet high. After traveling in five sections from Chicago to Albany on railroad flatcars, it was erected on top of the RTA (RCA distributor) Building in Albany, New York, in 1954. The steel-skeletoned statue is coated with weather-resistant materials. The people of Albany affectionately call it "Top Dog of Albany." In its right ear is a flashing beacon to alert low-flying planes, and pigeons build nests under its chin.

Nipper is still used as an official trademark by RCA on company trucks, television sets and television cameras. Not only that—Nipper, dead nearly a century, still gets fan mail.

Big Brothers of America

ONE SATURDAY MORNING in July 1903, Irvin F. Westheimer, a twenty-three-year-old tycoon, looked out the window of his office at his father's distillery in Cincinnati. The sight he saw—of a boy and a scruffy-looking dog searching garbage cans for food—changed his life and the lives of millions of children. As he described it, "I said to myself, 'God did not create all men equal.' I put on my hat—all properly dressed young men wore hats in those days—went down to the alley, and introduced myself to the boy. His name was Tom and his dog was named Gyp. The boy was frightened at first, but I took him to lunch." This simple act—an adult befriending a disadvantaged child—became the symbol of one of this country's great service organizations: Big Brothers/Big Sisters of America.

Westheimer's kindness did not stop with lunch. He helped Tom's mother find a better job and befriended her son. More than that, he persuaded his Cincinnati friends, mostly Jewish businessmen, to follow his example.

Meanwhile, in New York in 1904, Colonel Ernest Coulter, clerk of the Children's Court, quite independently began a Big Brother program for fatherless boys who came to court. It was one of the first juvenile delinquency prevention programs in the United States. Four years later, Mrs. W. K. Vanderbilt started Big Sisters, under the direction of Mrs. Willard Parker, to work with court-referred delinquent girls.

In 1915, Westheimer moved permanently to Cincinnati, where he headed Westheimer Investment Brokers. After his company merged with Hayden, Stone in 1963, he went into retirement—from business, not philanthropy.

When the New York group of Big Brothers was chartered by Congress in 1958, it was integrated racially and religiously, and in 1977, Big Brothers and Big Sisters merged into Big Brothers/Big Sisters of America. The group continues to provide its simple service—matching adults and children who need what an adult can give. The two meet four to six hours a week for a minimum of a year to help the child over the rough spots and troubles of childhood. Unlike the original New York group, the children are not necessarily delinquent. Neither are they necessarily neglected by their parent or parents. Instead, they have a special need for adult companionship from someone outside their immediate family.

Westheimer died December 31, 1980, at the age of 101. Big Brothers/Big Sisters then numbered 168,000 boys and girls.

10. Creative Thievery

Everything seems to be grist for the creator's mill—no matter how far-fetched. Yes, creators steal, but they also transform the plunder into something so new that they cannot truly be accused of thievery.

Are you aware of the less-than-grand beginnings of our national anthem? Did you know that a cartoon series celebrating the ridiculous originated in serious thoughts about a piece of serious scientific equipment used at a university? At least one cartoon character bears little resemblance to his pulp fiction model. A beautiful European dream city is tackily memorialized in a California resort town.

Often the borrower makes only a few major changes in what he has borrowed. For example, take Vaseline, which originated in the oil fields of Pennsylvania. A newspaper story inspired a best-seller and movie that match it in its ability to arouse fascinated horror, but went beyond it in characterization and art. The burr stripped to an essential characteristic—hooks—served in the design of an extremely useful fastening device.

Architects modeled two great buildings after well-designed but strange objects—a grapefruit half and a lily pad. The sight of mighty industry at work inspired a toy set.

In art and technology, even thievery can be creative.

Venice in a Duck Marsh

ON a barren salt marsh visited ordinarily only by ducks and those who hunted them, reeking with a swampy smell of decaying vegetation, whining with mosquitoes, visionary entrepreneur Abbott Kinney superimposed a dream city. Here, seventeen miles from Los Angeles, on the shore of the Pacific, he would build a city modeled after Venice, Italy. It would have canals, culture, and architecture like that of its archetype. What arrogance! Venice, the "Queen of the Adriatic," more than fifteen hundred years old, was called by French ambassador Philippe de Comines (c. 1447–c. 1511) "the most triumphant city I have ever seen." Its fantastic and whimsical buildings with their Byzantine spires, domes, and filigree, with their colonnades and arcades, were masterpieces built over centuries by architects known throughout the world. Kinney planned a few pavilions, a pier, and some three-story wooden hotels.

Yet it is easy to imagine young Abbott Kinney on a world tour in the late 1800s, drifting on the Grand Canal and staring down into the shimmering mirror of water where reflected marble quivered, turned ephemeral, danced in depths colored fantastically by a Venetian sunset. It would be beautiful enough for him to romantically ignore the garbage and swear never to forget the grandeur. And to try to reproduce it somewhere else.

Born in New Jersey in 1850 to a wealthy family, Kinney was educated in Europe, was fluent in several languages, and had already gone broke in the stock market once when he joined his brothers' tobacco manufacturing company, which made Sweet Caporal cigarettes. In 1878, he took a three-year world tour in search of a climate that would alleviate his poor health and insomnia. Finally he docked in San Francisco, intending to go east but was held up by snowpack that blocked rail travel in the Sierra Nevada. To while away the time, he traveled to the Sierra Madre Inn near Los Angeles. Because no rooms were available, he spent the night in the parlor, where he played billiards, then fell asleep on the game table. He called it the "best damn night's sleep" he had had and decided to stay in southern California. In 1884, he married Margaret Thornton, daughter of a supreme court justice. The couple went to live in Santa Monica.

Kinney was an old-fashioned liberal. He helped to establish free public libraries, allied himself with citrus growers to break up a "fruit trust" in orange and lemon prices, investigated the plight of the mission Indians with Helen Hunt Jackson (author of *Ramona*), and worked to preserve Yosemite. In his lifetime he was mentioned as a candidate for senator and president, though he never ran for office. A friend said of him, "Give him an oil lamp, a sack of tobacco, and a good heavy book, and he is satisfied." It was true. Kinney was a lover of arts, culture, and astronomy, and an expert in botany and horticulture. He did not own a car, horse, or house. His clothes were old and comfortable. He was a tall, handsome man, with blue-gray eyes and a reddish beard.

Though Kinney didn't worship money, he was shrewd and knew how to make it. His successful wheeling and dealing in real estate resulted in his ownership of the property south of Navy Street that later became Venice.

In 1904, work began on the dream city. As with most of Kinney's schemes, his plan for the canals of Venice had a hard, practical core. How else to drain a marsh? The fan-shaped design developed after a couple of false starts. In August, workmen and mules began excavating tons of dirt to dig the Grand Canal, which connected to the lagoon. It was half a mile long, seventy feet wide, and four feet deep, a short ditch compared to its prototype. The other seven miles of canals were connected to the ocean with two thirty-inch pipes, so that the canals would be flushed by tidal waters twice a day. Over the canals, builders erected wooden bridges decorated with reliefs depicting sea serpents and animals; they were designed by Felix Peano, an Italian sculptor.

On the main street facing Lion Canal (now Windward Avenue) was a row of three-story hotels, reminiscent of Venetian buildings with their arcades, colonnades, and reliefs of the lion of Saint Mark. On the northeast corner of Ocean Front Walk and the canal stood Saint Mark's Hotel. It was supposedly a loose imitation of the doge's palace, built during the Renaissance, a fairy-tale edifice from whose windows convicts were hung. The California namesake, built of wood, three-stories high, was to last only a few decades before it was torn down.

A miniature railroad circled Kinney's town. Its president was eight-year-old Carleton Kinney. A sixteen hundred-foot-long pier jutted out into the Pacific from the end of the Grand Canal. Alongside the pier floated a restaurant built like a Spanish galleon, and at its end was Kinney's pride and joy: a thirty-five hundred-seat auditorium which he hoped would be the seat of West Coast culture.

The city was destined to open in the summer of 1905. In March, a storm destroyed the pier, auditorium, and a pavilion. Kinney, after receiving federal approval to build a breakwater, carted in seventy tons of granite by rail to accomplish the task. Everything was rebuilt by herculean efforts, and Venice opened on time.

On June 30, 1905, Margaret Kinney turned a wheel on a valve and seawater started flowing into the canals. Light blazed from seventeen hundred lamps along the streets and canals.

The true grand opening came on the Fourth of July when forty thousand people, close to half the population of Los Angeles, arrived on the green cars of the Los Angeles Pacific Line railroad, fare twenty-five cents. Italian gondoliers imported by Kinney from Italy poled passengers in imported gondolas over the waters of the canals. A chorus of four hundred children sang "Hail, Columbia" and "Battle Hymn of the Republic."

Camels took visitors for a ride for a price. And the nearly five hundred lots that Kinney had put up for sale were going fast.

Kinney's ultimate dream had been not to make money, though he was certainly not averse to it, but to provide culture in his auditorium with its pipe organ (it could play a bird chorus) and curtain designed by Peano. That first year the auditorium hosted the Chicago Symphony, opera singers, the amazing Sarah Bernhardt, lectures by Helen Hunt Jackson, readings from *Macbeth*—and total failure. By the year's end, the culture program was $16,000 in debt. Visitors to Kinney's Folly wanted to ride in gondolas and have fun. Culture was not what they came for. Kinney shut the auditorium down and scrapped his plans for a botanical garden and for a college modeled after an ancient Greek academy.

Kinney's dream died.

But Venice-by-the-Sea (which was officially named in 1911) was an enormous success. Visitors and residents loved its bathhouse and seventy-foot-square plunge, its gondolas, and especially its amusements—like the honky-tonk Midway-Plaisance, where dancers did the hootchy-kootchy and shills beckoned suckers in to play at games of chance. People screamed as they rode in the roller coaster, Tom Prior's Race through the Clouds.

Through the years, Old Bill the Pelican, who patrolled the boardwalk, was witness to many attractions: pioneer surfer Duke Kahanmoku on his big wooden surfboard barreling in on the Venice waves, Charlie Chaplin making one of his first movies (*Kid Auto Races*), Barney Oldfield winning the accident-ridden first (and last) Annual Venice Grand Prix auto race, Chief Whitefeather hanging from a flying airplane by his long braid in a barnstorming exhibition.

During Prohibition, now known for "vice," Venice sprouted speakeasies reached by tunnels. The Citizen's Protective League railed against the bathing beauty contests, the Yama Yama girl parades, and the mock bullfights. The canals, which had not been flushed by the tides, were filling with algae, silt, and garbage. The miniature railroad shut down.

Evangelist Aimee Semple McPherson disappeared from Venice Beach one day in 1926. A month later, a solemn memorial service for her was held on the beach, and flowers were strewn on the sea. They had hardly sunk beneath the waves when McPherson showed up alive and well in Phoenix.

(Venice, Italy, a city of merchant princes, was also at times a pleasure city. Bold-painted ladies in low-cut dresses of luxurious jeweled cloth paraded its sidewalks, and Dante spoke of the "unbridled lasciviousness of Venetians," who indulged often in earthly pleasures and were known for their carnivals. In 1491, troops from Crete jousted on the frozen ice of the Grand Canal to entertain the populace.)

In 1925, Venice merged with Los Angeles, mostly to get street lights and other amenities, and Los Angeles promptly began to fill the canals north of Venice Boulevard with dirt, in spite of the protests of outraged citizens. Someone struck oil in 1929, and then derricks decorated the landscape. Sewage contaminated the beach. Gambling ships anchored offshore. The city was becoming a slum.

Venice's Renaissance came in a guise Kinney might not have recognized: the Beats, with their poetry readings, iconoclastic art, Zen Buddhism, and jazz. They built coffeehouses such as the Forty Thieves, Venice West, and the Gas House. The Gas House was owned by attorney Al Matthews and a six-foot, seven-inch artist, Eric "Big Daddy" Nord, who liked to "paint" nudes by swabbing women with paint and then pressing them into the canvas. Though the owners of the Gas House were supported by Christopher Isherwood, Mort Sahl, and Igor Stravinsky, they were unable to prize an entertainment license out of the Los Angeles Police Commission, were harassed by the vice squad and fire department, and finally closed down in 1960.

But art flourished in Venice. At one time murals on Venice walls, like Terry Shoonhoven's "Venice in the Snow," numbered about sixty. (Giorgione, at twenty-nine, first attracted attention in Renaissance Italy with a mural on a warehouse wall near the Rialto Bridge.)

Artists in residence in Venice, California, in the last few decades include Billy Al Bengston, Robert Rauschenberg, Ron Cooper, Larry Bell, Claire Falkenstein, De Wain Valentine, Alexis Smith, and Charles Eames. All part of a highly respected avant-garde, their works grace museums throughout the world. And while they cannot as yet lay claim to the fame and genius of a Titian or Bellini or Veronese, they, too, celebrate luscious women and sensuous colors. Ron Cooper creates photographs with metal-plate lithography and computer science, while Titian stuck with his brush, but their visions are not all that different.

(At the 1978 Biennale, an international art show in the public gardens of Venice, Italy, one of the most popular exhibits was a work by Antonio Paradiso which consisted of a Lombard bull and a fake cow made of a car chassis draped in a cow skin. A journalist alerted the Italian animal humane society, which termed it "an exploitive example of coerced masturbation." The bull, allowed to mount once, symbolically ejaculated in the dirt. Outrageousness still lives in the "Queen of the Adriatic.")

The hotels in the Pacific Venice have been mostly torn down. Ducks paddle in the remaining canals. On Ocean Front Walk, facing the ocean, roller skaters do their razzle-dazzle, improvisational drama troops act on the sand, street musicians wail tunes for a handout, and poets sell mimeographed poetry books. Along the beach is a living fantasy: drug freaks, tourists, hot dog vendors, crazies, beggars, and winos. It is a pageant of light, surface, texture.

And did Abbott Kinney, in some grotesque fashion, finally realize his dream? Venice, California, is a ramshackle parody of its namesake, as if seen in a reducing and distorting glass of a funhouse mirror. And yet . . .

Velcro: The Persistence of a Burr

ONE MORNING in the late 1940s, Swiss inventor George de Mestral went hunting in the Jura Mountains near Nyon. With him was his dog, an Irish pointer. Both brushed up against burdocks, which left burrs in the dog's fur and on the man's wool pants. De Mestral attempted to pull off the burrs, but they resisted. Anyone else might have cursed or shrugged, but de Mestral wondered why they clung with such tenacity. When he returned home, he examined them under a microscope and saw hundreds of tiny hooks that snagged into the flat matt of wool and fur. It occurred to him that as a fastener the burr was without equal—and, unlike a zipper, did not jam or catch.

Although he worked for years as an inventor, supported on an estate by a banker friend, he did not attack the idea for the fastener until many years later. A friend of the banker loaned de Mestral $150,000 to work on the idea. The inventor traveled to a textile center in Lyon, France, to find a way to manufacture the burr-inspired device. The only one of the six loom manufacturers he visited who took him seriously was Jacques Muller, who tried to design a loom with two ribbons to make a prototype of cotton; one ribbon had hooks, the other loops. It worked, but many problems remained. How could the hooks on machine-made tape be kept in line? How could hooks be produced? De Mestral tried heat, steam, ultrasonic sound, and finally infrared, which worked, to make loops of nylon thread. To find glue to set the loops, he consulted with experts from London and the United States.

One stubborn problem would not yield: how to cut every other nylon loop into a hook *by machine*. "This is one of the things I failed on over and over," de Mestral told an interviewer. His backer was about to stop financing him. Not until he went to an alpine hunting cabin to meditate did the solution occur to him: a machine based on a barber's thinning shears. On the way home, he bought a pair. The solution worked.

In 1956, Velcro S. A. was formed in Switzerland. A year later, French-born American Jean Rivaud organized and launched the business—Velcro Industries Ltd. (then Velok Ltd.)—with United States and Canadian rights for Velcro. By 1959, there were enough looms in operation to make one million yards of tape. In 1969, the company obtained worldwide rights.

Considered "the father of Velcro," de Mestral lives in a chateau in the village of San Saphorin near Lausanne and still hunts in the Jura Mountains. In his seventies, he has a broad face, lively blue eyes, and an even livelier wit. He says, quoting a French industrialist friend, "There are two ways to ruin—women and invention, with invention providing the more certain route." Though he has had the luck he deems necessary for every inventor, without his persistence Velcro might have remained just a good idea.

Velcro, the noisy fastener, is jam-proof, non-rusting, lightweight, and washable. It can be sterilized, glued, heat-sealed, stitched, stapled, and nailed. It sticks to almost all materials, including glass. The process by which it is made is one of the most sophisticated in the world.

Velcro can be used for camping equipment and in subarctic conditions, because it continues to function in cold weather. It is found in medical facilities (on blood pressure cuffs, cervical collars, and artificial hearts) and on military clothing and supplies. Astronauts use it to attach food packets to the wall and to keep their boots adhering to the floor.

Rube Goldberg and the Barodik

WEBSTER'S DICTIONARY defines "Rube Goldberg" as "accomplishing by extremely complex, roundabout means what seemingly could be done simply." The man behind the definition, Reuben Lucius Goldberg, born in San Francisco in 1883, was one of America's most versatile cartoonists. He began as a sports cartoonist but soon moved into mainstream humor, creating more than sixty cartoon series that appeared in hundreds of American newspapers. His most popular comic strips were "Foolish

Questions," "Boob McNutt," "Mike and Ike—They Look Alike," "I'm the Guy," and "The Inventions of Professor Butts." By the end of his career he had turned to political cartoons. His most acclaimed cartoon, "Peace Today," which shows a family precariously balanced atop an atomic bomb with world control on one side and world destruction on the other, won a Pulitzer Prize in 1948.

Goldberg, as suggested by the dictionary definition of his name, is best remembered for his elaborate, wacky inventions. Most of them were created with the help of the character Professor Lucifer Gorgonzola Butts. The ingenious professor could turn any simple task—like scratching a mosquito bite, swatting a fly, or sharpening a pencil—into a multistage process. His gadgetry boasted gears, wheels, pulleys, springs, magnets, hoses, mirrors, spigots, disks, saws, cups, rods, chains, corks, and ropes. And he rarely left out people or animals—from policemen, midgets, dentists, tramps, and dwarfs to hyenas, lovebirds, bears, woodpeckers, mice, sardines, crocodiles, whales, "peaceful" cockroaches, and Russian dancing bugs. The operating instructions for each outlandish device often consisted of more than fifteen maneuvers and were written in a very serious, trenchant style that only added to the hilarity.

The absurdly complicated inventions for simple chores were Goldberg's satiric commentary on the machine age, on the American public's fascination with, and naive trust in, the wonders of technology. He always contended that his clever contraptions were "symbols of man's capacity for exerting maximum effort to accomplish minimal results." While his only aim was to get a laugh, Goldberg did inadvertently predict several inventions years before their time, including a garage door opener, an olive extractor, and self-washing windows. Even so, he was astonished by the popularity of Professor Butts and his army of screwy devices. He once said, "The machine-age slant on human frailties has grown to be widely accepted out of all proportion to my original conception. I am credited with any machine that looks crazy. People coming into my studio expect me to be hanging from the chandelier."

To describe the apparatus Professor Butts used in the cartoon "Cooling a Plate of Soup," Goldberg begins with a chef who spills a large plate of scalding chili onto a porcupine. The chili burns the porcupine (sitting under a cane-bottomed chair), causing it to raise its quills. The sharp quills shoot through the chair, upon which sits the restaurant owner. He is propelled into the air and hits a shelf which is suspended above him. On the shelf is a beer stein. It falls and pulls a string that activates a bellows. The bellows inflates a large gas bag beneath a huge tray of dishes. As the size of the gas bag increases, it knocks over the dishes. The dishes crash to the floor, creating a ruckus that scares an alley cat. The cat races up and down a five-tiered circular metal fence. At the bottom of the fence is the bowl of soup. When the cat finally rests at the bottom of the fence, he huffs and puffs so hard that the soup cools off.

How did Goldberg dream up his gallery of cockeyed inventions? They stemmed from his college days as an engineering student at the University of California at Berkeley. An eccentric physics professor, Freddy Slate, started it all. Endowed with a red beard, egg-shaped head, and deadpan manner, Slate had but one mission in life: to weigh the earth with his personally crafted machine, the Barodik. Goldberg described the magnificent machine as "pipes and tubes and wires and chemical containers and springs and odd pieces of weird equipment, which made it look like a dumping ground for outmoded dentists' furnishings." Using the amazing concoction, each student had six months to figure out the earth's weight. No one succeeded, but everyone was awarded an A for effort. And the Barodik inspired a pen-and-ink genius.

The Airline Terminal Inspired by a Grapefruit

THE FAMOUS ARCHITECT Eero Saarinen (1910–1961) believed that buildings should express a bold unity. This philosophy shows in his design of the breathtaking arch of the Jefferson Westward Expansion Memorial at St. Louis. Reflected in the waters of the Mississippi, it soars 630 feet in the air. He built model after model to get it right. His buildings are very different from one another, true to site and spirit, yet each is a harmonious whole: the IBM building in Rochester, Minnesota, "eyeing the valley like a motionless eagle"; the General Motors Technical Center in Warren, Michigan, known as the "Industrial Versailles"; and all the rest.

Saarinen was born in Finland, the son of Eliel Saarinen, another famous architect. When Eero was twelve, he won a Swedish matchstick design contest, and his family moved to the United States, where his father set up the Cranbrook Academy of Art, a Bauhaus-like community of artists and craftsmen, in Michigan. Eero studied sculpture at the Grand Chaumiere in Paris and graduated with a degree in architecture from Yale University. After two years in Europe on a fellowship, he returned to the United States and joined his father's firm. His original training in sculpture may have contributed to his philosophy toward architecture and certainly influenced his sideline of chair design. He created the pedestal chair "to clear up the slum of legs in the U.S. house," as well as the famous womb chair.

Eero's friend, sculptor Charles Eames, said of him, "But with all of Eero's highly refined skills, he remained always like a puppy with big feet." He was unself-conscious. For example, he whipped out a list of recommended wine vintages from his pocket to check against wine lists at fancy restaurants. His sense of humor was legendary. He said of the functional school of architecture, "Strict functionalism was a necessary purgative, but, after all, there is nothing esthetic about an enema."

In 1959, he was invited with forty other architects to the University of California at Berkeley to participate in creativity tests, one of which involved working alone in a cubicle to construct a design from colored tiles. After the test, he said, he talked to fellow architect Philip Johnson: "I asked Philip what he did with the tiles, and he said, 'Oh, those colors were awful. I threw the colored tiles away and used only the black and white. What did you do, Eero?' I told Philip I had used only the white, and he was so jealous."

"You have to chase the problems," Saarinen said. "Once you have caught them, you can always solve them." To do the chasing, he often worked at night, littering his offices with Old Granger tobacco. If his draftsman found a heap of tobacco on his drafting board, he knew his work had undergone real scrutiny.

In 1956, Saarinen was commissioned to design a building for TWA at what is now New York's Kennedy Airport. As was his custom, he took a group of his colleagues to the site itself. There, using stopwatches and notebooks to record information, they collected data on plane arrivals and departures, the flow of passengers through the terminals, and other patterns of movement. The problem became clear. "The architecture would express the excitement of travel and reveal the terminal not as a static enclosed space, but a place of movement," said Saarinen.

The first design Saarinen created for TWA did not suit him; he called it "pigeon-toed, the Leonardo da Vinci flying machine." But he kept working, relying on models of cardboard and wire and other materials, instead of traditional flat drawings, to capture the curved shapes he was trying to envision.

One morning, in keeping with his unpretentious ability to use the materials at hand, he saw a solution in a most unlikely object—the curved shell of his breakfast grapefruit. As his wife watched, he turned it over and began carving arches in it. Then he carried the finished product off to work with him to add to the other models that contributed to the final design of the TWA roof—four intersecting barrel vaults like an umbrella over the passenger area.

Saarinen died tragically of brain cancer at fifty-one. Much of his best work was unfinished, including the TWA terminal. When it was completed in 1964, architectural magazines described it as a "bird in flight," "a totality of fluid form curving and circling within itself." The grapefruit wasn't mentioned.

A Drinking Song in Disguise:
The Story of "The Star-Spangled Banner"

IN the very early hours of Tuesday, September 13, 1814, thirty-four-year-old American lawyer Francis Scott Key, aboard a small cartel boat that bobbed in the shadow of the British frigate *Surprise*, watched the British navy bombard Fort McHenry, the seaport gateway to Baltimore. Key, accompanied by Colonel John S. Skinner, had been with the British for seven days, trying to persuade Vice Admiral Alexander Cochrane to free American prisoner-of-war Dr. William Beanes. Cochrane had agreed to the request, but he refused to let the Americans go until after the assault on Fort McHenry.

For twenty-three hours the British shelled the fort. The three Americans on the deck of their boat had a front-row seat to the spectacle and watched hundreds of bombs (some weighing as much as two hundred pounds) fall on the American garrison. Since the British refused to disclose information on the progress of the battle, Key had to use his telescope to search through the dense smoke and fog, hoping to see the huge American flag (32 feet by 40 feet) that flew over Fort McHenry. As the bombing continued into the night, the Americans felt reassured that the United States had not yet surrendered. Then the deafening explosions suddenly stopped. Key, Skinner, and Beanes began to worry and to pray that the Americans had not given up. Key's good friend Roger Taney (later to become Chief Justice of the United States) described the scene: "They paced the deck for the residue of the night, in painful suspense, watching with intense anxiety for the return of the day, and looking every few minutes at their watches, to see how long they must wait for it; and as soon as it dawned, and before it was light enough to see objects at a distance, their glasses were turned toward the fort, uncertain whether they should see the stars and stripes or the flag of the enemy." When he saw that the American flag was still flying, the emotionally-charged Key pulled a paper from his pocket and began to write a poem—verses conceived during the silence of the few hours before dawn.

On September 14, when the British naval commanders learned that their land forces had been defeated, they ceased fire on the fort (only four Americans were killed), boarded their wounded, and prepared to head out to sea. The cartel boat was set free and proceeded toward shore. Later that evening Key, unable to sleep in his room at the Fountain Inn in Baltimore, continued work on his poem/song. A week later, on September 21, it was published in the newspaper *The Baltimore Patriot* under the title "The Defense of Fort McHenry." Printed beneath the title was the name of a tune, "To Anacreon in Heaven," to which the poem was to be sung.

A devoted music lover and member of the glee club in Georgetown where he lived, Key was talented at composing words, not music, which is why he took the melody for his song, later to be called "The Star-Spangled Banner," from "To Anacreon in Heaven," an English drinking song. The tune, which had already been adopted to other American patriotic songs, had become very popular after Robert Treat Paine used it for his well-known song, "Adams and Liberty," in 1798. From the taverns of Georgetown to the army posts west of the Alleghenies, the tune was a familiar one.

"To Anacreon in Heaven" (words by Ralph Tomlinson, music by John Stafford Smith) was written in the 1770s for London's Anacreontic Society, a music and social club named after the ancient Greek poet Anacreon whose verses extolled the virtues of love and wine. The society, "a sprightly class of citizens," had no other purpose than to eat, drink, and fraternize. Members met about every two weeks in private rooms at the Crown and Anchor Tavern, where they enjoyed a two-hour concert followed by an elegant dinner. After indulging in numerous culinary delights, the all-male group would continue their "meeting" with more drinks, spirited conversation, and amateur entertainment provided by the members themselves (jokes, imitations, a song or two). The evening inevitably concluded with a boisterous rendering of the society's official hymn, "To Anacreon in Heaven." The first stanza of the six-stanza song:

> To Anacreon, in Heav'n, where he sat in full glee,
>   A few sons of harmony sent a petition,
> That he their inspirer and patron would be;
>   When this answer arriv'd from the jolly old Grecian—
>   Voice, fiddle, and flute,
>   No longer be mute;
> I'll lend ye my name, and inspire ye to boot;
> And, besides, I'll instruct ye, like me to intwine
>   The myrtle of Venus with Bacchus's vine.

Despite its official adoption as the national anthem in 1931, "The Star-Spangled Banner" has been the brunt of jokes and insults from music connoisseurs. The song, with its wide range of notes and complicated rhythm, is difficult for most people to sing. The *New York Herald Tribune* summed up the complaints in an editorial that claimed that the song had "words that nobody can remember, to a tune that nobody can sing." But Americans have enshrined the song, next to baseball and apple pie, even though most can only remember the first verse.

The Crystal Palace: Fit for a Frog Prince

THE CRYSTAL PALACE, a shimmering marvel of glass and wrought iron, built for the Great Exhibition of 1851 in London's Hyde Park, was a sensation. But few knew the real story behind it. Joseph Paxton, a gardener who had never studied architecture, was inspired to design the palace (the first prefabricated modular building ever built) by, of all things, a colossal lily pad.

The story began when Paxton, who worked for the Duke of Devonshire, rescued a sickly seedling of the water lily *regia Victoria* from the Royal Botanical Gardens at Kew. It languished when it was away from its native habitat in lake waters of South America, so Paxton put it in a tank and bathed it in constantly moving warm water. His ingenuity gained him a Frankenstein's monster in six months: eleven six-foot-wide leaves which, floating, could support the weight of his seven-year-old daughter. In November 1849, Paxton presented an enormous flower, the *regia's* first in England, to its namesake, tiny Queen Victoria. That year his lily produced 140 great leaves—a total of 4,000 green square feet. Twice it outgrew its tank. A man with less inventiveness and grandiosity might have run for his life, but not Paxton. He built for his plant queen an elegant glass house of his own design, based on the wonderfully engineered understructure of the lily leaf—technology copying nature. He said, "Nature has provided the leaf with longitudinal and transverse girders and supports that I, borrowing from it, have adopted in this building." He called it the Lily House.

In 1850, architects submitted 240 designs for the huge hall that was to be the centerpiece of the Great Exhibition of the Works of Industry of All Nations to be held the following year. Paxton entered the contest late. He presented a plan, on pink blotting paper, for a gigantic tiered variation on the Lily House. It was too daring for the building committee to accept immediately. While they hesitated, Paxton, who had a sophisticated grasp of the power of publicity, talked the *Illustrated London News* into printing his design. It set London's imagination on fire, and when an inspired editor of *Punch* came up with the magical title Crystal Palace for it, the public's enthusiasm mounted to a pitch the committee could not ignore. Paxton's design won.

The Palace was completed in thirty-eight weeks, its prefabricated modules bolted together floor by floor. It was a glittering transparent palace. The world fell in love with it.

Though the building was lacy and airy, it had the incredible strength of the leaf that served as its model. Withstanding even the shattering high B-flat sung by a soprano during opening ceremonies when it was moved to Sydenham after the Exhibition, it lasted for eighty-five years, succumbing to fire in 1936. The two remaining towers were demolished during World War II because they presented too clear a target for German bombers.

Chesebrough's Versatile Petroleum Jelly

VASELINE PETROLEUM JELLY, a household staple in most American homes, originated in the oil fields of Pennsylvania in 1859. In that year a twenty-two-year-old Brooklyn chemist, Robert Augustus Chesebrough, was busy building up his own company, which refined kerosene from cannel oil, when he heard of the country's first big oil strike in Titusville. Certain that the newly discovered fuel would put him out of business, he traveled to the oil fields to see if his refining skills might adapt to the petroleum industry.

As Chesebrough watched the pumps draw up the oil from the earth, he heard the oilmen complain about "rod wax," a paraffinlike residue that collected on the steel rods of the pumps. The residue had to be cleaned from the rods often so that the pumps would not malfunction. Despite their complaints about rod wax, the field workers admitted that the troublesome substance did have a major benefit: it was a soothing, healing salve for burns and cuts. Intrigued by the medicinal properties of the oil residue, Chesebrough collected samples of the rod wax and took them home with him to Brooklyn.

For eleven years he worked at refining and purifying the residue. At that time most ointments, which were made from animal greases and vegetable oils, spoiled if kept for too long a period, and Chesebrough reasoned that his nonrancid petroleum-base ointment would become a product in demand. Diligently and confidently, he transformed the rod wax into a salable commodity. To test the effectiveness of the substance, he cut, scratched, and burned his own body. When his work was completed in 1870, Chesebrough set up his first manufacturing plant for the new balm—a nonsticky, colorless, odorless, tasteless, semisolid healing wonder which he named Vaseline. Convinced of its imminent success, he gave free samples to Brooklyn's manual laborers and sent bottles of the jelly to doctors and druggists.

The less than enthusiastic response resulted in very few orders. So the ambitious young chemist hitched up a horse and buggy, filled it with one-ounce bottles of Vaseline, and headed into upper New York State. In his extensive travels through the countryside as well as the cities and towns, he gave away samples of his product, extolling its virtues. It was not long before New Yorkers started to ask their local druggists for Vaseline, and the druggists began to stock it. Chesebrough, delighted with the success of his grassroots campaign, hired twelve salesmen to carry on the horse-and-buggy marketing program in New Jersey and Connecticut. In a few years orders for Vaseline were pouring in at the rate of one jar a minute.

In 1912, when fire swept through the Equitable Life Assurance Society's headquarters in New York, large quantities of Vaseline were used to treat burn victims. Thirty years later the product was again used to treat the injured in Boston's Cocoanut Grove fire. During World War II the U.S. Army Surgeon General asked executives in the Chesebrough company to develop gauze burn pads saturated with petroleum jelly for shipment to European battlefields.

The success of Vaseline is not, however, due solely to its medicinal benefits. Consumers at home and abroad have found thousands of uses for the versatile product. Fishermen put globs of it on their hooks as bait. Women use it to remove eye makeup. Baseball players smear it on their gloves to soften the leather. Swimmers coat their bodies with it before jumping into icy waters. Housewives apply it to traverse drapery rods to make them slide more easily. Car owners dab it on automobile battery terminals to stop corrosion. Skiers put a thin layer of it on their lips to prevent chapping. Company reports claim that natives in remote jungle areas of the world once used jars of Vaseline as money because it didn't turn rancid in high temperatures.

Endorsements and praise from the famous have also enabled Vaseline sales to soar. Admiral Robert Peary took it with him on Arctic expeditions because it didn't freeze at forty degrees below zero. President Calvin Coolidge instructed his aides to rub his head with Vaseline as he ate his breakfast in bed. In 1981, *Esquire* magazine reported that Doris Day coated her body with the product at least once a week before she slipped into bed at night.

Today, Vaseline petroleum jelly, with its familiar blue-and-white label, is part of the corporate empire of Chesebrough-Pond's Inc., which markets its wide assortment of products to 140 countries around the world. Not surprisingly, Vaseline is in the forefront of company sales. Robert Chesebrough, who died in 1933, would not have been surprised. No one believed in the product more than he did. For the last thirty-five years of his life he swallowed a spoonful of Vaseline daily, believing that it could cure any number of ailments. And when he was ill, he smothered himself from head to toe with the balm. Before he died he said that his long life of ninety-six years was directly attributable to Vaseline.

An All-American Boy Invents an All-American Toy

A. C. GILBERT, inventor of the Erector Set, was the consummate achiever. An Olympic gold medal champion, toy manufacturer, and doctor (though he never practiced medicine), Gilbert possessed endless reservoirs of optimism, determination, and energy. A self-made millionaire, he enjoyed talking about his many achievements and often spoke of the merits of competition: "I love the spirit of competition. It teaches boys to do their very best in everything and to know that they cannot win unless they prepare themselves. It makes them better businessmen—it teaches them to be fair and square and always alert."

Born in Salem, Oregon, in 1884, Gilbert entered his first sports contest at the age of five or six. It was a tricycle race for which he trained for two weeks. That triumph was only the first in a long line of sports victories that earned him fifty silver cups and over one hundred medals.

By the time Gilbert was eleven, his family had moved to Moscow, Idaho. Their new home had a huge barn that A. C. converted into a gymnasium equipped with a horizontal bar, punching bag, makeshift tumbling mats, body-building weights, a boxing and wrestling ring, and even a flying trapeze. The enterprising boy invited all his friends to work out in his gym, and soon he formed the Moscow Athletic Club. Before long the persuasive A. C. talked school officials into sponsoring a track and field meet in Moscow. The young athlete organized and supervised all aspects of the meet, right down to making medals for the winners. (He punched holes in the backs of old watches, pulled colored felt through the holes, and fastened the felt with a safety pin.) The meet was a huge success, especially for A. C. who walked off with top honors in six of seven events including the strenuous shot put and hammer throw. Of his sole defeat, the youngster said: "I lost the mile run. That was the last event, and I was a little tired. I came in second. Not so good."

Gilbert's interest in athletics was equaled only by his love for magic. At seven A. C. won a set of magic tricks for selling subscriptions to a children's magazine and spent many hours in front of a mirror practicing the sleight-of-hand maneuvers. When noted magician Hermann the Great came to town, wide-eyed A. C. sat close to the stage and shot up his hand as soon as the call went out for volunteers. He was chosen, and in a state of near ecstasy helped the magician perform an array of feats that delighted the audience. At the end of the performance Hermann turned to his boy helper and said, "Well, son, don't you wish you could do things like that?" The precocious A. C. answered, "I can," and proceeded to skillfully execute a few card tricks. In front of the audience the professional praised the amateur, and A. C. walked home that night repeating, "Gilbert the Great, Gilbert the Great." At that time he had no idea that his magician's skills would help pay his way through college.

At Yale, to supplement his shoestring budget, Gilbert put together a magic show, which he performed at children's parties as well as in local nightclubs. And when he wasn't studying or pulling rabbits out of a hat, he was dazzling everyone with his prowess on the athletic fields. Not gifted with a herculean physique, Gilbert worked hard to make the best of what he had—a 5-foot, 7-inch, 135-pound body—and earned the university's coveted "Y" letter in track, gymnastics, and wrestling. In 1908, he reached the peak of his sports career when he traveled to London for the Olympic Games and came home with a gold medal in pole vaulting.

By the time graduation arrived in June 1909, Gilbert had decided to devote full time to the mail-order business he had set up earlier that year. For the next two years, with characteristic Gilbert determination, he made and sold Mysto Magic Sets from a small town outside of New Haven. But his firm showed only a small profit. To increase business, Gilbert opened a small store on Broadway in New York City. To get to New York from New Haven, he rode on the New York, New Haven, & Hartford Railroad.

In the fall of 1911 the railroad was converting from steam power to electricity. One morning, as Gilbert watched the construction crews at work, the proverbial light bulb went on in his head. He described that moment in his autobiography: "I looked out the window and saw steel girder after steel girder being erected to carry the power lines. I found it interesting to watch their progress from week to week, and most other travelers did too. It seems the most natural thing in the world that I should think about how fascinated boys might be in building things out of girders. . . ."

It was not long before Gilbert's magic company was stamping out the girders and wheels for Erector Sets. There were other construction toys on the market, but Erector boasted axles, gears, pinions, and an electric motor. Soon the company had an advertising slogan, "Hello, Boys! Make

Lots of Toys," and an official newsletter, *Erector Tips.* The free publication invited boys to send in pictures of their models and offered prizes for the most original. At that time Erector Sets ranged in price from one dollar to twenty-five dollars, with the five-dollar set being the most popular.

After the magic company changed its name to the A. C. Gilbert Company in 1916, it branched out to make new products. Among the vast array of scientific and educational toys was everything from tool chests and chemistry sets to a Hydraulic and Pneumatic Engineering Set (which enabled a child to raise sunken toy ships), a Weather Bureau (complete with aneroid barometer), an Atomic Energy Lab (with Geiger counter and uranium-bearing ore), plus sets for civil engineering, astronomy, mineralogy, and glass blowing. In addition, Gilbert bought an electric train company, American Flyer Trains, which became an important part of his toy empire. While Gilbert was proud of many of his innovative toys, the Erector Set remained his favorite. He loved to tell the story of how the first model of the Bailey Bridge, an engineering marvel of World War II, was designed by Sir Donald Bailey of the British Ministry of Supply, using a No. 10½ Erector Set.

Gilbert, as expected, became very rich. He and his wife bought a 600-acre estate in Hamden, Connecticut, which had its own game preserve of about one hundred white-tailed deer, twenty-five hundred pheasants, and scores of mallard ducks. Appropriately called "Paradise," the property also featured a dairy farm and two small lakes stocked with trout. Shortly before his death in 1961, Gilbert wrote what was to become his epitaph: "I've never worked at anything that wasn't fun. If I had my life to live over, I don't think I'd change it. Except maybe to take up mountain climbing."

Spiderman: Genesis of the Web Slinger

IN THE 1950s, teenager Stan Lee was fascinated by a character named the Spider, hero of a pulp magazine called *The Spider, Master of Men.* The sophisticated Spider, in his slouch hat, did not have superhuman powers; instead, he felled his enemies by an old-fashioned method—a punch in the mouth. But, like all good heroes, he left his mark: on his finger was an engraved ring that pressed an impression of a spider on the victim's flesh.

When Lee grew up, he did not forget his idol. As a writer for *Marvel Comics*, he longed to create a character different from the usual superhero. His offbeat hero would be a flawed teenager and sometime loser—and his memories of the Spider proved a perfect source. Of course he altered the character: not only were there changes in age and personality, but Lee's hero had superhuman spiderlike powers.

When Lee suggested the idea to a Marvel executive, he was told that people are repelled by spiders and that there was no place for the character in the mainstream strips. After much work, Lee finally found a place for his Spiderman in the last issue of *Amazing Adult Fantasy*, which was going under because superhero strips were outselling it.

Surprisingly, the strip was a big hit, and Spiderman was off on his fabulous career. He became a cult hero—with his teenaged identity crisis, his sweet Aunt May, his love problems, and his fantastic spider powers. Evidently, the executive was dead wrong; evidently, not everyone hates spiders.

The Exorcist

IN 1949, when he was a junior at Georgetown University, William Peter Blatty read an account of an exorcism in the *Washington Post*. Written by reporter Bill Brinkley, the story involved a fourteen-year-old boy in Mt. Rainier, a Maryland town in the suburbs of Washington, D.C. The case of demonic possession and the resulting exorcism (the first exorcism to be performed in that area in more than 100 years) kept Blatty spellbound. As he later recalled, "The reports and the rumors truly captured me. I had trust in my Catholic beliefs, but it was then more a hope than a true conviction. Like [Doubting] Thomas, I had to put my fingers through the wounds."

At the suggestion of a Jesuit professor at Georgetown, Blatty started to investigate demonic possession as his topic for an upcoming oratorical contest. Though Blatty lost the contest, he remained interested in his subject, and twenty years later, in 1969, he began writing *The Exorcist*, which was published in 1971 and entrenched itself on the *New York*

Times best-seller list for fifty-five weeks. In 1973, it became a movie that played to packed audiences across the United States and received ten Academy Award nominations.

When interviewed about the origins of *The Exorcist*, Blatty freely refers to the 1949 case, which he says "was really the seed that led to the book." While researching the case he was given free access to the diary kept by the real-life exorcist, a St. Louis Jesuit priest in his fifties, but Blatty always refused to disclose the identity of the priest, the Mt. Rainier boy, or anyone else who participated in the exorcism.

The 1949 exorcism was permitted by the Catholic church only after extensive medical and psychiatric treatment had failed to cure the boy of his afflictions. The ancient ritual to cast out the devil was performed over a period of two months, mostly in a St. Louis hospital. During that time observers were shocked, amazed, and thoroughly frightened by the phenomena they witnessed.

The boy (call him David) seemed to be surrounded by a strong field of electric current. At school his desk moved about the floor whenever he sat in it. Sometimes when he got into his bed it moved across the room—five to six feet at a time—and shook violently. In one instance, when the boy was sitting in a heavy armchair with his knees tucked under his chin, the chair tilted to one side and fell over, spilling David onto the floor. The power, or "invisible force" as one priest called it, seemed to fill whatever room the boy was in. On one occasion, prior to the start of the exorcism, two clergymen visited David at his home in Mt. Rainier. As the men entered the boy's bedroom, they were immediately struck by the force and were laid flat on the floor.

In the boy's presence, objects flew about in the air. One day, pieces of fruit rose from atop a refrigerator, sailed across the kitchen, and crashed into the wall. It was not unusual for David's bedside table to rise to the ceiling, hover and slowly descend. Called in to help analyze the mysterious happenings, Dr. J. B. Rhine, director of the parapsychology laboratory at Duke University, labeled them "the most impressive example of poltergeist phenomena I have ever come across."

Two other bizarre manifestations totally perplexed medical experts and church authorities: The first was David's shocking language, filled with obscenities and Latin phrases (he had never studied Latin), which was interrupted by fits of screaming. The second was the boy's dermal brandings. As author Blatty concluded from his research: "The brandings were lines and markings, some single, some double and even triple, that resembled claw marks and appeared spontaneously on the flesh of the boy each day and as many as thirty times in the day. Their appearance was accompanied in every instance by screams of anguish and pain from the boy. Once, when the exorcist was sitting on the bed no more than two feet from the boy, a branding appeared even as he watched. It extended from the boy's inner thigh to his ankle. Near the ankle the skin was broken, and droplets of blood appeared. Sometimes the brandings were images and words. Some of the words that appeared were SPITE, HELL, and EXIT. When the latter appeared, it was particularly clear and in letters a little more than two inches high. It did not vanish, staying vivid for another four hours. It was on the boy's back. At no time were there coverings on the bed. The boy wore only undershorts. And his hands, in each case, were reported in sight."

After the rite of exorcism had been performed some twenty to thirty times, each taking about forty-five minutes, the devil was finally driven from David's body. His parents, who were not Catholic, converted to the faith that had saved their son. As for David—he retained no memories whatsoever of the diabolic forces that had controlled both his mind and body in his fourteenth year.

11. Fakes, Mistakes, and Accidents

So what if Newton, watching an apple fall, did not experience the great aha! attributed to him? The story of the Newton myth-making is fascinating in itself. If Watt didn't envision his invention while watching steam lift a teakettle lid, he did realize great and interesting breakthroughs as a scientist. Little Jack Horner was neither so innocent nor so little as the nursery rhyme would have you believe, and his plum was an expensive one.

Some creators deliberately put us on. Irrepressible liars tell us lies for cussedness or fun, as did Frank Baum (author of *The Wizard of Oz*) and songwriter Cole Porter, or for self-promotion, as did Mary Baker Eddy, the strange founder of Christian Science.

Far more scientists than can be included in this chapter discovered great principles and created great inventions—by accident. A spike driven by mistake into the head of a workman was the precursor of a sophisticated operation. Clumsiness can pay off: a piece of rubber held too close to a stove gives clues to a valuable process; wipe-ups after spills bring amazing results; a piece of equipment left carelessly near a demonstration registers odd readings leading to an important discovery.

Things, then, are not always what they seem.

The Creation of Oz

SURROUNDED by a group of wide-eyed children, including his own sons, L. Frank Baum—unanimously voted the neighborhood's best storyteller—spun another yarn. This time he told about a girl named Dorothy who had been swept away from her home in Kansas and deposited in a strange but magical land. Before long she met up with a Scarecrow, a Tin Woodsman, and a Cowardly Lion. At a pause in the narrative, one little girl, Tweety Robbins, pleaded to know the name of the fairyland. Baum hesitated as his eyes scanned the room, looking for a quick answer. He glanced at the headlines on the May 7, 1898, *Chicago Journal* which lay on the floor, but it offered no help. Suddenly his face lit up, and he burst forth with the answer—the characters lived in Oz, the marvelous land of Oz.

Years later, in an interview published in the May 10, 1903, issue of the *St. Louis Republic*, Baum divulged the source that gave him the name for his fairyland. As the newspaper quoted him:

I have a little cabinet letter file on my desk in front of me. I was thinking and wondering about a title for my story, and I had settled on "Wizard" as part of it. My gaze was caught by the gilt letters on the three drawers of the cabinet. The first was A–G; the next drawer was labeled H–N; and on the last were the letters O–Z. And Oz it at once became.

This delightful story, popularized in the Baum biography *To Please a Child* by Frank Joslyn Baum and Russell P. MacFall, is almost certainly not true. When Baum first submitted the manuscript to his publisher, the George M. Hill Company, in 1899 (a year after the supposed file-cabinet incident), the book was called *The Emerald City*. At that time Oz was not the name of the *land* but of the *ruler*, or wizard, of the land. When the publisher complained about the title, because of a superstition that a jewel in the title of a book was bad luck, Baum was forced to create another title. After numerous submissions, including *From Kansas to Fairyland* and *The City of the Great Oz*, he finally came up with an acceptable one, *The Wonderful Wizard of Oz*. Then, since he had changed Oz into a place, Baum hurriedly went through the book and made a few last-minute changes to indicate that the Emerald City was located in the *land* of Oz.

The apocryphal inspiration story was but one of the little white lies that Baum so loved to tell, always with a straight face. One of his friends, poet Eunice Tietjens, told of his verbal extravagances in her auto-biography, *The World at My Shoulder*: "L. Frank Baum was a character. He was tall and rangy, with an imagination and vitality which constantly ran away with him. . . . Constantly exercising his imagination as he did, he had come to the place where he could honestly not tell the difference between what he had done and what he had imagined. Everything he said had to be taken with at least a half pound of salt. But he was a fascinating companion."

Despite Baum's fictitious file-cabinet tale, he did invent the word Oz. But where he got it is still a matter of conjecture. Oz historians, however, have come up with at least four plausible theories:

1. Baum slightly altered "Boz," the pseudonym of Charles Dickens, whose works he greatly admired.
2. Oz could have been an adaptation of the biblical land of Uz, where Job lived.
3. Baum claimed that a truly good story elicited "Ohs" and "Ahs" from readers. (Oz can be pronounced either way.)
4. Fond of two-letter combinations, Baum simply tossed together vowels and consonants until he arrived at a pleasant sounding name.

While the story behind the word Oz will remain ambiguous, the origins of two of Dorothy's three adventurous friends—the Scarecrow and the Tin Woodsman—are more certain. According to author Russell Mac-Fall, Baum had recurring nightmares in which a scarecrow chased him. Just as Baum was within the pursuer's reach, the scarecrow fell down and was reduced to a pile of straw. The Tin Woodsman stemmed from Baum's early life. Prior to his success as a writer, Baum worked at a number of jobs, including chinaware salesman and window-display designer for a hardware store. It was during his hardware store days, according to a story in the *Indianapolis Times*, that the metal man became implanted in Baum's brain. As the newspaper reported the incident: "He wanted to create something eye-catching, so he made a torso out of a washboiler, bolted stovepipe legs and arms to it, and used the underside of a saucepan for a face. He topped it with a funnel hat, and what would become the inspiration for the Tin Woodsman was born."

The Cowardly Lion, unfortunately, is without a tantalizing origins story. If Baum had only known the extent to which his Oz story would be dissected and analyzed, he surely would have reached into his bag of little white lies and pulled out a praiseworthy inspiration for the Cowardly Lion.

Charles Goodyear: The Rubber Man

WHEN inventor Charles Goodyear spotted the life preservers in the salesroom windows of the Roxbury India Rubber Company one day in the early 1800s, he was so intrigued that he went inside to investigate them. He even took one home to try to invent a better valve for it. Hardly a neophyte, he had already taken out several patents: on inventions for a

safe-eye button, steel spring fork, spring lever faucet, and spoon manufacturing. But the work with the life preserver consumed his interest for
quite a while.

After devising a better valve, Goodyear took the life preserver back to
the rubber company. The proprietor was pleasant but not enthusiastic
about the inventor's work and soon switched the conversation to a related
topic—problems with the rubber that composed the life preserver. Although it had invaluable characteristics for those interested in making
raincoats, gum shoes, and life preservers, rubber was exasperating stuff.
Yes, it was water-repellent, but it became sticky in hot weather and stiff in
cold weather. It stretched when it shouldn't. It could stink. In fact, the
proprietor of the Roxbury India Rubber Company had just had to bury a
whole lot of gum shoes returned by an angry customer because they
started to smell bad. The proprietor then advised Goodyear to work on the
problem of rubber itself. It was a casual suggestion, but Goodyear took it
seriously.

When he arrived home in Philadelphia, he was arrested for a debt—a
hardware store he and his father ran had just failed—and set free on the
orders that he work within a certain geographical limit of the jail. So he
set up a laboratory in his kitchen to invent a better quality of rubber.

Goodyear had no special background in chemistry and took a shotgun
approach to his experimentation, mixing the gum with everything from
cream cheese and quicklime to bronze powder, magnesium, and various
acids. He kneaded his mixtures and rolled them out with his wife's rolling
pin on a marble slab.

Finally, he took some uncoagulated latex as it came from a tree and
tried that. One of his workmen tried it too—by dipping his pants in it to
waterproof them. Thinking himself superior to his boss in inventiveness,
the man sat down to mix rubber in front of the fire. To the man's great
chagrin, as Goodyear wrote in his autobiography: "On attempting to get
up again a few minutes after, he found that he was not only cemented to
his seat, but that his legs were cemented together. On being extricated
from his improved trousers, to the no small merriment of the bystanders,
he subsequently manifested no further inclination for invention."

An inveterate showman, Goodyear always courted publicity. Among
other things, he threatened to send Queen Victoria a rubber dress and
asked a newspaper to print its pages on rubber. He himself advertised his
enterprise by wearing a rubber suit. As he later told in his book, someone
asking how to recognize him was told: "If you meet a man who has on an
India rubber cap, stock, coat, vest and shoes, with an India rubber money
purse, without a cent of money in it, that is he."

When in 1839, he received a government contract to make 150 mail-bags to keep mail from getting wet, he wasted no time in telling the papers about it. It was a mistake, for, to his chagrin, the mailbags repelled water all right, but they also sagged and stretched, even though they were treated with his new acid-gas process. Contract cancelled.

It was in that same year that he made his greatest discovery—by accident. As Goodyear tells it, putting himself in the third person: ". . . at the dwelling where he stopped whenever he visited the manufactory at Woburn, the inventor made some experiments to ascertain the effect of heat upon the same compound that had decomposed in the mail-bags and other articles. He was surprised to find that the specimen, being carelessly brought in contact with a hot stove, charred like leather. He endeavored to call the attention of his brother, as well as some other individuals who were present, and who were acquainted with the manufacture of gum-elastic, to this effect, as remarkable, and unlike any before known, since gum-elastic always melted when exposed to a high degree of heat. This occurrence did not at the time appear to them to be worthy of notice; it was considered as one of the frequent appeals that he was in the habit of making, in behalf of some new experiment.

"He however directly inferred that if the process of charring could be stopped at the right point, it might divest the gum of its native adhesiveness throughout, which would make it better than the native gum."

It was easier said than done. Again and again he succeeded, using small pieces of rubber. As his daughter Ellen recalled: "As I was passing in and out of the room, I casually observed the little piece of gum, which he was holding near the fire, and I noticed also that he was unusually animated by some discovery which he had made. He nailed the piece of gum outside the kitchen door in the intense cold. In the morning he brought it in, holding it up exultingly. He had found it perfectly flexible, as it was when he put it out."

However, the process he was experimenting with, called vulcanization for the ancient god of the forge, needed a great deal of perfecting. In addition to heat, it involved the addition of sulphur to the latex as a curing agent. But it was tricky. Goodyear heated rubber over a candle flame, in his wife's oven, in boiling water, in front of a teakettle spout. Finally he found the money to build a brick oven, and eventually he was successful enough to win some acclaim. But the price had been high: debtor's prison, his illness, his children's hunger. When his two-year-old son died, the family took the boy's body to the grave in a wagon, being able to afford nothing better.

However, he remained a rubber enthusiast to the end. He saw a thousand uses for rubber: carpets embossed with maps, blackboards, water beds for the ill, linings for reservoirs, inflated "bat-clubs," boxing gloves, skating jackets, parasols, rubber bank notes, plugs for stopping up cannon holes in ships. Many ideas prevented people from being hurt—for example, the fording dress in the "form of pantaloons with boots attached, and a large tube around the top which is inflated with air. They are used for fording rivers, and by the aid of a cord to pull the dress back across the stream, a party of any number may cross a river with one dress." Only in a few cases could Goodyear see little or no use for rubber: "Although the native Indians may drink it in the form of sap, with impunity, he is not so infatuated with the subject as to recommend it as an article of food. It should not be worn next to the skin. . . . Nor should one sleep enveloped by it. . . ."

We give Goodyear the final word on his accidental discovery: "While the inventor admits that these discoveries were not the result of *scientific* chemical investigations, he is not willing to admit that they were the result of what is commonly termed accident; he claims them to be the result of the closest application and observation. . . . It may, therefore, be considered as one of those cases where the leading of the Creator providentially aids his creatures by what are termed accidents, to attain those things which are not attainable by the powers of reasoning he has conferred on them."

A Fall on the Ice: Mary Baker Eddy and Christian Science

IT WAS an item that—deservedly—made only the inside pages of the local newspaper. Who could have foretold its incredible metamorphosis into myth, part of a religion—Christian Science—that has affected thousands of people?

The item: On February 1, 1866, forty-five-year-old Mary Patterson (Mary Baker Eddy) slipped and fell on the ice on the corner of Market and Oxford streets in Swampscott, Massachusetts. She was taken into a house nearby, and Dr. Alvin Cushing was called in to treat her. He reported that she was "nervous, partially unconscious, semi-hysterical, complaining by word and action of severe pain in the back of her head and neck." When he visited her the next morning she was conscious but still "complaining of severe pain, almost spasmodic, on moving."

A few days after the accident, Mrs. Patterson wrote a description of her accident:

I fell on the sidewalk and struck my head on the ice and was taken up for dead, came to consciousness amid a storm of vapors from cologne, chloroform, ether, camphor, etc., but to find myself a helpless cripple. . . .

The physician attending said I had taken the last step I ever should, but in two days I got out of my bed *alone* and will *walk.* . . .

The myth was taking shape.

In five years, in her mind it had ballooned into an even more dramatic event: The doctor had said she could not live for more than three days but she had risen from bed on the third day.

In a 1904 deposition, the doctor contradicted her story, stating that he had never said she would not recover or that she was in a critical condition or that she had three days to live. By February 13, he said, she had gotten well.

In an official biography of 1907, the myth emerged full-blown, its heroine a female Christ rising from the dead:

After the doctor's departure on Friday, however, she refused to take the medicine he had left, and as she has expressed it, lifted her heart to God. On the third day, which was Sunday, she sent those who were in her room away, and taking her Bible, opened it. Her eyes fell on the account of the healing of the palsied man by Jesus. . . .

A spiritual experience so deep was granted her that she realized eternity in a moment, infinitude in limitation, life in the presence of death. . . . In that moment all pain evanesced into bliss, all discord in her physical body melted into harmony, all sorrow was translated into rapture. She recognized this state as her rightful condition as a child of God. Love invaded her, life lifted her, truth irradiated her. God said to her, "Daughter, arise!"

Mrs. Patterson arose from her bed, dressed, and walked into the parlor where a clergyman and a few friends had gathered, thinking it might be for the last words on earth with the sufferer, who they believed was dying. They arose in consternation at her appearance, almost believing they beheld an apparition. . . . She stood before them fully restored to health.

Mary Baker did more than experience a cure. She in that hour received a revelation for which she had been preparing her heart in every event of her life.

The central figure in this florid account, Mary Baker Eddy, *had* been preparing for that moment, though not quite as her biographer meant.

Her inspirations for Christian Science—mostly related to her indomitable will and enthusiasm—occurred at various times in her life, before and after her fall. Many arose from her pecularities.

Even as a child, Mary was prone to illness and obsessed with her health. She often went into fits, kicking the floor spasmodically or lying limp; sometimes she was cataleptic. Her father, who adored her to distraction, would shout, "Mary is dying!" and leap for the horse and wagon to race for the family doctor. Even then she was a master at dramatic death scenes. To cure her, the doctor hypnotized her. He once said, "I can make that girl stop in the street any time, merely by thinking."

She used her delicate condition to manipulate others. When she was twelve, her father tried to force her to accept predestination, the Calvinist belief that those elected to heaven are chosen before they are born. It was a gargantuan struggle of souls. When her intellectual resistance did not succeed, she resorted to a raging fever. She later wrote, "I prayed, and a soft glow of ineffable joy came over me. The fever was gone, and I rose and dressed myself in a normal condition of health. . . . The physician marveled, and the 'horrible decree' of predestination . . . forever lost its power over me."

After she lost her first husband, George Glover, and bore his son in agony, all within the space of months, she collapsed into a protracted illness. All that helped was rocking: Her father rocked her in his arms, the neighborhood boys in a swing. Twelve years later, at her wedding to Daniel Patterson, an itinerant dentist and ladies' man, she was so ill that she had to be carried up and down stairs.

One man was able to cure her: Phineas Parkhurst Quimby, a self-educated ex-clockmaker-turned-healer, and if there was a real inspiration in her life, he was it. Quimby had begun as a believer in mesmerism and animal magnetism, and he developed a theory which had all the rudiments of psychosomatic medicine: that illness was real but existed because the patient believed in it. In 1862, after failed water cures and other attempts to regain her health, Mary came under Quimby's care at his establishment in Portland, Maine.

When she arrived she needed help to mount his office steps, but in a week or two she was able to climb the 182 steps of the New City Building in town. When her errant husband escaped from a Confederate prison and made his way home, he found her in the thrall of Quimby as his disciple and pupil. Her marriage was over.

By 1863, she, too, had become a healer, inspired by her mentor's ideas and the drama of her own miraculous recovery. Quimby had enormous influence over her. Once she even saw him as a ghost, in hat and dress coat, in her parlor at high noon. When she greeted him, he left. However, later, when her religion of Christian Science was established, she forgot her considerable debt to Quimby and claimed many of his ideas as her own. He died in 1866, shortly before her fateful fall.

After her divorce from Patterson in 1873, Mary dedicated herself to practicing and teaching the precepts that lay behind Christian Science and to adopting young disciples. A charismatic woman with intense dark eyes, she was not easy to live with and often displayed bizarre behavior. When she broke with her disciples, as she invariably did, she feared their psychic influence, their "malicious mesmerism," on her. Against her enemies she levied magic incantations, called "taking up the foe." For example, she ordered one of her group to deal with an ex-disciple: "Say to him, 'Your sins have found you out. You are affected as you wish to affect me. Your evil thought reacts upon you. You are bilious, you are consumptive, you have liver trouble, you have been poisoned by arsenic.' " It is possible that her third husband, Gilbert Asa Eddy, a retiring ex-sewing machine salesman with a perpetual smile, and a slick hanger-on named Arens helped her to conspire to kill a former pupil, Daniel Spofford, by hiring a Boston saloon keeper to do the job. The case was dismissed, possibly because witnesses were bought off.

When Gilbert Eddy died at the relatively tender age of fifty-one from heart disease, it was an embarrassment to her. She solved the problem by claiming he had been metaphysically poisoned with arsenic. When, after an autopsy, one doctor refused to list this cause, she found another who would.

Her inspirations lay in her illnesses and eccentric personality. Yet, no matter how strange she was, she was an early expert at psychosomatic medicine, and the religion she began became enormously successful. This obsessed woman changed the lives of thousands.

Porter's Tall Tales

WHETHER sailing the South Seas, sunning on the French Riviera, hiking in the mountains of northern Italy, or entertaining in his palazzo in Venice, Cole Porter made headlines. A man born into an affluent family, he married a rich American divorcée and then multiplied their combined fortunes after becoming a successful songwriter. The *Coleporteurs*, as the French dubbed them, lived in a style befitting their wealth. Amid servants, swimming pools, grand pianos, custom-made furniture and clothing, Porter reveled in his glamorous, hedonistic image. Newspapers of the 1920s and 1930s gleefully reported the escapades of the American composer as he romped around the globe in search of adventure and good times, as he mingled with the elite of the worlds of art, politics, and business. As one columnist wrote: "It is really the simple things of life which give pleasure to Mr. Porter—half-million-dollar strings of pearls, Isotta motor cars, cases of double bottles of Grand Chambertin '87, suites at Claridge's, brief trips aboard the *Bremen*, a little grouse shooting."

Porter loved to discourse on his lavish parties, especially those at the Palazzo Rezzonico in Venice (once the home of Robert and Elizabeth Barrett Browning). At one such affair six hundred guests were given red-and-white crepe-paper costumes which they donned as they danced around the palazzo's grand ballroom; for additional merriment the group was treated to a performance by tightrope walkers who entertained in the courtyard amid a kaleidoscopic array of colored lights. At another soirée Porter featured Sergei Diaghilev's ballet company, complete with full orchestra, a fifty-foot statue of Venus, 200,000 candles, and fireworks. However, the composer's favorite and "most vulgar," as he called it, extravaganza was the summer evening aboard his *galleggiante*, a barge which he had converted into a nightclub. Boasting a wine cellar, a French chef, and a Dixieland band, the gala would have been a rousing success except for one oversight—Porter had forgotten to install bathrooms. Rough waters caused many partygoers to get seasick, resulting in a mass exodus to the rails where many of the 150 elite guests threw up together.

Porter spent his life avoiding his personal demon, boredom, and when facts of his life diminished his image, he embellished them before feeding them to an ever eager press. He delighted in claiming that he was younger than he was and suffered no shame when he altered the height category on his passport—making himself five feet, eight inches instead of five feet, six inches. Even his tragic horse riding accident in 1937, which resulted in more than thirty operations and the amputation of his right leg, spawned a fabricated story: Porter claimed that while he waited for help to arrive, he took out pencil and paper and completed the lyrics to "You Never Know."

His greatest exaggeration was that he joined the French Foreign Legion during World War I and even received the Croix de Guerre from the French government. But there is no documentation to back up his supposed service in the French Foreign Legion nor is there any proof that he was ever decorated by the French government. During the war years, however, he was spotted on the streets of Paris in a variety of military uniforms which he alternately wore as he leisurely strolled the streets. One day he was an aide-de-camp, the next day a captain, then a colonel. The confusion over Porter's actual military service has never been sorted out. As one reporter put it, "Porter's war record is a case for Scotland Yard."

As Porter jumbled the facts of his personal life, he also scrambled the facts of his professional life. He maintained that he wrote fifteen hundred songs in his lifetime, an extravagant total even considering the fact that he did write the scores for thirty-three musical comedy shows. His seemingly endless string of hit songs includes "What Is This Thing Called Love?" "I Get a Kick out of You," "I've Got You Under My Skin," "Let's Do It," "I Concentrate on You," "In the Still of the Night," "From This Moment On," "You Do Something to Me," and "Just One of Those Things."

In countless interviews reporters invariably asked Porter where he got the ideas for his songs. "My inspiration, whatever that may be, doesn't come out of the thin air," he once said. Then he added, "It comes from people and places." The stimulus for "The Kling-Kling Bird on the Divi-Divi Tree" was the bird and the tree of the same names which he observed on a trip to Jamaica. "You're the Top" was a result of a party aboard a *faltboot* on the Rhine—a party in which all the upper-crust guests gushed over each other with compliments. "I Love You" grew out of a five-dollar bet with friend and director Monty Woolley that Porter could not concoct a hit tune out of a banal title like "I Love You." The beat and rhythm of "What Is This Thing Called Love?" evolved from the music and dancing of the local natives in Marrakesh. The stories abundantly poured forth. However, sometimes Porter gave conflicting accounts—different stories for the same song.

"Night and Day" (1932), probably his most popular song, had three origins stories:

1. Porter composed the melody one Saturday while living at the Ritz-Carlton in New York. Shortly afterward he left for Newport, where he was the guest of Vincent Astor. On Sunday most of the words came to him while lying on the beach. Then a rainstorm forced Porter indoors, and when Mrs. Astor complained of the "drip, drip, drip" of a faulty eaves spout, he filled in the one phrase that the song lacked, "the drip, drip, drip of the raindrops."

2. "Night and Day" was inspired by "the monotonous wail of Moroccan music."
3. The song was born in Morocco after listening to a priest summoning worshipers to their daily prayers.

The story behind "Begin the Beguine" (1935) is of a similarly confusing nature. The two versions of its genesis:

1. A war dance which he heard in the Dutch East Indies moved him to write the song.
2. It emerged after Porter watched a folk dance, the beguine, performed in Paris. To quote the composer: "There was a special dance hall on the Left Bank where the French Negroes from Martinique used to dance every night, and I went often to see them."

Porter's songs, wherever they came from, were tremendous money-makers. During one candid interview "the supreme sophisticate of American song" gave an incisive, no-nonsense account of how his prodigious mind worked: "My sole inspiration is a telephone call from a producer. If he phoned me today and asked me to write a new song for a spot, I'd just begin thinking. First, I'd think of an idea, and then I'd fit it to a title. Then I'd go to work at the piano, spotting the title at certain moments in the melody, and then write the lyric—the end first; that way it has a strong finish. It's important for a song to have a strong finish."

The Soap That Floats

IN 1878, the Procter & Gamble Company in Cincinnati, Ohio, developed a creamy white, delicately scented soap that it hoped would compete with the finest soaps of the day, imported white castiles. Procter & Gamble's soap, called the White Soap, produced a rich lather, even in cold water, and had a pleasant, even consistency. An accident one afternoon at the factory gave it yet another desirable quality and turned it into what we know today as Ivory Soap.

Procter & Gamble claims that a factory worker, in charge of the mixing vats, left for his lunch break and forgot to turn off the machinery. When he returned he noticed that too much air had been whipped into the soap mixture. Reluctant to throw away the soap, he poured it into the hardening and cutting frames, and the batch was subsequently sent out to nearby stores. Weeks later requests for the "soap that floats" began to arrive at company headquarters. Whether bathing in murky river water or murky bathtub water, consumers were happy that they no longer lost their soap—it always popped up to the surface of the water. Realizing that they had been the beneficiaries of a lucky accident, the Procters and the Gambles ordered that from then on White Soap was to be given a good, long beating.

Next came the search for a new name. White Soap was too common a label for such an innovative product. The man who came up with the solution was Harley T. Procter, one of the five sons of the company's cofounder William Procter. The elusive name came to him one Sunday in 1879 while he was in church. During a reading of the Forty-fifth Psalm, his mind wandered, but his attention quickly focused on the words, "All thy garments smell of myrrh and aloes and cassia out of ivory palaces whereby they have made thee glad."

All the product now needed was a good advertising campaign. In an effort to confirm his belief that Ivory was a high quality soap, Harley Procter sent bars of soap to chemistry professors and independent laboratories, asking for a complete analysis. One report particularly impressed him. It stated that the soap had very few impurities—56/100 of one percent. With a simple mathematical calculation, Procter turned the negative statement into a positive one. It became the hallmark of the company's advertising: Ivory Soap was 99 and 44/100 percent pure.

The first printed ad for Ivory appeared in 1882. It read:

> The "Ivory" is a Laundry Soap, with all the fine qualities of a choice Toilet Soap, and is 99 44/100 percent pure. Ladies will find this Soap especially adapted for washing laces, infants' clothing, silk hose, cleaning gloves, and all articles of fine texture and delicate color, and for the varied uses about the house that daily arise, requiring the use of soap that is above the ordinary in quality. For the Bath, Toilet or Nursery, it is preferred to most of the Soaps sold for toilet use, being purer and much more pleasant and effective, and possessing all the desirable properties of the finest unadulterated White Castile Soap. The Ivory Soap will "float". . . . The price, compared to the quality and size of the cakes, makes it the cheapest Soap for everybody and every want.

In 1979, Ivory Soap celebrated its 100th anniversary. At that time more than 30 billion cakes of the floating soap had been sold.

Jack Horner Was Not Such a Good Boy

RICHARD WHITING, the abbot of Glastonbury, the last remaining religious house in the county of Somerset, England, knew it was only a matter of time before his monastery, too, would be dissolved under the orders of Henry VIII, as many others in England already had been. To placate the king and hold off the inevitable, he sent a Christmas pie to the palace. It was an unusual pie, for under its crust were title deeds to twelve monastery lands.

Chosen to deliver the pie was the steward of Glastonbury, Jack Horner. On the way from Glastonbury to the palace, Horner reached in the pie and took out a "plum"—the deed for the manor of Mells, which he kept for himself.

Whiting was later put on trial on a trumped-up charge of embezzlement, and in the jury was Horner, the thief. In 1539, pronounced guilty by that jury, the hapless Whiting was hanged, drawn, and quartered. A Richard Pollard wrote Thomas Cromwell that Whiting took "hys deathe very pacyently" and recommended Horner, among others, for his service to the king "according to hys dewtye and ryght."

As for Jack Horner, not only did he get away with his crime, but he was immortalized in a nursery rhyme as a "good boy." So much for poetic justice.

Big Bangs in the Kitchen

IN THE THIRTEENTH CENTURY, Roger Bacon discovered the recipe for gunpowder, foundation of modern warfare, and rightly fearing the harmful use of it, wrote it down in a code not broken until 1904. Others, however, also came upon the secret, and gunpowder was well known when Professor Christian Friedrich Schoenbein, chemistry teacher at the University of Basel, Switzerland, came upon an improvement for it by accident in 1845.

271

One evening he was conducting experiments at home in the kitchen. It has been said that his wife objected to this practice of his. If so, you can't blame her. In any event, she was out that evening when he set about distilling nitric and sulfuric acids.

Unfortunately, the flask containing the acids broke and spilled all over the kitchen floor. Frantically, the distraught Schoenbein searched for a mop or rag to clean it up, finally grabbing his wife's cotton apron from a hook to blot up the acid before it did damage. Then he washed the apron and hung it to dry by the stove. To his great consternation, after it dried the apron exploded into flames and quickly burned to ashes.

What had happened? Neither nitric acid nor sulfuric acid are explosive or flammable, Schoenbein knew, and while cotton will burn, it rarely blows up. Like a good scientist, he repeated the scenario and attained the same result—with the loss of another apron. What was happening was this: The acid added NO_2 to the cellulose in the apron to produce nitrocellulose, or nitrated cotton, an explosive like gunpowder. He called his discovery *Schiessbaumwolle*, "shooting tree wool," but it came to be called by the far simpler name of guncotton.

Schoenbein described it as follows: "One pound of guncotton is as effective as two to four pounds of black powder. . . . Cotton so treated does not leave any residue when exploded and produces no smoke. The manufacture is not attended with the least danger."

His first statements were true. Before guncotton, gunpowder blackened gunners when it went off, mucked up cannons, and turned battlefield atmosphere into a fog of sooty mist, rendering things almost invisible.

However, his last boast turned out to be untrue, as a European fabricator, John Hall, found out to his sorrow. In 1847, he rented a factory in Kent and started making guncotton. At 11:00 A.M. on July 14, a huge explosion shook the plant and killed twenty-one people inside. The *London Times* reported: "The roofs of all the buildings within about a quarter of a mile of the explosion are completely stripped of their tiles, and the walls are much shaken. Even in the town of Faversham, fully a mile distant from the scene of the disaster, windows were broken." Other such explosions occurred in France, Russia, and Germany. So the discovery was tabled until modifications made it safer.

Perhaps Schoenbein, watching the apron explode, should have taken a leaf from Bacon's book. If he had, the destruction from his mistake would have remained at just a piece of cloth.

Watt's Teakettle—The Story Doesn't Hold Water

WHEN James Watt was about twelve, his aunt scolded him for spending so much time watching a kettle boil. "For the last hour you have not spoken a word, but have taken the lid off that kettle and put it on again, holding now a cup and now a silver spoon over the steam, watching how it rises from the spout, and catching and connecting the drops it falls into. Are you not ashamed of spending your time in this way?" The little story, probably true, made a fine anecdote for the textbooks of how a Scottish schoolboy's fascination with steam lifting the lid of a teakettle inspired the invention of the steam engine. The story became even better when we learned that the boy was sickly and dull in school, even considered retarded, though he had shown talent in mathematics.

Unfortunately, the teakettle story, closely examined, does not hold water.

First, Watt was not the first to recognize the power of steam. The ancients knew of it.

Second, decades before Watt was born in 1736, the first crude but working steam engine was invented by Thomas Newcomen. Watt improved it, but he didn't invent it.

Third, Watt's engine actually obtained its power from the force of atmospheric pressure. Steam in the cylinder was condensed to create a vacuum into which, pushed by the weight of air above, the piston "fell." The Newcomen engine operated the same way. Neither obtained power from the expansive power of steam, so, strictly speaking, neither was a steam engine as we would define it.

Fortunately, the real story of Watt is much more interesting. Watt, who combined an understanding of theory with practical mechanical ability, was Mathematical Instrument Maker to the University of Glasgow when, in 1764, Professor John Anderson asked him to repair a Newcomen model. Watt was intrigued because he had already performed experiments with high-pressure steam and was itching to investigate how it worked. In fixing the engine he began to envision improvements that he later incorporated into the vastly more efficient and versatile steam engines that he made to sell to mining companies and factories. By 1790, the Watt engine had replaced the Newcomen engine; a decade later in England, there were 500 Watt engines, representing driving forces in the Industrial Revolution.

One of Watt's improvements involved a functional paradox. For ideal operation, the piston cylinder should be kept hot to avoid wasting heat; yet, at the same time, the piston had to be cooled so that the steam would condense to form the vacuum. Watt's improvement was ingenious, and it came to him through a genuine inspiration:

"It was in the green of Glasgow," he told a fellow engineer, "I had gone to take a walk on a fine Sabbath afternoon. I had entered the green by the gate at the foot of Charlotte Street and had passed to the old washing house. I was thinking upon the engine at the time, and had gone so far as to the herd's house when the idea came into my mind that, as steam is an elastic body, it would rush into a vacuum, and if communication were made between the cylinder and an exhausted vessel, it would rush into it, and might there be condensed without cooling the cylinder. . . . I had not walked further than the golf house when the whole thing was arranged in my mind." The "whole thing" was the first condenser.

The next day he made a model of the condenser, using tinplate, solder, and a sewing thimble. Simply stated, his solution was to segregate the unwanted effects of condensation from the engine itself by having the condensation take place separately.

Not one of his own solutions for leaky pistons—cow dung, felt cloth used in hats, or "chewed paper" (papier-maché)—worked, so he went to ironmaster John Wilkinson for the answer. Wilkinson was the right man—he was so in love with iron that he had made himself a coffin of it and was the first person to launch an iron boat. For French cannon makers, he had created a method of precisely boring iron with a tolerance the width of a shilling's edge. He had no trouble solving Watt's leaky piston problem.

Watt's advanced designs included devices to convert piston movements into rotary motion, which meant they could be used not only for pumping water, all that the Newcomen engine was capable of, but also for crushing ore and numerous other tasks. Perhaps Watt's most important contribution was to apply a governor to the engine to control the output of steam and regulate the engine's motion. For this Watt deserves the title of Father of Automation.

The Invention of Rayon

WHILE assisting Louis Pasteur in investigating the problem of stopping a silkworm epidemic, Comte de Chardonnet, Louis Marie Hilaire Bernigard, became intrigued with the question of how the silkworms produced silk. Could an artificial process also produce such fibers?

Though he tabled the problem for a while, he happened upon an answer some years later while he was trying to develop gunpowder, an explosive involving nitrocellulose, for the French Government.

In a darkroom developing photographic plates, de Chardonnet spilled a bottle of collodion (a solution of nitrocellulose in ether and alcohol), but did not clean it up right away. When he did, much of the solvent had largely evaporated, but what was left was thick and tacky. The cloth he used to wipe it up lifted long strands of collodion from the table surface. They looked remarkably like silk threads. Thus he was inspired to make the first popular artificial fiber—rayon. When he forced solutions of nitrocellulose through holes and allowed the solvent to evaporate, fibers resulted.

Independently wealthy, he financed his experiments himself. By 1884, he had perfected his "textile material similar to silk" from a solution of cellulose nitrate mixed with alcohol and ether. At first it was called artificial silk or Chardonnet silk, then later rayon, because it shone in rays of light. At the Paris Exposition of 1891, it was a sensation. (One problem shadowed its popularity—his rayon was at first highly flammable. For this reason it was nicknamed "mother-in-law silk"; it was said in a macabre joke that a good present for a hated mother-in-law was a rayon dress with a kitchen match.) In his hometown of Besançon, de Chardonnet built the first commercial rayon factory, the prototype of all the synthetic fiber factories that followed.

Murder of the Mind

THE WORLD'S first recorded lobotomy was the result of a bizarre accident that happened on a railroad construction site near Cavendish, Vermont, on September 13, 1848. On that day the victim of the accident, Phineas Gage, unknowingly became a part of medical history.

Gage, the twenty-five-year-old foreman of a crew working on the Rutland & Burlington Railroad, was setting black powder charges into the rock of a steep mountain grade when one exploded. As the smoke cleared, his fellow workers raced to the site to find Gage still conscious, though somewhat dazed, with a trickle of blood running out of his head. About fifty feet away lay his tamping iron (used to compact the powder)— an iron spike 3½ feet long and 1¼ inches in diameter—covered with blood and brain tissue. Apparently the spike blasted its way through Gage's left cheek, then followed a path behind his left eye, and exited through the top of his skull.

The doctors caring for Gage predicted that any man with a hole in his head would surely die. Instead, Gage made a remarkable recovery and after seven months seemed completely healthy, free of pain, and ready to return to work. But he was a different man. Prior to the accident Gage was a mild-mannered, church-going man; he didn't gamble, swear, smoke, or drink. After the accident, however, he became unreliable, boisterous, irritable, foul-mouthed, and frequented a number of saloons where he spun extravagant tales that not even the most inebriated would believe. When he reapplied for his foreman's job, he was rejected.

Gage's peculiar experience would have been forgotten except that one of Gage's doctors had the foresight to record the case in a Boston medical journal and later presented the case before the Massachusetts Medical Society. As for the man with the altered personality: Four years after the accident he moved to Chile to build railroads through the Andes, but he returned to the United States in 1860 and settled in San Francisco, where he died on May 21, 1861, following a series of epileptic attacks. Less than ninety years after Gage's accidental lobotomy, thousands of human beings were undergoing personality changes—only these transformations took place in hospitals and doctors' offices.

Lobotomy, the cutting off of the two frontal lobes of the brain, was designed to help patients suffering from a variety of mental disorders—including schizophrenia, neurosis, depression, anxiety, and suicidal states; it was an alternative procedure for patients who did not respond to conventional psychiatric therapy. The controversial operation was first performed on human patients in 1935 under the direction of a Portuguese neuropsychiatrist, Dr. Antonio de Egas Moniz. After only twenty operations, the Portuguese government, distressed by the drastic behavioral results, outlawed any further lobotomies. For his work Moniz received the 1949 Nobel Prize in medicine "for his discovery of the therapeutic value of prefrontal lobotomy in certain psychoses." The brilliant doctor, however, was later to suffer at the hands of the very monster he helped to create when one of his "successful" lobotomized patients went mad and shot him. The bullet entered Moniz's spine, and the injury made him a hemiplegic (one side of his body was paralyzed).

The leading proponent of lobotomies in the United States was a Washington, D.C., neurologist, Dr. Walter Freeman. He personally performed or supervised four thousand such operations and through his lectures and writings may have been directly responsible for an additional twenty thousand lobotomies. It was Freeman who abandoned the standard prefrontal technique in favor of a "transorbital" variation.

In the early lobotomies a doctor drilled holes in a patient's temples, inserted a surgical knife into the holes, then manipulated the knives until he cut the appropriate nerve passageways. This standard operation was performed only in a hospital and took more than an hour. Freeman perfected a transorbital—or "ice-pick"—method which took only ten minutes and could, if necessary, be performed in a doctor's office. One eyewitness account of the "improved" technique: "Strapped to an operating table, patients got three quick jolts of electricity—enough to start violent, involuntary convulsions before they lapsed into anesthetic coma. Next, a thin, ice-pick-like leucotome was inserted under each eyelid, hammered home through the eye socket and into the brain. Carefully manipulating the two ice picks, the doctor severed the connection between thalamus and frontal lobes in the patient's brain."

What were the results of lobotomies? First of all, many patients slipped into a passive, sedated state, although some experienced "perpetual overactivity." All human functions related to the frontal lobes, which had been cut, were affected: emotional response, judgment, sensitivity, insight, empathy, and self-awareness. Patients became indecisive, lethargic, irritable, irresponsible, rude, profane. In addition, there were

more severe repercussions like epileptic seizures and cerebral hemorrhage.

While the operations allowed many mental patients to leave the back
wards of institutions and return to their families, those who opposed
lobotomies claimed that the operations did little more than create a small
army of "vegetables" and "zombies." Dr. Freeman often commented on
the changed personalities. On one occasion he wrote: "Lobotomized patients seldom come into conflict with the law precisely because they lack
the imagination to think up new deviltries and the energy to perpetuate
them."

About fifty thousand Americans were lobotomized between 1936 and
1956. Full ramifications of the operations will never be known because
doctors did not keep careful records, and very few follow-up studies were
ever commissioned. Neither the government nor the medical establishment ever officially condemned lobotomies. By the mid-1950s lobotomies
were on the decline, mostly due to the development of new tranquilizing
drugs.

The Needle Swung—The Wrong Way!

IN 1819, Danish professor Hans Oersted was giving a private class-
room demonstration that involved heating platinum wire with electric
current. There exist several different versions of what happened during
the demonstration. One says that a compass needle left under the wire by
chance reacted to the current. Another says that Oersted was deliberately
testing the needle, expecting it to move parallel to the current. In any
case, instead of doing so, the needle twitched, moved, then steadied—*at
right angles to the current!* When Oersted reversed the current, the
needle swung around 180 degrees but still at right angles. Later, a perplexed Oersted repeated the experiment with a bigger conductor and
stronger battery, and obtained the same results. This was the first demonstration of the relationship between electricity and magnetic fields, and
Oersted probably came upon it by accident.

Oersted, who published news of the discovery in a four-page Latin
tract, *Experimenta circa Effectum Conflictus Electrici in Acum Magnet-
icam*, told the story this way, as hindsight, giving himself credit for more
foresight than he had actually had.

I resolved to test my opinion by experiment. The preparations for this were made on a day in which I had to give a lecture on the same evening. There I showed Canton's experiment on the influence of chemical effects on the magnetic state of iron. I called attention to the variations of the magnetic needle during a thunderstorm, and at the same time I set forth the conjecture that an electric discharge could act on a magnetic needle placed outside the galvanic circuit. Since I expected the greatest effect from a discharge associated with incandescence, I inserted in the circuit a very fine platinum wire above the place where the needle was located. The effect was certainly unmistakable, but it still seemed to me so confused that I postponed further investigation to a time when I hoped to have more leisure. At the beginning of July these experiments were resumed and continued without interruption until I arrived at the results which have been published.

He eventually concluded that an electric current in a conductor creates a magnetic field and that a magnetic needle coming into the field moves tangent to it. Above the field, it points in one direction; beneath it, in the opposite one. If the direction of the current is reversed, so is needle direction.

Oersted, a friend of Hans Christian Andersen, was highly regarded in his time. Astronomer John Herschel praised him: "In science there was but one direction which the needle would take when pointed toward the European continent, and that was toward [his] esteemed friend Professor Oersted. . . . The electric telegraph and other wonders of modern science were but mere effervescences from the surface of this deep recondite discovery, which Oersted had liberated and which was yet to burst with all its might force upon the world. If we were to characterize by any figure the advantage of Oersted to science, we would regard him as a fertilizing shower descending from heaven, which brought forth a new crop delightful to the eye and pleasing to the heart."

The Case of the Falling Apple

ON a warm summer afternoon in 1666, twenty-four-year-old British physicist and mathematician Sir Isaac Newton sat in the shade of a tree in the garden of his home in Woolsthorpe. His contemplative mood was broken when an apple fell from an overhead branch, perhaps hitting his head. Suddenly, Newton's eyes rested on the fallen apple, and a new theory came into focus, the law of universal gravitation. Charming as the story may be, it is almost certainly untrue.

The source for the often repeated tale is *Elements de Philosophie de Newton* by Voltaire. He got the story from Newton's niece, Catherine Barton Conduitt, who lived with Newton and managed his household for twenty years. Some historians speculated that she did not intentionally lie, but that Newton might have tried to explain gravity to her by using the example of a falling apple and that she mistook the example for an actual occurrence.

Newton never recorded the story in either his published works or personal letters. One of his friends and biographers, Dr. William Stukeley, claimed that Newton personally told him about the apple incident one evening in 1726. However, two other Newton contemporaries, physician Henry Pemberton and mathematician/theologian William Whiston, interviewed him extensively on the origins of his gravity theory, and in their writings about Newton neither mentioned the falling apple. One of the cleverest explanations for the apocryphal apple came from German astronomer Karl Friedrich Gauss who scoffed: "The history of the apple is too absurd. Whether the apple fell or not, how can anyone believe that such a discovery could in that way be accelerated or retarded? Undoubtedly, the occurrence was something of this sort. There comes to Newton a stupid importunate man who asks him how he hit upon his great discovery. When Newton had convinced himself what a noodle he had to do with and wanted to get rid of the man, he told him that an apple fell on his nose; this made the matter quite clear to the man, and he went away satisfied."

Nevertheless, in 1820, when the famed apple tree fell victim to decay and had to be cut down, parts of it were carefully preserved as historical relics.

A GALLERY OF QUOTES

ABOUT INSPIRATION

Socrates [470?–399 B.C.]

"All good poets, epic as well as lyric, compose their beautiful poems not by art, but because they are inspired and possessed."

Cicero [106–43 B.C.]

"No man was ever great without a touch of divine afflatus (*adflatu divino*)."

William Law [1686–1761]

"Perpetual inspiration is as necessary to the life of goodness, holiness, and happiness as perpetual respiration is necessary to animal life."

George Christoph Lichtenberg [1742–1799]

"There is something in our minds like sunshine and the weather, which is not under our control. When I write, the best things come to me from I know not where."

Johann Wolfgang von Goethe [1749–1832]

"At times . . . my poems . . . have been preceded by no impressions or forebodings, but have come suddenly upon me, and have insisted on being composed immediately, so that I have felt an instinctive and dreamy impulse to write them down on the spot. In such a somnambulistic condition, it has often happened that I have had a sheet of paper lying before me all aslant, and I have not discovered it till all has been written, or I have found no room to write any more. I have possessed many such sheets written diagonally; but they have been lost one after another, and I regret that I can no longer show any proofs of such poetic abstraction."

Wolfgang Amadeus Mozart [1756–1791]

"When I am, as it were, completely myself, entirely alone, and of good cheer—say, traveling in a carriage, or walking after a good meal, or during the night when I cannot sleep—it is on such occasions that my ideas flow best and most abundantly. Whence and how they come, I know not; nor can I force them. Those ideas that please me I retain in my memory, and am accustomed, as I have been told, to hum them to myself. If I continue in this way, it soon occurs to me how I may turn this or that morsel to account, so as to make a good dish of it. . . . All this fires my soul and, provided I am not disturbed, my subject enlarges itself, becomes methodized and defined, and the whole, though it be long, stands almost complete and finished in my mind, so that I can survey it, like a fine picture or a beautiful statue, at a glance. Nor do I hear in my imagination the parts *successively*, but I hear them, as it were, all at once. . . . What a delight this is I cannot tell!"

Robert Burns [1759–1796]

Explaining how he sometimes got ideas for poems from music: "I consider the poetic sentiment correspondent to my idea of the musical expression; then choose my theme; begin one stanza; when that is composed, which is generally the most difficult part of the business, I walk out, sit down now and then, look out for objects in Nature around me that are in unison or harmony with the cogitations of my fancy and working of my bosom; humming every now and then the air with the verses I have framed. When I feel my Muse beginning to jade, I retire to the solitary fireside of my study and there commit my effusions to paper, swinging at intervals on the hind legs of my elbow-chair, by way of calling forth my own critical strictures, as my pen goes on. Seriously, this, at home, is almost invariably my way."

Percy Bysshe Shelley [1792–1822]

"The mind in creation is as a fading coal, which some invisible influence, like an inconstant wind, awakens to transitory brightness; this power arises from within. . . . Could this influence be durable in its original purity and force, it is impossible to predict the greatness of the result; but when composition begins, inspiration is already on the decline, and the most glorious poetry that has been communicated to the world is probably a feeble shadow of the original conceptions of the poet."

Victor Hugo [1802–1885]

"Inspiration and genius, one and the same."

Edgar Allan Poe [1809–1849]

"Most writers—poets in especial—prefer having it understood that they compose by a species of fine frenzy—an ecstatic intuition—and would positively shudder at letting the public take a peep behind the scenes, at the elaborate and vacillating crudities of thought—at the true purposes seized only at the last moment—at the innumerable glimpses of idea that arrived not at the maturity of full view—at the fully matured fancies discarded in despair as unmanageable—at the cautious selections and rejections—at the painful erasures and interpolations—in a word, at the wheels and pinions—the tackle for scene-shifting—the stepladders and demontraps—the cock's feathers, the red paint, and the black patches, which, in ninety-nine cases out of the hundred, constitute the properties of the literary *histrio*."

William Makepeace Thackeray [1811–1863]

"I have been surprised at the observations made by some of my characters. It seems as if an occult power was moving the pen. The personage does or says something, and I ask, how the dickens did he come to think of that?"

Feodor Dostoevsky [1821–1881]

"You evidently confuse the inspiration, that is, the first instantaneous vision or emotion in the artist's soul (which is always present), with the *work*. I, for example, write every scene down at once, just as it first comes to me, and rejoice in it; then I work at it for months and years."

Gustave Flaubert [1821–1880]

As for my frenzy for work, I will compare it to an attack of herpes. I scratch myself while I cry. It is both a pleasure and a torture at the same time. And I am doing nothing that I want to! For one does not choose one's subjects, they force themselves on one."

Hermann Ludwig von Helmholtz [1821–1894]

"After investigating a problem in all directions, happy ideas come unexpectedly, without effort, like an inspiration. So far as I am concerned, they have never come to me when my mind was fatigued or when I was at my working table. . . . They came particularly readily during the slow ascent of wooded hills on a sunny day."

Alfred Russel Wallace [1823–1913]

"No one deserves either praise or blame for the *ideas* that come to him, but only for the actions resulting therefrom. Ideas and beliefs are certainly not voluntary acts. They come to us—we hardly know how or whence."

Samuel Butler [1835–1902]

"Inspiration is never genuine if it is known as inspiration at the time. True inspiration always steals on a person, its importance not being fully recognized for some time."

Pëtr Ilich Tchaikovsky [1840–1893]

"If that condition of mind and soul, which we call *inspiration*, lasted long without intermission, no artist could survive it. The strings would break and the instrument be shattered into fragments. It is already a great thing if the main ideas and general outline of a work come without any racking of brains, as the result of that supernatural and inexplicable force we call inspiration."

Thomas Alva Edison [1847–1931]

"Genius is one percent inspiration and ninety-nine percent perspiration."

Jules Henri Poincaré [1854–1912]

"Often when one works at a hard question, nothing good is accomplished at the first attack. Then one takes a rest, longer or shorter, and sits down anew to the work. During the first half hour, as before, nothing is found, and then all of a sudden the decisive idea presents itself to the mind. . . . These sudden inspirations . . . never happen except after some days of voluntary effort which has appeared absolutely fruitless and whence nothing good seems to have come, where the way taken seems totally astray. These efforts then have not been as sterile as one thinks; they have set agoing the unconscious machine, and without them it would not have moved and would have produced nothing."

Alfred Edward (A. E.) Housman [1859–1936]

"Having drunk a pint of beer at luncheon—beer is a sedative to the brain, and my afternoons are the least intellectual portion of my life—I would go out for a walk of two or three hours. As I went along, thinking of nothing in particular, only looking at things around me and following the progress of the seasons, there would flow into my mind, with sudden and unaccountable emotion, sometimes a line or two of verse, sometimes a whole stanza at once, accompanied, not preceded, by a vague notion of the poem which they were destined to form part of. Then there would usually be a lull of an hour or so, then perhaps the spring would bubble up again. . . . When I got home I wrote them down, leaving gaps, and hoping that further inspiration might be forthcoming another day. Sometimes it was, if I took my walks in a receptive and expectant frame of mind; but sometimes the poem had to be taken in hand and completed by the brain, which was apt to be a matter of trouble and anxiety, involving trial and disappointment, and sometimes ending in failure."

Anton Chekhov [1860–1904]

"To deny that artistic creation involves problems and purposes would be to admit that an artist creates without premeditation, without design, under a spell. Therefore, if an artist boasted to me of having written a story without a previously settled design, but by inspiration, I should call him a lunatic."

John Galsworthy [1867–1933]

"Writers—not merely spinners of yarns to pocket pennies—require to be moved before they can write; some match must strike against the surface of their hearts or eyes. As a rule it is the unexpected, the peculiar, the—so to say—dramatic, that moves them; or it is something that violates their sense of proportion, or sets free emotions of love, of admiration, of anger, or of pity."

Amy Lowell [1874–1925]

"A common phrase among poets is, 'It came to me.' So hackneyed has this become that one learns to suppress the expression with care, but really it is the best description I know of the conscious arrival of a poem."

Edgar Wallace [1875–1932]

"They [ideas] keep coming all the time. But I get most from sitting here by my window and watching people go by. Especially people on the tops of buses, at midnight. I wonder about them, what kind of work they do for a living, what kind of houses they live in."

Dorothy Canfield Fisher [1879–1958]

"Everybody knows such occasional hours or days of freshened emotional reponses when events that usually pass almost unnoticed suddenly move you deeply, when a sunset lifts you to exaltation, when a squeaking door throws you into a fit of exasperation, when a clear look of trust in a child's eyes moves you to tears, or an injustice reported in the newspapers to flaming indignation, a good action to a sunny warm love of human nature, a discovered meanness in yourself or another to despair. I have no idea whence this tide comes, or where it goes, but when it begins to rise in my heart, I know that a story is hovering in the offing."

Henry Louis (H. L.) Mencken [1880–1956]

"It is impossible to state categorically what produces the stimulus to write. I assume that it is inborn. Some people have it and others do not. Ideas for books and articles come to me. . . . I always have in hand at least one hundred times as many as I could conceivably execute."

Igor Stravinsky [1882–1971]

"Just as appetite comes by eating, so work brings inspiration, if inspiration is not discernible at the beginning."

Jean Cocteau [1889–1963]

"[Inspiration is] the result of a profound indolence and of our incapacity to put to work certain forces in ourselves. These . . . work deep within us, with the aid of the elements of daily life, its scenes and passions, and . . . when the work that makes itself in us . . . demands to be born, we can believe that this work comes to us from beyond and is offered us by the gods."

Henry Miller [1891–1980]

"Who writes the great books? It isn't we who sign our names. What is an artist? He's a man who has antennae, who knows how to hook up to the currents which are in the atmosphere, in the cosmos; he merely has the facility for hooking on, as it were. Who is original? Everything that we are doing, everything that we think, exists already, and we are only intermediaries, that's all, who make use of what is in the air. Why do ideas, why do great scientific discoveries often occur in different parts of the world at the same time? The same is true of the elements that go to make up a poem or a great novel or any work of art. They are already in the air;

they have not been given voice, that's all. They need *the* man, *the* inter-preter, to bring them forth."

William Faulkner [1897–1962]

"I don't know anything about inspiration because I don't know what inspiration is; I've heard about it, but I never saw it."

Thomas Wolfe [1900–1938]

On writing: "It was a process that began in a whirling vortex and a creative chaos and that proceeded slowly at the expense of infinite confu-sion, toil, and error toward clarification and the articulation of an ordered and formal structure. . . . I cannot really say the book was written. It was something that took hold of me and possessed me, and before I was done with it—that is, before I finally emerged with the first completed part—it seemed to me that it had been done for me. It was exactly as if this great black storm cloud . . . opened up and, mid flashes of lightning, was pouring from its depth a torrential and ungovernable flood. Upon that flood everything was swept and borne along as by a great river. And I was borne along with it."

Jean Anouilh [1910–   ]

"Inspiration is a trick that poets have invented to give themselves importance."

David Mackenzie Ogilvy [1911–   ]

"The creative process requires more than reason. Most original think-ing isn't even verbal. It requires 'a groping experimentation with ideas, governed by intuitive hunches and inspired by the unconscious.' The majority of businessmen are incapable of original thinking, because they are unable to escape from the tyranny of reason. Their imaginations are blocked."